ECO-MONEY

The Green Party's Roadmap to Monetary Reform

ZAID ALASAD

NOVAVIA Publishing

NOVAVIA Publishing

ISBN: 9798872576006

Dedication

To my wife and children: This book is dedicated to you, my unwavering foundation and most incredible support. Your patience and encouragement have guided this journey of words and ideas. I am eternally grateful for all this and the love that binds our family.

To the People of England and the United Kingdom: I extend a heartfelt dedication and thanks to you, the community that has warmly embraced me as one of your own. This great nation possesses more fortitude and capability than you often imagine. I have bound my fate to yours when I embarked on my journey to settle and take roots in this country, one where each step is a stride towards building a brighter, more sustainable future for our children.

Table of Contents

Introduction

To the esteemed reader, your decision to engage with this book signals a crucial step towards understanding and addressing the existential crises we face today. *Eco-Money* ventures into the heart of an urgent need to rethink our monetary system to effectively confront the climate emergency and the broader systemic challenges of our times. This call is echoed by the Green Party of England and Wales and the Green Party of the US as an answer to the affordability problem. Still, there is a need to develop the literature on how the economic plans of the UK and US Greens will work and how the transition to a new monetary system might be possible. This book is a first step towards that common goal.

The genesis of this work lies in a transformative moment for the author, a former banker with substantial experience in risk oversight for a treasury desk at a depository institution. His expertise in commercial banking operations, especially the mechanism through which banks create deposits through loan issuance, provides a unique vantage point for this exploration of the monetary reform proposed by the Green Party of England and Wales and the Green Party of the US. The author's research into proposals in US Congressional legislation, which outlined an alternative monetary system proposed by the Green Party, sparked a journey leading to the creation of this book. This legislation, presented in 2011, offered a coherent remedy to the systemic risks that precipitated the 2008 Global Financial Crisis (GFC) and resonated deeply with the author's philosophical inclinations and professional insights from his experience during that crisis.

This text offers the Greens' proposals as a critical examination of Modern Money Theory (MMT), acknowledging its accuracy in depicting the operational reality of the money system while scrutinising its inadequacies, particularly concerning the private credit system. The book emerges in the context of the post-pandemic world, where massive fiscal spending by governments in developed markets has inadvertently provided a real-world testbed for MMT. However, as the author points out, implementing MMT without fundamental monetary reform presents significant flaws. The book ventures into these complex issues, advocating for a reform aligned with broader humanistic goals, especially pertinent to the green transition.

This book aligns with certain MMT tenets, such as the advocacy for free-floating currencies and the central bank's balance sheet consolidation with the Government's financial balances. However, it expands on MMT by acknowledging the role of private credit in influencing demand in the economy. The Greens attract many MMT advocates to their ranks, and this book is an attempt to open a dialogue on what needs to be revised to address the limitations of relying on fiscal policy to rectify imbalances caused by private credit. The text presents evidence of the current monetary system's subservience to market-driven interest rates despite claims that interest rate policy is a political choice. The reality is that we are operating under legislative constraints that enshrine central bank independence in law. These are not imagined constraints, and many MMT advocates would gladly rid governments of central bank independence.

Eco-Money challenges the reader to rethink the foundations of our monetary system. It argues for the necessity of reform, not just in the operational understanding of money but in its structural and policy implications, particularly in light of the climate crisis and societal challenges. The book is set against the backdrop of the United Kingdom's institutional structure. Yet, its insights are relevant to the US and other major developed economies with free-floating currencies and sovereignty over currency issuance. It also applies to the reform-minded Greens in the Eurozone, who must first grapple with the challenge of a fiscal union before considering the solutions presented in this text.

As humanity grapples with significant crises requiring unprecedented mobilisation of resources, this book posits that the first step for any Green Party, and indeed for society at large, is to reform our modern monetary system. The question of affordability for green initiatives must be reframed in real terms beyond the constraints of current fiscal paradigms. This is a premise that the Greens' monetary reform advocates and MMT economists agree on. Many financial constraints are self-imposed and imagined, but the real constraints in the ecosystem's capacity to support current human activity are unaccounted for. The Greens' reforms aim to achieve what MMT purports to do by reinforcing the state's position as the currency issuer in the economy. The misunderstanding of the Greens' reforms is often due to the scarcity of discussion about the operational consistency and accounting treatment under the MMT model.

The monetary reform initiatives advocated by Green Parties globally align with the monetary system's fundamental accounting principles and operational mechanics, as described by the original thinkers of MMT. However, relying on fiscal policy as a reactive measure (ex-post) to counterbalance the imbalances introduced by the private banking sector's credit creation and destruction legitimises the extreme boom and bust cycles motivated by pro-cyclical private credit creation. MMT economists call for fiscal policy and automatic stabilisers to play a more significant role in reducing the variability of economic cycles. The Greens argue that this approach seeks to address the symptoms rather than the root causes of economic volatility, viewing price bubbles as preventable if governments had more say on the level of private credit expansion.

MMT is correct that reserves are not currently a constraint for lending because the central bank operates a separate money circuit to set interest rates in the economy, and managing the price and quantity of bank reserves is its prerogative. In a reserve-constrained system, a central bank must provide sufficient reserves to the member banks; otherwise, it will lose control of its target interest rate because banks must source these reserves from one another in the absence of a central bank borrowing facility. When the system is not reserve-constrained, i.e. banks carry excess reserves in their accounts at the central bank, interest rates are set by making interest payments on excess reserves.

However, the MMT framework often downplays the role of monetary policy as a constraint on government fiscal power. It overlooks the significant influence wielded by the private banking sector, which necessitates central banks to accommodate the financial institutions' demand for credit. A credit boom creates the self-reinforcing mechanisms for higher valuations, more eligible collateral, higher income, and more credit expansion. A credit bust works in reverse and can lead to a deflationary spiral without fiscal intervention.

It is easy to say that fiscal fine tuning can moderate and offset any excessive credit expansion or contraction by the banking sector. real-world scenarios reveal the complexity and challenges in such applications. Accurate fiscal adjustments rely on precise economic measures like GDP, which are inherently uncertain. Even perfect accuracy does not guarantee successful intervention due to complexities of fiscal spending and tax rate adjustments. Less discussed is the misalignment of state-controlled fiscal levers with the broader market influences on interest rates. Notably, in the wake of large-scale economic disruptions, this misalignment spills into the public realm and pressures governments into increased deficit spending. This incongruity leads to a regressive fiscal outcome, as the state seeks to recoup costs by reaching into the pockets of the public, with those less affluent bearing the disproportional burden of systemic inefficiencies.

The difference of opinion between the Greens and MMT economists is often driven by the inability of the current monetary system to reduce the collateral damage from conducting fiscal policy under MMT. The proposition that fiscal policy adjustments can effectively counterbalance the banking sector's excessive credit expansions or contractions is more easily stated than executed. In practice, governments face substantial challenges in implementing such adjustments. This difficulty is exemplified by the complexities inherent in accurately estimating GDP or actual governmental expenditures, not to mention the intricate task of projecting government deficits, which forms a fundamental prerequisite for adjusting tax rates.

Furthermore, a critical aspect absent from the discourse surrounding MMT is the current monetary system's dependency on market-driven interest rates set for the state's sovereign currency. This dependency was particularly evident in the post-pandemic scenario, where Western governments experienced escalated deficit spending, driven primarily by interest expenses determined by the banking sector. The situation creates a dichotomy where private sector creditors receive remuneration for funding government deficits, while simultaneously, the Government is compelled to rationalise increased taxation on the populace, disproportionately affecting those in lower income brackets.

MMT proponents, while adept at delineating the mechanics of the money system, often overlook the critical nuances of its practical application and the legislative realities governing monetary creation. This theory predominantly focuses on the operational aspects of money creation yet does not fully encompass the perception of reality by its participants or the legislative frameworks that permit private entities to challenge the state's prerogative in money creation. Warren Mosler, a prominent figure in the MMT community, has articulated the view that the natural rate of interest should be zero. However, MMT has not presented a concrete proposal or advocacy for systemic reform to address this fundamental issue and rectify the system's vulnerability to private sector influence over interest rates on government debt.

Therefore, the theoretical foundation of MMT is at odds with the Green Party's economic proposals because it does not provide practical solutions to prevent the creation of detrimental feedback loops, where state deficit spending escalates due to interest rates being significantly influenced by external financial market forces. This gap in the MMT framework has led to internal conflicts within the school of thought, especially in explaining the unintended consequences of their proposed financial solutions. Such shortcomings in MMT proposals potentially jeopardise the progress made in educating the public about the true nature of money and the state's unique role in its creation.

Crucially, the influence of the banking system extends far beyond mere credit provision; it profoundly impacts fiscal policy, influences asset prices, alters income distribution, affects unemployment rates, and steers interest rate flows throughout the entire economic system. The book argues that the Green Party's more proactive (ex-ante) approach to monetary reform is essential to mitigate these systemic issues, advocating for a restructuring that pre-empts and prevents the inherent instabilities caused by private credit dynamics.

Furthermore, a just monetary system should not allow the privatisation of profits and socialisation of losses. MMT continues to defend a system that will allow losses to be absorbed by taxpayers by placing the responsibility for such a loss on a failure to regulate and enforce appropriate capital requirements. The Greens have proposed alternatives that not only limit this open-ended liability to the taxpayer but also reduce the scourge of liquidity and interest rate risk in the monetary system. These proposals are MMT-compatible and can be reconciled with the national accounting framework if both sides agree on a common language. This book uses the operational language of MMT to communicate the logic and coherence of the Greens' monetary reform plans, ensuring that if there is any disagreement about the methods, it is not due to misunderstanding the operational realities of modern money.

Eco-Money aims to be more than an academic exploration; it seeks to overcome the policy paralysis that hampers serious government action in combating climate change and social dysfunction. By presenting a framework for a new monetary system, the book offers tangible solutions to these formidable challenges. It looks at historical precedents, such as the monetary system in Colonial America, to illustrate the potential of these reforms. The reader is guided through the complexities of transitioning to a new monetary framework, the operational and technological implications of this transition, and the prospect of a Central Bank Digital Currency (CBDC) where the state becomes a depository institution for the non-financial sectors of the economy.

In addressing the affordability question that often stifles discussions on green initiatives, this book reframes the debate in real terms, challenging the constraints imposed by current fiscal paradigms. It emphasises the ethical and moral imperatives that should guide our actions, advocating for a compassionate standard that recognises our shared ecosystem and the interconnectedness of all life.

The world stands at a crossroads, with pivotal elections, shifting global dynamics, and technological breakthroughs reshaping our future. Our choices today will have profound implications on humanity's future, including how we design our future money system. *Eco-Money* is an essential read for anyone committed to fostering a more ethical, sustainable, and cooperative world. This book is not just a call to read and understand; it is an invitation to spread the word about the Green Party's vision in the UK, the US and beyond as we collectively navigate these transformative times.

PART I

Architecture of Modern Money

In Part I of this book, we undertake a comprehensive exploration of the contemporary monetary system, seeking to unravel the complexities of its structure and the historical trajectories that have culminated in its present form. This journey into the heart of our financial architecture is far more than an academic exercise; it is a vital quest to grasp the underpinnings of the current economic landscape before laying the groundwork for the monetary reforms proposed by the Green Party of England and Wales. While the book uses the United Kingdom's institutional structures for concrete examples, the monetary structure is similar to that of the US and other countries with legislative powers to issue their sovereign currencies, making many of this book's policy prescriptions relevant for the broader global green movements. The Green Party of the US shares many of the same policies and objectives, and it benefits from very active economic researchers with years of research and detailed documentation of what a future monetary system might look like to better serve the public and protect the environment.

We begin by examining the intricate mechanisms and evolution of money and aim to shed light on how our monetary system has become a pivotal factor in shaping economic policies and outcomes, societal dynamics, and individual livelihoods. This foundational understanding is essential, as it equips us to confront and address the multifaceted economic challenges that our society faces today, from inequality and financial instability to the broader impacts of monetary policy on social welfare and environmental sustainability. Thus, Part I serves as a historical review and a critical analysis, laying the groundwork for a deeper understanding of the contemporary financial world and its far-reaching implications.

Chapter One takes us through the historical evolution of money, tracing its roots back to ancient agrarian societies. This historical perspective is vital for contextualising the nature of modern fiat currencies. Far from being an aberration, today's monetary systems represent a continuum of financial innovations that have unfolded over millennia. By viewing money through this historical lens, we anchor our understanding of its fundamental nature, setting the stage for a more informed discussion about the monetary challenges and solutions pertinent to our current economic landscape.

Chapter Two delves into the role of government debt as a cornerstone in creating financial assets for various sectors of the economy. This chapter elucidates the concept of convertibility – the Government's promise that enables the seamless interchangeability of privately-issued money (such as bank deposits) with state-issued money. We examine instances where this convertibility could falter and assess the risks inherent in our current monetary framework. The chapter also introduces the distinction between exogenous and endogenous money, offering a comprehensive view by aggregating the financial balance sheets of both the Government and financial sectors.

Chapter Three presents an in-depth analysis of the modern operations of a central bank, with a specific focus on the BoE. As stated earlier, the choice of a UK context is not pertinent to the overall objectives because most of the world's major central banks operate similarly – the exception being the ECB, which is designed as an external authority without subservience to the legislative bodies of the individual states. Parliament grants the BoE authority, and its role extends beyond mere monetary issuance; it is instrumental in steering the economy through its influence on spending and investment, primarily by setting the price of money. The chapter explores these functions within the broader objectives of maintaining monetary and financial stability.

Chapter Four examines the genesis and importance of central bank independence as a mechanism to temper governmental fiscal excesses. While the monetary system permits the direct issuance of state currency, the Government predominantly finances its operations through market-driven interest rates, issuing gilts and thus diffusing fiscal authority to non-government interests. This diffusion involves a wide range of stakeholders, from legislative bodies and financial markets to international investors, intricately weaving them into the fabric of fiscal decision-making.

Chapter Five scrutinises how central banks react to market dynamics, particularly in the context of pricing government debt – essentially, the cost of money issued by the state. A critical case study is presented: the fall of Liz Truss's government amidst the Liability-Driven Investment (LDI) crisis. This event serves as a microcosm, illustrating the complexities and ramifications of allowing market forces to determine the price of government debt. The narrative unravels the intricate sequence of events – from the BoE's stance on liquidity provision to the market's reaction to fiscal policy announcements – culminating in the political upheaval that led to the fall of the Truss administration.

Chapter Six delves into the ascendancy of Neoliberal ideology and its profound impact on economic policies and structures. This chapter contextualises central bank independence within the broader Neoliberal agenda of market liberalisation and the diminution of fiscal authority. It critically examines how this ideological shift fostered an environment where market-driven policies and the financialisation of the economy became dominant forces, often at the expense of public welfare. The chapter elucidates how the principles of deregulation, privatisation, and free-market supremacy led to the systematic rollback of state involvement in critical sectors, propagating the belief that market mechanisms could more efficiently allocate public resources than state-directed initiatives. Central bank independence is explored as a component of this ideology, positioned as a safeguard against government fiscal excesses but, in effect, serving as a catalyst for the retrenchment of state economic intervention.

As we dissect the outcomes of these Neoliberal policies, the chapter reveals a series of unintended consequences and policy failures.

The aggressive push for privatisation and market solutions significantly eroded the quality and accessibility of essential public goods and services, such as healthcare, education, housing, and utilities. These sectors, once bastions of state responsibility, were increasingly subjected to market dynamics, often leading to costlier and less equitable access for the public. The financialisation of the economy exacerbated economic disparities by increasing the influence of financial markets on policy, facilitating a wealth transfer from the real economy to the financial sector. The chapter argues that this shift contributed to heightened income and wealth inequality and externalised costs by offloading risks associated with market-driven strategies onto the general public, particularly in instances of financial bailouts and environmental damage.

Throughout these chapters, Part I aims to provide a comprehensive understanding of the structure and dynamics of the current monetary system in the context of the United Kingdom. This exploration is relevant for the Green Parties worldwide, and understanding the existing monetary architecture is essential if we are to succeed in overcoming the wall of fiscal prudence that is deeply ingrained in the establishment's mindset. This predisposition towards fiscal conservatism invariably leads to a do-nothing approach, where the urgency of environmental action is acknowledged but not acted upon due to perceived financial constraints. The current monetary framework often fails to internalise environmental and social costs, leading to continuous disappointment and suboptimal outcomes with detrimental effects on the planet. Green Parties can actively prioritise fiscal action with ecological considerations by reforming the monetary system first. Monetary reform is not just an economic imperative but a crucial step towards ecological sustainability, enabling a shift from short-term market-driven profiteering to long-term environmental stewardship.

Chapter One

What is Money?

The standard economic storyline traces a neat path from barter to precious metals to state-backed currencies, finally arriving at today's fiat money – a currency that depends on government say-so for its value and nothing more. But scratch the surface of history, and you'll find a more complicated, fascinating story. It is a story as old as civilisation itself, about the development of agriculture, writing, and the state.

Contrary to this stylised progression from barter to banknotes, historical and archaeological scholarship reveals an alternative narrative in which the concept of money has often been about debts and credits rather than direct trade in physical goods. The moment humans began to organise agrarian societies to increase food production, debt became a necessity in as much as the daily necessities for the first farmers could not align with the seasons. The promise to deliver a physical good in the future is embedded in the concept of money, a tradeable promise that can be exchanged from person to person.

In the archetypal agrarian societies that formed the bedrock of civilisation, the currency of trust was as vital as the crops that sprouted from the soil. In many respects, money evolved as a formalisation of the age-old promises made between farmer and consumer, landowner and labourer. Even before the concept of money as we know it, a farmer's pledge to deliver grain after the harvest was a de facto financial instrument, a proto-promissory note that held value and could be traded or used to pay taxes.

According to anthropologist David Graeber, the author of the book *Debt: The First 5000 Years*, debt was the basis for conceptual underpinnings and the historical evolution of economic transactions. Debt was the primary mechanism with which archaeologists first documented early trade. The invention of writing itself was a necessity for recording transactions, with the tablets promising delivery becoming a form of money in and of themselves. An early form of cuneiform can be seen on the clay tablet in Figure 1 from the period between 3100 and 2900 BCE, depicting an early form of accounting for an amount of barley owed to an official. The official stamp is represented by a cylinder seal impression of a male figure, hunting dogs, and boars.

Figure 1: Ancient Sumerian Cuneiform Tablet for Receipt of Barley[1]

Central to Graeber's thesis is the exploration of the Sumerian civilisation, dating back to approximately 3500 BCE, identified as possessing the earliest recorded instances of debt systems. In this ancient society, debt was not merely a financial instrument but also a social construct that could have profound and often deleterious effects on the lives of individuals. Farmers, as Graeber notes, frequently found themselves ensnared in a web

---

[1] Metropolitan Museum of Art, "Proto-Cuneiform tablet with seal impressions: administrative account of barley distribution with cylinder seal impression of a male figure, hunting dogs, and boars," ca. 3100–2900 BCE, Mesopotamia, https://www.metmuseum.org/art/collection/search/329081.

of debt, a circumstance so dire that it sometimes resulted in their offspring being thrust into debt peonage.

Graeber's treatise embarks on an expansive journey, tracing the lineage of debt from its embryonic stages as a rudimentary credit system, a form of accountancy that emerged well before the inception of coinage, which was a much later development around 600 BCE. Graeber's exploration is not confined merely to the economic realm; instead, it traverses a myriad of social institutions such as marriage, friendship, slavery, law, religion, war, and governance, thereby illustrating the intricate interplay between debt and the societal constructs within which it operates.

This historical context is pivotal in understanding the evolution of economic systems and debt's role in shaping societal structures and relationships. Graeber's work serves as a historical account and a critical analysis of how debt, as an economic and social construct, has been instrumental in developing civilisations from antiquity to the present. It is a compelling narrative that challenges conventional perspectives on economic history, asserting the primacy of debt as an agent of trade and societal organisation, a notion that resonates with the contemporary economic discourse.

When we delve into today's derivatives markets, we see an advanced form of this early agrarian concept in futures contracts for agricultural commodities. Here, money is made manifest not in gleaming coins or the print of banknotes but in contracts written on the promise of corn, soybeans, or pork bellies to be delivered at a later date. These contracts, which are traded actively on futures exchanges, are modern-day descendants of ancient promises made at the time when the planting season began and the harvest was only a hope on the horizon.

In many cases, these financial obligations were not just personal but sovereign, embedded within the state's ability to tax its citizens. Indeed, in the annals of history, it is not uncommon to find the state – or its stand-ins, like the ancient temples – not just enforcing debt contracts but actively creating and managing them. Temples of the ancient world, serving as the quasi-financial hubs, did not merely serve the gods but also played bankers, tax collectors, and ledger keepers.

Furthermore, those who assume that the intricacies of financial valuation – the discounting of future cash flows or the pricing of credit risk – are modern inventions might be surprised to learn just how far back these practices go. Long before the advent of modern banking and even before the widespread use of gold and silver as money, there was *fey tsien*, an 8th century Tang Dynasty invention for transferring state debts over long distances.[2] Arab merchants were also known to have used bills of exchange in the 8th century. By the 13th century, Lombard traders were spreading the use of bills of exchange across Europe,[3] a precursor to the standardised regulations we saw solidified in Britain's 1882 Bills of Exchange Act.[4]

This arc from past to present underscores a fundamental truth: that money, in any form, has always been fundamentally about trust in receiving something of value later for something given up now. Whether it is the farmer's informal IOU or a complex financial derivative, the basic principle that underpins the concept of money is the assurance that a physical good or service will change hands at some point in the future. The abstraction of this promise to deliver something of value evolved to become a unit of value in and of itself, a token that can also be used to pay debts and settle taxes levied by the state. This enduring promise gives money its utility and its reason for existence.

---

2 "Origin of Bills of Exchange," Canadian Bar Review 4, no. 7 (1926): 443, CanLIIDocs 39, accessed 26 November 2023.

3 The Editors of Encyclopaedia Britannica, "Bill of Exchange | Negotiation, Acceptance & Payment Definition," Britannica Money, 2023, https://www.britannica.com/money/bill-of-exchange.

4 Bills of Exchange Act 1882, c. 61, 45 & 46 Vict. (18 August 1882), accessed 6 November 2023, https://www.legislation.gov.uk/ukpga/Vict/45-46/61.

Coinage in the Roman Empire

The fall of the Roman Empire is often attributed to its debasement of currency over time, a perspective notably espoused by Austrian economists, who assert that the chronic and progressive dilution of the precious metal content in Roman coinage was a critical factor in the empire's decline. They argue that the Roman government, facing mounting expenditures on military campaigns, welfare, and public works, resorted to reducing their coins' silver and gold content to extend their fiscal reach. In the Austrian view, this currency manipulation undermined the trust and stability of the monetary system, leading to inflationary pressures, a reduction in the purchasing power of the populace, and an eventual economic crisis. The resultant financial turmoil eroded the economic foundation of the empire, exacerbating other socio-political and military challenges and contributing to the gradual disintegration of Roman authority, illustrating, for Austrians, the perilous long-term consequences of irresponsible monetary policies.

Advocates of physical money, such as the Austrian school, often criticise state currencies for lacking intrinsic value. Austrian economists extol the virtues of gold and silver as monetary bases due to their inherent properties that guard against the whims of governmental currency issuance, thereby preventing debasement and ensuring long-term stability. These precious metals are championed for their intrinsic value, limited supply, and historical role as dependable stores of wealth. These properties starkly contrast fiat currencies, which are vulnerable to inflation and may become subject to the detrimental effects of arbitrary increases in the money supply. The Austrian view holds that the natural scarcity of gold and silver imposes a discipline on monetary policy, thereby constraining the Government's capacity to manipulate the economy through currency inflation.

Moreover, using precious metals is seen as a promoter of economic predictability and a bulwark against the volatility resulting from the unfettered manipulation of fiat money supplies. Austrians argue that adopting gold and silver as monetary standards would foster a self-regulating monetary system where market forces determine the money supply instead of central bank policies. This perspective embraces the idea that a precious metal standard would minimise government intervention in the economy, thereby aligning with the laissez-faire principles central to Austrian economic thought and providing a solid foundation for international trade without the instability of fluctuating exchange rates.

However, this narrative attributing the fall of the Roman Empire to currency debasement does not account for the empire's longevity following its initial fiscal malpractices. Indeed, despite significant debasement of its coinage, the empire endured for centuries after that, suggesting that the intrinsic resilience and adaptive capacity of Rome's administrative and economic structures played a role in sustaining the empire in the face of monetary dilution. The continued survival and, at times, thriving of the Roman Empire post-debasement implies the presence of mitigating factors such as the strength of its military, the administrative cohesion provided by a complex bureaucracy, and a deeply entrenched system of taxation that, collectively, could support the empire's socio-economic framework. These aspects, alongside Rome's integration of conquered peoples and continuous territorial expansion, which often led to the influx of new wealth and taxes, helped to cushion the impacts of currency devaluation.

Indeed, in the inception of its monetary system, the Roman Empire employed coinage that was imbued with a substantial content of precious metals such as gold, silver, and bronze. These coins bore intrinsic value commensurate with their metal content, facilitating trade within the empire's vast expanse and in its external commercial engagements. However, as the empire expanded and solidified its dominion, it increasingly leveraged the power of state-issued currency to assert its economic sovereignty and streamline the administration of its imperial economy.

The pivotal transition to a currency system underpinned by the state's authority, rather than the value of the metal content alone, was catalysed by the practical exigencies of maintaining a sprawling empire. The state decreed that its issued currencies – the denarius, the aureus, and their successors – were valid for the discharge of public obligations such as taxes, tributes, and public dues, which conferred upon these currencies their essential utility and acceptability.

The Roman state meticulously cultivated trust and confidence in its currency, ensuring that its coinage remained a robust representation of the economic might and stability of the empire. In this milieu, the Roman currency transcended its role as a mere medium of exchange; it became a tool of statecraft through which Rome could project its influence, consolidate its power, and regulate the economic lifeblood of its territories.

Rome's insistence on accepting its state-issued currency for settling debts and taxes was a conscious strategy that endowed it with significant control over its economy. This mechanism of monetised taxation meant that all economic actors within the empire were inexorably bound to the state's financial system, as participation in the market economy necessitated the acquisition and expenditure of state-sanctioned coinage. The utility of Rome's currency was thus not solely a reflection of the precious metal it once held; it was increasingly a manifestation of the economic and administrative prowess of the state.

Moreover, the ability to mint coinage afforded Rome the flexibility to respond to fiscal and monetary challenges. It could adjust the supply of money – through methods such as debasement – to meet the empire's financial obligations and to manoeuvre through periods of fiscal strain. However, this power was not without consequence, as it required a delicate balance to maintain the currency's credibility and avoid the pitfalls of inflation, which could erode the trust upon which the system was predicated.

The Roman Empire's utilisation of state currency thus exemplifies a sophisticated understanding of money as a construct of political authority and economic control. The strength of Rome's currency lay in the infrastructure of the state – its ability to levy and collect taxes, enforce its monetary policies, and command the resources necessary to uphold the currency's standing. In this context, Rome's state currency served as a medium for economic transactions and an instrument of imperial cohesion, facilitating the integration of diverse peoples and regions into a singular economic and political entity.

International Currencies

This narrative does not claim that gold and silver have no role as value tokens; there are times when they serve a helpful role in history. In a global landscape devoid of a hegemonic power to disseminate a standard currency – unlike the epochs dominated by the Roman Empire's denarius, the British Empire's sterling, or the US dollar in the 20th and 21st centuries – the exigency for gold and silver as mediums of international trade became markedly accentuated. The absence of a universally imposed state currency compels the reliance on alternative stores of value that carry intrinsic worth and are accepted by disparate economic agents independent of a centralised issuing authority. A debt contract can substitute for money under an authority with the power to enforce it, but it has no enforceability where this authority's jurisdiction and power are not recognised.

In the theoretical absence of an international hegemon – or mutually recognised group of political powers – there would be no sovereign currency with the requisite ubiquity and trust to function as the global standard for trade. Hence, the recourse to gold and silver emerges not merely for convenience but as an economic imperative. These precious metals accrue their stature as vehicles of international trade through their intrinsic characteristics; they are rare but not so rare as to become unobtainable, they are virtually indestructible, and they enjoy a consensus of value across different cultures and societies.

Without a hegemonic monetary standard, the fragmentation of state currencies would likely result in heightened volatility and uncertainty in international exchange rates, exacerbating the risk associated with currency conversion and potentially inhibiting trade flows. Gold and silver, in this context, provide an anchor of stability in international trade; their value is not predicated on the economic health or policies of any single nation-state but on a more universally shared recognition of their worth.

The historical reliance on gold and silver in such a decentralised international monetary system would also reflect their role as equalisers of political power. Rather than accruing economic influence by exporting a national currency, states would be driven to accumulate these metals to secure their financial standing and trade capabilities. The metals' universality ensures that no single state could unduly influence or manipulate their value to achieve hegemonic economic control.

This state of affairs would foster a system where bilateral and multilateral trade agreements necessitate payments in these precious metals or currencies pegged to their value to facilitate trade with assurances against the vicissitudes of currency fluctuations. Indeed, precious metals would function as the denominator for such agreements, providing a common language for international economic discourse in a world without a hegemonic fiat currency.

Deflationary Bias of Precious Metal Currencies

It is important to note that states relying on gold and silver for internal trade within their borders only survived a short time. Their strengths as currencies for international trade become their weaknesses for building lasting nation-states. Using gold and silver as the basis of a monetary system within a state's borders can engender a deflationary bias, primarily due to the metals' limited supply and the challenges associated with mining and acquisition. In an economy where currency issuance is tied to the stock of these precious metals, the natural scarcity and the fluctuating rates of new gold and silver extraction can lead to a situation where the money supply does not align with the economy's growth or potential. When economic productivity outpaces the growth of the money supply, deflation can ensue, reducing prices and potentially stifling spending and investment as consumers and businesses anticipate further price declines. In a world where doing nothing is rewarded with increased purchasing power, no state can dream of surviving on its taxing powers, let alone building anything significant. This deflationary pressure also exacerbates economic downturns, leading to deeper and more prolonged recessions as a part of the boom-and-bust cycle.

In such a monetary regime, credit expansion and contraction become predominantly dictated by private entities, the moneylenders, who hold the authority to issue loans based on their gold and silver reserves. The ability of these private hands to extend or withhold credit becomes a potent economic force; during times of optimism, they may extend credit liberally, amplifying economic booms by enabling increased investment and consumption. Conversely, in periods of pessimism or financial distress, they sharply contract credit, withdrawing liquidity from the market and precipitating or deepening economic busts. This concentration of power in private credit issuers' hands can lead to over-expansion cycles followed by sudden contractions as banks respond to market signals and risk assessments rather than a central monetary authority's directives to maintain economic stability.

Furthermore, this system can yield a credit environment prone to shocks and panics. In times of economic uncertainty or crisis, the public's trust in the money system may waver, leading to runs on moneylenders – or modern-day banks – as individuals seek to redeem their deposits for the underlying gold and silver. Such events can compel moneylenders to liquidate assets and call in loans to meet redemption demands. This process can precipitate a cascade of defaults and asset price collapses, thereby contracting credit further and intensifying economic downturns. The centralisation of credit control within private hands, coupled with the inherent limitations on money supply growth imposed by a precious metal standard, can thus serve to amplify the intrinsic cyclicality of market economies, rendering them far more susceptible to boom and bust dynamics.

Chapter Two

Modern Money is an IOU

Money is a debt of the issuer. It always has and always will be a promise to pay. This enduring truism that has characterised its function throughout history continues to endure and is unlikely to change. In essence, money embodies a pledge to remunerate, serving as a contractual medium of deferred payment across various sectors, from governmental to non-governmental spheres and between members of the non-government sectors. This financial instrument, under modern economic systems, manifests as an acknowledgement of debt – an *I-Owe-You* – that is systematically recorded: on the one hand, as a liability on the balance sheet of the issuer, and the other, as an asset to the holder. The conceptualisation of money, however, is a matter of considerable debate among economists. There is a divergence in thought, where some experts advocate for a more restricted interpretation, focusing on a narrower band of monetary aggregates. In contrast, others support a broader perspective, acknowledging the significance of a more expansive range of financial assets and liabilities within the economy's monetary base.

Expanding upon the conventional understanding, a broader definition of money could encompass net financial assets, as revealed through analysing the flow of funds statistics and national accounts of many modern nations. These government publications, which aggregate data on financial transactions and balance sheet positions across different sectors of the economy, offer a more expansive view of financial liquidity by encompassing a spectrum of assets and liabilities. Net financial assets, within this context, embody the residual value of an entity's financial claims after all its obligations have been accounted for. This perspective acknowledges that the liquidity of an economy hinges not merely on the traditional forms of money supply – such as currency in circulation and demand deposits – but also on the broader array of financial instruments that can be rapidly converted into purchasing power.

Consider the consolidated financial statements of a nation's economy to delineate these monetary aggregates. The United Kingdom's Office for National Statistics (ONS) meticulously compiles and maintains comprehensive financial and balance sheet accounts that encapsulate every economic sector within the country. The ONS's Flow of Funds report, issued quarterly, serves as the financial tableau of the United Kingdom's economy, aggregating the currents of financial flows within the financial account alongside the intricacies of the balance sheet positions. These data furnish a granular insight into the financial obligations in the British economy and facilitate a more transparent comprehension of the accounting identities that underpin the definition of money within the prevailing financial architecture.

The "whom-to-whom" figures further imbue the discourse with a transparency that illuminates the impact of policy decisions on the financial interplay and market valuation of financial assets and liabilities across the diverse segments of the UK economy. This extension includes interactions beyond domestic confines to encompass financial transactions with international counterparts. Within this systematic financial ledger, each transaction in a financial asset or liability is offset by an opposite and balancing transaction. The framework of the Flow of Funds highlights the relational dynamics between debtors and creditors within the financial system and chronicles the temporal progression of financial assets and liabilities.

A stacked time series representation of the aggregate net assets and liabilities derived from the Flow of Funds report elucidates the intrinsic character of these financial entities as balancing accounting identities. The aggregate net financial assets invariably serve as the counterpoint to the aggregate net financial liabilities across all economic sectors, with the discrepancy representing the net financial assets attributable to the *Rest of the World* (*ROW*). This portrayal accentuates the interconnectedness and equilibrium inherent within the financial domain of the economy.

Figure 2: UK Financial Assets & Liabilities by Sector[5]

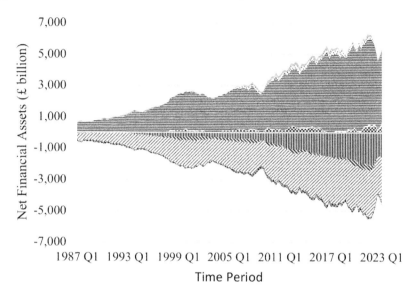

Figure 2 exhibits a symmetrical relationship between aggregate net financial assets and aggregate net financial liabilities. This is consistent with

5 Office for National Statistics, "UK Economic Accounts: flow of funds," 29 September 2023, chart, accessed 6 November 2023,

https://www.ons.gov.uk/economy/nationalaccounts/uksectoraccounts/datasets/unitedkingdomeconomicaccountsfl owoffunds.

accounting identities and the requirement for a credit transaction in the system for every debit transaction. These debits and credits must offset each other on one side of the aggregate economy's balance sheet or be matched identically as a concurrent increase or decrease in both the asset and liability sides of the aggregate economy's balance sheet. Overall, the aggregate net financial assets constitute the mirror reflection of the aggregate net financial liabilities across all sectors of the economy. The reciprocal depiction is not merely a happenstance but an embodiment of the accounting principle that presides over the entire system of tracking ownership of financial assets. Except for gold and silver, financial assets are unlike real assets because they are contractual promises to deliver something of value rather than being the object of intrinsic value. This principle remains valid for any chosen breadth of money definition.

The Flow of Funds report includes assets and liabilities appraised at market valuations wherever feasible, thus clarifying the influence of private credit expansion and monetary policy on the current valuation of the financial wealth within the non-governmental sectors. For example, in 2023, the net financial assets within the *Households* sector had a marked drop, a consequence stemming from a diminished market valuation of *Private Non-Financial Corporations* and a depreciation in the valuation of *Central Government* debt, aligning with the economic principle that the net present value of cash flows from corporate profits is reduced with a higher discount rate and with the mathematical certainty that sovereign debt prices inversely correlate with rising interest rates.

This symmetry between assets and liabilities is the basis for understanding Modern Money Theory, and it is why the political language revolving around government deficits needs to change if we are to have an honest discussion about affordability. Hence, it is imperative to comprehend this inverse relationship for a coherent analysis of financial health and the policy impacts on wealth distribution and fiscal capacity. Moreover, the connection between rising interest rates and the diminishing market value of government debt often eludes the awareness of many economists, media analysts, and political figures. It also leads to misrepresentations of government debt and its role in the current monetary system in the state's creation of sovereign currency.

The Purpose of Government Debt

The official measure of government debt is calculated at face value, which is the amount promised to be paid to bondholders at maturity, not the market price for those bonds at the time of valuation. The face value of debt is used for international comparisons and to guide fiscal policy decisions. Consequently, when government debt is presented as a percentage of GDP, a methodological incongruity emerges: GDP figures are typically adjusted for inflation to reflect real values, whereas government debt is frequently quantified at its nominal value, ignoring the market assessment that would account for variations due to interest rates and inflationary effects.

The interpretation of financial ratios can, at times, yield counterintuitive results. Consider the June 2023 data, which presents a perplexing scenario: the market valuation of gross general government debt stands at £2,319 billion, as defined by the Maastricht ESA 95 standards, while the nominal value of the Government's debt, using the same constrained measure under Maastricht ESA 10 guidelines, is quantified at £2,637 billion. If the Government engages in a strategy to repurchase its undervalued debt in the open market – financing this repurchase with the issuance of new gilts bearing higher interest rates – the conventional government debt-to-GDP ratio remarkably decreases from 101% to 89%.

Further confounding policymakers is the equally absurd notion of basing fiscal decisions on the market value of this narrowly defined debt in proportion to GDP. Such a practice could lead to pro-cyclical policy-making amidst rising inflation and interest rates, potentially exacerbating inflationary pressures in a self-perpetuating cycle. A more insightful approach to assessing government debt is to consider the creditor's perspective, the non-governmental economic sectors. For these entities, gilts represent a form of monetary asset that yields interest, akin to the function of a fixed-term deposit. These highly liquid securities carry negligible credit risk and obviate the necessity for deposit insurance because they are perceived as proxies for money.

Over an extended temporal horizon, the aggregate of UK Government debt tends to expand with the private sector's demand for excess savings. The private sector's appetite for secure assets typically dictates the trajectory of government debt issuance. In economics, one incontrovertible truth governed by the accounting identity for calculating GDP is that aggregate *Saving* must equal aggregate *Investment*. This is not merely a theoretical construct but an accounting axiom, wherein an act of investment invariably signifies the assumption of a financial asset by one economic participant from another. Herein lies a dichotomy: on one flank of this transaction, the investor possesses equity stakes, bond holdings, or creditor status vis-à-vis a nascent corporate entity. On the opposing flank, the debtor is encumbered with the obligation of either debt or equity as a mechanism to acquire real assets or other financial assets, the ultimate aim being the generation of a financial return in the form of dividends, interest or capital gains.

As the population ages, demand for *Saving* intensifies, expanding the economy's absorptive capacity for heightened sovereign indebtedness without proportionately depreciating the national currency's value. *Saving*, fundamentally characterised by an abstention from consumption, necessitates an offset through governmental dis-saving to avert a contractionary economy and mass unemployment. Absent this counterbalance, an ageing cohort's unfulfilled ex-ante saving inclination persists and escalates, further entrenching into precautionary financial behaviours and a persistent economic downturn. For example, an ageing society like Japan can only have its desire to increase aggregate *Saving* by a counterbalancing increase in government debt or increased financial liabilities by the rest of the world. In this case, a significant government debt level is needed to maintain a stable monetary system.

The phenomenon of governmental dis-saving emerges not as a matter of volitional elective policy but as an inexorable response to the alternative — economic contraction of a magnitude that compels state intervention. As elected officials face the prospect of being ousted from office, political survival instincts render such fiscal responses inevitable. Concurrently, the economic machinery is buffered by built-in mechanisms: automatic stabilisers activate, expanding welfare provisions and unemployment benefits, among other forms of socio-economic support. These systemic responses function as a countervailing force to the downward gravitational pull of the contracting economy, serving to preserve the socio-political fabric while mitigating the severity of economic retrenchment.

It is this very dynamic that elucidates the economic enigma of Japan: the nation's ability to sustain a currency exhibiting enduring stability and subdued inflationary pressures, even while shouldering a government debt-to-GDP ratio that has soared beyond the 200% mark for a protracted duration. It also explains the ability of the US to sustain such high valuations for its currency despite the persistently high government deficits. The desire by the rest of the world to save in the US dollar can only be met by US government dis-saving or a contraction in the US domestic economy.

Figure 3 illustrates two important points that lead to a misunderstanding about the fiscal capacity of the Government sector. 1) The market valuation of government debt goes down as interest rates rise. The last data points in 2023 illustrate the effects of the rise in interest rates on market prices. 2) The other and more important characteristic is that both market and nominal values of government debt are growing steadily over time to meet the demand for *Savings* by the non-government sectors.

Figure 3: Nominal vs Market Value of National Debt[6]

General Government consolidated Maastricht debt at market prices (Maast ESA 95)
General govt. gross consolidated debt at nominal value (Maastricht ESA10)
Expon. (General Government consolidated Maastricht debt at market prices (Maast ESA 95))

A close examination of the y-axis of this chart reveals an added insight into the language around debt sustainability. Compounding growth rates over time lead to exponential curves when plotted on an arithmetic y-axis, and the growth in debt often needs to be understood in the same context as growth in GDP. It is inconsistent to expect GDP to grow steadily and panic when seeing the same happening to the Government debt. To illustrate the stability of this growth rate over time, the chart uses a logarithmic scale. This linear transformation of the exponential growth data

_____

6 Office for National Statistics, "Government debt and deficit," published October 27, 2023, https://www.ons.gov.uk/economy/governmentpublicsectorandtaxes/publicsectorfinance/datasets/governmentdefi citanddebtreturn.

can be utilised to understand and interpret the scale and patterns of growth over time without equating the time values of the national debt.

Defining Modern Money

In honing our conceptualisation of money, it is imperative to distinguish between the state's obligations – guaranteeing convertibility into sovereign legal tender – and those non-governmental financial assets that lack a commensurate promise of conversion. Instruments such as government bonds, savings deposits, money market funds, and short-term debt securities, while not customarily functioning as mediums of exchange, nonetheless offer a degree of liquidity. These financial assets hold the potential for rapid transformation into immediately spendable forms, such as zero-maturity monetary instruments or currency, thus blurring the lines in the spectrum of monetary assets.

The delineation of money should be expansive enough to encompass privately created credit, a bank asset that augments aggregate liabilities in the form of bank deposits. In essence, when financial institutions extend credit, they concurrently create deposits, an act tantamount to money creation within the private sector. While originating from private contractual agreements, these deposits are no less spendable than those directly issued by government mandate. They are woven into the monetary fabric of the economy, circulating with similar liquidity to state-sanctioned currency.

Private credit possesses a dualistic character; it is both an asset to the depositor and a liability to the bank. The interplay of credit creation and deposit expansion is a powerful dynamic force in monetary economics. It substantially influences the money supply and, by extension, the economy's overall liquidity. Recognising this private facet of the money supply is indispensable for a comprehensive understanding of how the modern financial system operates and for formulating effective monetary policy. It is also the source of much of the contention between the advocates for monetary reform among the Greens and MMT economists who do not believe reform is needed.

Privately-created money is convertible to state-issued money on a 1:1 ratio. For example, the modern money system allows a depositor to walk up to an ATM and convert bank deposits into notes issued by the central bank; these notes can also be exchanged for coins issued by the central government at their mandated conversion values. Depositors can also pay taxes owed to the state by transferring bank deposits to the Government's account at the central bank, effectively converting bank money to sovereign money. However, it is essential to note that convertibility is not without risk. Any form of money with future convertibility carries interest rate risk. Money held with private intermediaries carries credit risk. Some forms of money are also exposed to liquidity risk, which is the risk that an asset cannot be sold or converted into cash quickly without a loss in value.

Government bonds, or gilts, may experience a decline in market value if interest rates rise. This market risk reflects the opportunity cost of holding a lower-yielding security when newer issues offer higher returns. However, these instruments guarantee redemption at their face value upon maturity, thus ensuring convertibility into the issuing state's currency for the amount initially promised on a 1:1 ratio. Therefore, a government debt security is treated as money by MMT economists, serving the same economic payoff for its holder as that provided by a fixed-term deposit issued by the same government.

Bank deposits, while generally perceived as a safe form of money, are not without credit risk. The risk arises from the possibility that the banking institution may face solvency issues, thereby jeopardising the depositors' ability to recover their funds fully. To mitigate this risk, deposit insurance schemes are provided by many governments, safeguarding the convertibility of deposits up to a certain threshold. Furthermore, regulatory bodies enforce stringent capital requirements and oversight protocols to ensure that banks maintain adequate capital buffers and liquidity to honour their obligations to depositors, mitigating risk for any deposits above the insured limits. These protective measures underscore the state's role in maintaining confidence in various forms of money, thereby preserving the stability and functionality of the monetary system.

Even gilts can face liquidity challenges during financial stress or market turbulence. Investors seeking to sell gilts may find less market appetite for these securities, which can drive down their price, particularly if the need to sell is urgent. Fixed-term deposits, which are bank deposits with a specified term to maturity, can also carry liquidity risk, especially if they come with break clauses that penalise the depositor for early withdrawal. These penalties can take the form of reduced interest or principal, acting as a deterrent to early cash-out and reflecting the cost associated with the bank re-establishing its liquidity position before the deposit's premature termination.

Within the framework of modern monetary systems, money can be defined as financial liabilities with a sufficiently low risk of failing to convert into state-issued currency upon demand. These financial liabilities encompass a spectrum of assets, ranging from physical cash, which is a direct obligation of the state, to demand deposits at commercial banks, which are convertible into state currency on demand and backed by government insurance schemes up to a certain amount.

The essential characteristic of money is its general acceptability as a medium of exchange, a unit of account, and a store of value, underpinned by the public's confidence in its ability to be converted into the legal tender of the realm without significant loss. This reasonable reassurance of convertibility and confidence in the various forms of money is often supported by institutional arrangements, such as central bank policies, deposit insurance schemes, and regulatory frameworks, which collectively work to minimise the risk of conversion failure.

In this sense, money is not merely an abstract unit of exchange but also an accounting identity, a legal and social construct that reflects the stability and credibility of the issuing authority and the effectiveness of the regulatory environment in which it circulates. Therefore, the "moneyness" of an asset is determined not just by its liquidity and ease of transferability but also by the systemic safeguards that ensure its near-certain convertibility into the fiat currency provided by the state.

This categorisation of money provides a measure of liquidity that can quickly become spendable balances. As such, the demarcation of money is extended to reflect a more integrated understanding of financial assets within the economic circuitry. Consequently, money, when delineated as net financial assets, transcends the simplistic ledger entries of liabilities and assets, assuming a role as the lifeblood of the economy's circulatory system, channelling funds through the various sectors – households, businesses, government, and the foreign sector – and thereby orchestrating the rhythmic flow of economic activity. This conception reflects an economy's broader financial health and capacity for sustaining consumption, investment, and economic growth.

Estimating Quantity of Money

Estimating the quantity of money within an economy necessitates an examination of the aggregate balance sheets of economic sectors, primarily the *Central Government* and *Monetary Financial Institutions* (*MFI*). By analysing the liability side of the *Central Government*'s balance sheet, one can discern the volume of state-issued currency in circulation – notes and coins issued directly by the *Central Government*. Additionally, the *MFI* balance sheet provides crucial insights into the amounts of demand deposits and other liquid financial instruments that can be promptly converted into cash and are, therefore, part of the broader money supply. These datasets collectively reveal the multifaceted nature of money in the modern economy, reflecting physical currency and digital representations of its purchasing power.

Figure 4: Central Government Financial Assets & Liabilities in Q1 2023

Central Government Balance sheet

Figures in £ millions: 2023 Q1

Assets	Liabilities
Monetary gold and special drawing rights 49,332	Monetary gold and special drawing rights 32,014
Currency and deposits 63,842	Currency and deposits 244,749
Debt securities 83,897	Debt securities 2,070,431
Loans 226,880	Loans 36,401
Equity and investment fund shares/units 53,630	Insurance, pension and standardised guarantee schemes 686
Financial derivatives and employee stock options 2,464	Financial derivatives and employee stock options 2,167
Other accounts receivable/payable 146,497	Other accounts receivable/payable 45,752

The UK's *Central Government* balance sheet in Figure 4 provides insight into the different forms of financial assets and liabilities that compose the state's monetary and fiscal resources. While loans, accounts payable, insurance, pension, and derivative obligations are free of credit risk, we will maintain our definition of money to those instruments benefiting from immediate convertibility. Note that this balance sheet excludes the Bank of England (BoE), which is included in the aggregate *MFI* balance sheet.

Monetary gold and special drawing rights (SDRs) totalling £32,014 million represent the Government's gold liabilities and reserve positions in the International Monetary Fund (IMF). These figures reflect the monetary obligations of the UK in gold and SDRs to foreign governments. This is an international position and a monetary asset held by the *Rest of the World*. This external liability on the *Central Government*'s balance sheet is covered by an external asset of £49,332 million in monetary gold and SDRs vis-à-vis the *Rest of the World*. From the MMT perspective, the UK is not constrained in spending by a concern for its default probability because it issues debt denominated in pounds sterling, a currency that can only be issued by the sanction of the British Parliament. However, as MMT agrees, it is constrained by inflation if deficit spending creates more money than the economy's capacity to absorb. The UK exercises full sovereignty over fiscal and monetary policies by matching its minimal foreign currency liabilities.

The *Central Government* issues currency and deposits directly amounting to £244,749 million. It is important to note that both the BoE and the *Central Government* are currency issuers. The BoE issues currency backed by the debt securities it purchases while conducting monetary policy. The broader definition of money under MMT includes gilts, which makes these gilt purchases by the BoE a simple exchange of money issued by the central bank as zero-maturity notes (pound sterling notes) for *Central Government* longer-maturity money (gilts). Aside from gilts, the *Central Government* issues coins, national savings certificates, SAYE contracts, income bonds, deposit bonds, premium savings bonds, national savings stamps, gift tokens, and other deposits at the National Savings Bank (NSB) and Trustee Savings Banks. Most national savings instruments are claims by the *Households* sector on the *Central Government* sector.

Gilts are tracked in the debt securities account, found on the liabilities side of the *Central Government*'s balance sheet in Figure 4. Debt securities totalled £2,070,431 million, representing the most significant portion of the *Central Government*'s balance sheet and signifying the total market value of government bonds and other debt instruments issued by the *Central Government*. These securities are obligations that the Government is committed to repaying at maturity and include both short-term and long-term maturities. They are utilised to finance budget deficits and manage the national debt, reflecting the cumulative borrowing by the state to meet expenditures above its income.

Figure 5: MFI Financial Assets & Liabilities in Q1 2023

Monetary Financial Institutions Balance Sheet

Figures in £ millions: 2023 Q1

Assets	Liabilities
Currency and deposits 4,690,020	Currency and deposits 9,699,223
Debt securities 1,547,374	Debt securities 929,548
Loans 4,462,715	Loans 3,369
Equity and investment fund shares/units 217,501	Equity and investment fund shares/units 265,393
Insurance, pension and standardised guarantee schemes 12,565	Insurance, pension and standardised guarantee schemes 8,676
Financial derivatives and employee stock options 3,524,900	Financial derivatives and employee stock options 3,479,102
Other accounts receivable/payable 665	Other accounts receivable/payable 5,806

The *Central Government*'s balance sheet does not include the currency and deposit liabilities issued by the BoE. The central bank is included in the *MFI* balance sheet in the Flow of Funds Report. Figure 5 illustrates the pivotal role financial intermediaries, such as the BoE and its commercial banking counterparts, play in creating the nation's monetary supply. When commercial banks and building societies extend credit, they concurrently generate corresponding deposits, manifesting as opposing entries within the aggregate banking ledger. Collectively, the entirety of loans originated by a banking institution will correlate with deposits within the financial system.

It is crucial to acknowledge that the power to create currency and deposits is not without its bounds; indeed, banking operations are circumscribed by a constellation of regulatory restrictions. Such constraints encompass capital adequacy rules, which serve as a bulwark against insolvency and liquidity stipulations, ensuring that short-term obligations can be met. Additionally, banks must navigate interest rate exposure, credit quality considerations, market volatility, and foreign exchange fluctuations, which collectively inform the prudent management of the institution's balance sheet and constrain the propensity to create money without limits. The liabilities from this sector for constructing the money aggregates are currency and deposits of £9,699 billion. Note that this figure ignores cross-holdings in the government sector, the BoE and banks owned by the Government.

Figure 6: ROW Financial Assets & Liabilities in Q1 2023

Rest of the World Balance Sheet

Figures in £ millions: 2023 Q1

Assets	Liabilities
Monetary gold and special drawing rights 32,014	Monetary gold and special drawing rights 33,374
Currency and deposits 3,708,929	Currency and deposits 3,502,900
Debt securities 1,678,541	Debt securities 1,253,177
Loans 1,837,354	Loans 2,316,263
Equity and investment fund shares/units 3,858,512	Equity and investment fund shares/units 3,622,501
Insurance, pension and standardised guarantee schemes 92,844	Insurance, pension and standardised guarantee schemes 174
Financial derivatives and employee stock options 2,826,286	Financial derivatives and employee stock options 2,755,614
Other accounts receivable/payable 8,790	Other accounts receivable/payable 17,510

The foreign sector, as tracked by the *Rest of the World*'s balance sheet within the Flow of Funds accounts, constitutes another critical segment in the issuance of monetary instruments (see Figure 6). This sector primarily comprises foreign sovereign entities and banking institutions domiciled abroad. Given the United Kingdom's status as a global finance hub, this sector's imprint is markedly pronounced. The monetary liabilities of this sector include monetary gold and special drawing rights (SDRs) amounting to £33 billion, alongside currency and deposits totalling £3,503 billion. Including these elements underlines the extensive reach and interconnectivity of the UK's financial system with the global economy, demonstrating the intricate web of financial relationships that underpin the issuance and flow of money across borders.

The "currency and deposits" classification aggregates all transactions involving money owned (assets) and issued (liabilities) by the foreign sector, encompassing all foreign and domestic currency and deposit accounts. The *Rest of the World*'s balance sheet is disproportionately large because the UK is a global centre for foreign currency funding. These activities in foreign currencies operate as a service to the *Rest of the World* and should not be confused with the economy's domestic supply of money. Despite its status as a financial centre, foreign currency banking services transactions do not create any material uncovered foreign currency liabilities for the domestic sectors. Currency mismatches between the assets and liabilities of *MFIs* are minimal because directional open positions on banks' balance sheets consume regulatory capital. Furthermore, while the British pound sterling retains its stature as a reserve currency, the proclivity for international savings in sterling constitutes a fiscal outflow, effectively reducing the pool of pound sterling available for the domestic UK market. Against this backdrop, the consolidated balance sheet of the UK's domestic sectors emerges as our focal point of analysis.

Figure 7: Total Economy Financial Assets & Liabilities in Q1 2023

Total Domestic Economy Balance Sheet

Figures in £ millions: 2023 Q1

Assets	Liabilities
Monetary gold and special drawing rights 49,332	Monetary gold and special drawing rights 32,014
Currency and deposits 9,773,608	Currency and deposits 9,979,637
Debt securities 3,655,739	Debt securities 4,081,103
Loans 6,479,331	Loans 6,000,422
Equity and investment fund shares/units 6,998,863	Equity and investment fund shares/units 7,234,874
Insurance, pension and standardised guarantee schemes 3,870,504	Insurance, pension and standardised guarantee schemes 3,963,174
Financial derivatives and employee stock options 6,369,149	Financial derivatives and employee stock options 6,439,821
Other accounts receivable/payable 551,879	Other accounts receivable/payable 543,159

The total domestic economy balance sheet in Figure 7 also includes the much smaller contributions to currency and deposits from non-bank financial institutions classified as *Other Financial Intermediaries and Financial Auxiliaries* in the Flow of Funds Report. What is important to note is that the bulk of the currency and deposits are liabilities of the *MFIs*, which are owed to the asset holders of currency and deposits by every other sector in the economy. The deposits that a person perceives as money in a bank account acquire this status under the Government's assurance of convertibility – a guarantee that these deposits will be accepted as payment for tax obligations and are exchangeable on a one-to-one basis with state-minted currency. It is also essential to understand the true nature of this money as an accounting entry to track an IOU to another actor in the economy.

While the magnitudes in question might invoke a sense of awe, a critical delineation must be made between money engendered as an obligation to the state and that spawned as a debt to a banking institution. The former is a manifestation of public policy, sculpted by the governing bodies elected to represent and serve the citizenry's welfare. The latter, conversely, is driven by the private, profit-oriented endeavours of banking establishments, whose operative decisions may not align with the currency users' best interests. The mechanics of private credit both swell and wane in a pro-cyclical manner, spurred by the banks' pursuit of profit, which naturally incites them to amplify credit issuance in flourishing economic periods and to retract it amidst downturns.

In contrast, governmental actions typically exert a counter-cyclical influence. In economic adversity, the Government injects liquidity into the system through augmented transfer payments and deficit spending. Fiscal automatic stabilisers are given that name because they inject money into the economy automatically even if the politicians do nothing; a severe recession precipitates a rise in deficit spending on unemployment insurance and welfare benefits, creating the currency needed to sow the seeds for the next expansion. Conversely, during periods of economic exuberance, the Government often indirectly curtails the money supply through automatic stabilisers that work through the tax code; progressive tax regimes inherently siphon off greater revenue from the increased individual and corporate earnings.

Equally noteworthy is the intricate web of cross-holdings that pervade the various sectors of the economy. Financial institutions create currency and deposits when funding debt and rely on these instruments as assets for their liquidity needs, making a complex interplay between their roles as both creditors and debtors. This duality can amplify the perceived size of currency and deposit liabilities on balance sheets. Additionally, the cross-holdings involving the *Central Government* substantially influence these figures. For instance, when considering consolidated accounts, the BoE's positions can be subsumed within the broader government balance sheet, thereby adjusting the overall currency and deposit liabilities estimate.

This consolidation is pertinent because it eliminates internal transactions that otherwise inflate the aggregate financial statistics, providing a more accurate representation of the net financial position. The cross-holdings between a central bank and government entities are particularly significant. When the BoE holds gilts or provides an account for government deposits, these amounts, though substantial on the BoE's balance sheet, are not offsetting assets and liabilities in the *Central Government*'s balance sheet. Thus, a careful examination that accounts for these cross-holdings is essential to distil an accurate measure of the state's monetary liabilities within the economy.

Money created as a byproduct of fiscal policy and coinage can be estimated by aggregating the net financial liabilities of the Government that enjoy some degree of convertibility. This aggregate estimate of state money is the sum of debt securities and the issued currency and deposits; we exclude monetary gold and SDRs from this aggregate, given their peripheral impact on the domestic economy. This state-issued money is estimated at £2.3 trillion at the 2023 Q1 market valuations (see Figure 4 for *Central Government* balances).

This aggregation includes gilts held by the BoE because its open market purchases create money in the form of bank reserves within the accounts of commercial banks. However, it also necessitates adjustments to reflect the gains or losses consequent to the BoE's market operations in gilts and the broader activities within the Asset Purchase Facility, consistent with valuing these debt instruments at market values and not at their nominal worth. For this calculation, it is assumed that these adjustments materialise in subsequent reporting periods as a change in the level of *Central Government* debt. The mechanism by which this is reflected is the BoE's engagement in open market operations involving transactions executed at prevailing market prices, which yield profits remitted back to the Government or, conversely, incur losses that necessitate governmental funding.

Some economists often classify money issued by the Government and central bank as exogenous, defined as money created by an external authority. In contrast, endogenous money is issued by the non-government financial sector as a byproduct of bank credit. Collectively, the issuance of a loan by a bank concurrently results in the creation of a deposit within the financial system. The *MFI* aggregate balance sheet also includes currency and deposit assets of £4,690 billion in pounds sterling, of which £12 billion are foreign currency assets belonging to the BoE, leaving £4,678 billion in currency assets on the *MFI ex BoE* balance sheet. Netting this sector's assets against its currency liabilities of £9,699 billion, we estimate a net currency issuance of £5,021 billion. The BoE's share of these liabilities is £995 billion in pounds sterling, per the central bank's report on reserve balances and notes in circulation on March 2023. Excluding the BoE's currency issuance, the *MFIs ex BoE* issued a net of £4,026 billion in currency and deposits in the asset accounts of the non-*MFI* economic sectors. Their portfolios of loans and corporate debt securities underpin such a proliferation of endogenous money supply.

This internally generated money engenders its own demand as the principal and interest on loans necessitate repayment – a financial obligation that transfers net money from the non-financial sectors to the financial sector. The expansion phase creates a feedback loop where more credit is extended as money flows through the economy. As debt repayments dominate and endogenous money contracts, the non-financial sector's debts can only be discharged through debt forgiveness, redemption, or the infusion of exogenous money into the economic system. Figure 8 illustrates how money is created exogenously by the Government and central bank and endogenously by bank issuance as a byproduct of the credit creation process.

Figure 8: Exogenous and Endogenous Money Flows

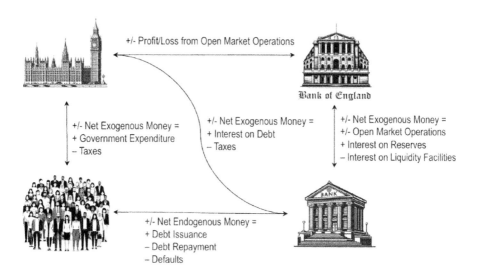

This is how the monetary system is designed today. Money comes into existence in one of two ways: as exogenously created state-issued money and as an offsetting balance to bank credit. The flow diagram illustrates the flow of money between the Government, the central bank, the banking system, and the general public. Net government expenditure refers to the purchase of goods and services, which include public consumption and public investment, and transfer payments consisting of income transfers (pensions, social benefits) and capital transfers. Government expenditure in excess of taxes collected creates exogenous money in the monetary system. Interest on reserves, interest in government debt, liquidity facilities and open market operations also impact the levels of exogenous money. Net endogenous money is determined by the net flows in interest, credit creation and credit destruction between the financial and non-financial sectors. By including the stock of gilts in the broad money estimate, the exogenous money that the MMT literature defines as money is £2.3 trillion. MMT refers to this as the non-government sector's Net Financial Assets, which are ultimately the liabilities of the government sector. The net endogenous money created by *MFIs ex BoE* adds another £4 trillion to this estimate of the quantity of money. MMT economists do not treat this as money and net it against the assets on the aggregate *MFI* balance sheet. Therefore, the delineation of money in MMT literature includes only the exogenous money described earlier.

However, in the spirit of starting a dialogue, let us adopt a broader definition of money to include the endogenous kind created in the private banking system. This will allow us to harmoniously integrate the Green Party's proposals within the national accounting framework, provided there is a consensus on a shared linguistic framework. This book strategically employs the operational terminology of MMT to elucidate the rationale and consistency of the monetary reform proposals advocated by the Green Party. By doing so, it aims to ensure that any potential disagreement regarding the proposed methods arises not from a misunderstanding of the operational realities of modern money but rather from differing perspectives on the application and implications of these realities within the context of the proposed reforms. This approach facilitates a more informed and nuanced discourse on monetary policy, bridging theoretical understanding with practical policy considerations.

Chapter Three

Central Bank Operations

E stablished in 1694, the BoE was nationalised after WWII and today serves the modern functions of a central bank for the United Kingdom, a key feature of most modern financial systems. The primary objectives of the BoE are to ensure monetary stability and foster financial stability. These twin pillars form the bedrock of its operations and mandate, underpinning the broader economic framework within which it operates. The central bank is given powers to set the base interest rate, which influences the cost of borrowing and the saving rate, indirectly affecting consumption and investment decisions across the economy. It is also tasked with safeguarding the financial system against systemic risks that can precipitate financial crises. It does this ex-ante by serving as a regulator of banking activities and ex-post by employing a range of funding facilities to mitigate the risk of financial instability.

The rationale behind Parliament vesting such significant powers in the BoE is predicated on the critical role of monetary and financial stability in the economy's overall health. The stated goal is a stable monetary environment that ensures predictable and stable prices, essential for consumer confidence and business planning. Financial stability is crucial for maintaining trust in the banking system, ensuring that it functions effectively as a conduit for capital and as a haven for deposits. This chapter explains the scope of the BoE's operations and the reasoning behind these activities – however flawed or misguided they may be.

Dual Mandate

The BoE, the United Kingdom's central Monetary Authority, has a dual mandate that charges it with the pivotal task of ensuring monetary and financial stability. This mandate primarily entails the stewardship of inflation rates within the economy. This twin imperative commands the institution to navigate the delicate balance between fostering conditions conducive to economic growth and vigilantly containing the inflationary pressures that may accompany such expansion.

The BoE employs monetary policy tools to control inflation, with interest rate adjustments as its principal lever. By modulating the cost of borrowing, the Bank influences the levels of spending and investment within the economy, thereby affecting aggregate demand and, ultimately, the price level of goods and services. An increase in interest rates typically serves as a brake on economic activity, tempering inflation, whereas a decrease can stimulate spending and production, provided inflation remains within acceptable bounds.

The Bank's inflation targeting framework is designed to provide clear guidance to markets and policymakers alike, anchoring inflation expectations and fostering an environment of price stability. This approach ensures that inflation does not erode the currency's purchasing power and that the economy does not succumb to the distortive effects of hyperinflation or deflation. The explicit inflation target, set by the Government, obliges the BoE to maintain vigilance over price stability, which, in turn, underpins the overall health and stability of the nation's financial system and economy.

In the aftermath of the 2008 financial crisis and again during the COVID-19 pandemic, the BoE found it imperative to extend temporary facilities as part of its monetary policy toolkit. These extraordinary measures were necessitated by the urgent need to stabilise financial markets, ensure the flow of credit to households and businesses, and buttress the economy against the seismic shocks of systemic liquidity crunches. The 2008 crisis exposed critical vulnerabilities in the financial system, prompting the central bank to inject liquidity to avert a complete market freeze. Similarly, the pandemic's unprecedented global economic disruption required swift and expansive monetary interventions to prevent financial collapse, support economic activity, and mitigate the adverse economic consequences of widespread lockdowns and the ensuing demand shock. These temporary facilities, tailored for crisis conditions, were pivotal in maintaining economic stability during acute stress, highlighting the Bank's proactive and responsive role in safeguarding the UK's economic resilience.

Temporary Emergency Facilities

The BoE's temporary emergency facilities epitomise a distinctive form of endogenous money creation, distinguished by its transient nature. These facilities are designed to inject liquidity into the financial system during periods of acute stress, operating under the premise that the funds provided are not a permanent expansion of the money supply but a provisional bulwark against systemic liquidity shortfalls. As such, the capital furnished by these mechanisms is endogenous in that it arises from within the banking system's architecture, tailored to meet specific demands for liquidity rather than a permanent money creation operation by the state.

This contrasts with exogenous money, which typically takes the form of permanent additions to the monetary base, such as the issuance of new currency by a central bank. Exogenous money, once introduced, becomes a durable part of the money supply, altering the monetary landscape in a more lasting fashion. It is money created outside the current credit system, often reflecting broader policy objectives such as long-term economic stimulus or structural adjustments to the monetary framework.

The temporary nature of the BoE's emergency facilities underscores their role as a responsive tool rather than a foundational component of the monetary supply. They are calibrated to retract as stability returns, with their presence on balance sheets diminishing with the restoration of normal credit flows. The repayable nature of these facilities means that, while they provide essential liquidity in times of need, they are not designed to leave a lasting imprint on the overall quantity of money exogenous within the economy.

Monetary Stability Tools

In a reserve-constrained system, reserve requirements do not constrain bank lending due to the operational framework within which central banks, like the BoE, set interest rates. Reserve constraints do not limit bank lending like capital requirements do because each new loan creates a deposit within the banks' aggregate balance sheet. The BoE's primary aim is not to control the quantity of reserves but rather to influence the price of money, namely the interest rate. To achieve its target rate for overnight lending, the Bank engages in open market operations, buying or selling securities to adjust the level of reserves in the system and thus steer the market rate towards its policy rate. This process inherently means that the quantity of reserves becomes a byproduct of the interest rate target rather than a binding constraint on banks' lending activities, as might be implied by reserve requirements.

The financial crisis of 2008 marked a paradigm shift in this operational framework. The advent of quantitative easing saw the BoE and other central banks embark on large-scale securities purchases, a policy designed to inject liquidity into the banking system and lower longer-term interest rates. As a result, banks found themselves awash with excess reserves – deposits that far exceeded the levels needed to meet reserve requirements or day-to-day liquidity needs. This environment – where excess reserves no longer incentivised banks to borrow reserves at the policy rate – meant that the market rate for inter-bank lending was far lower than the central bank's intended target.

In this new environment, where banks hold excess reserves, the traditional tool of open market operations to influence market rates becomes ineffective. To maintain control over the target interest rate, the central bank must instead remunerate those reserves, paying interest on the excess. By setting the rate paid on reserves, the central bank can establish a floor below which banks are disinclined to lend to each other, as they can earn at least that rate by holding reserves at the central bank. This mechanism of paying interest on reserves has become a key instrument for central banks to maintain their policy rate, even in abundant liquidity, ensuring that their monetary policy stance is effectively transmitted to the broader economy.

In conjunction with the Operational Standing Facilities (OSFs), the Reserves Account constitutes the cornerstone of daily liquidity management within the banking system, enabling financial institutions to deposit or procure funds to reconcile their overnight balance objectives. The Reserves Account is a pivotal node in the UK's monetary framework, allowing banks to manage their liquidity positions by holding reserve balances with the BoE. This facility assures that banks possess adequate reserves to meet their short-term obligations and payment system needs.

The OSFs serve as a complementary mechanism, providing a safety valve for the banking system by offering deposit and borrowing options. These options help banks manage unexpected fluctuations in their liquidity levels, ensuring that they can align their end-of-day balances with the BoE's requirements. By setting the rates for these facilities, the BoE effectively places a ceiling and a floor on overnight interest rates, framing the corridor within which these rates fluctuate.

Together, the Reserves Account and the OSFs are critical for the smooth functioning of the payment system and are integral to the stability of short-term money markets. They play a decisive role in disseminating monetary policy signals, influencing market interest rates and guiding them towards the policy rate set by the Bank's Monetary Policy Committee. This infrastructure ensures that the BoE's policy stance is accurately and efficiently transmitted throughout the financial system, affecting lending and borrowing behaviour across the economy and helping steer aggregate demand in the desired direction.

Short Term Repo (STR) operations are a critical tool used by central banks to ensure the provision of overnight liquidity to financial institutions, with the collateral offered as a safeguard. These operations are integral to the smooth functioning of the money markets — where short-term funds are lent and borrowed and where the liquidity needs of financial institutions are met. The STR mechanism allows banks facing temporary liquidity shortages to borrow against collateral, usually high-quality securities, thus preventing disruptions in their operations and maintaining the continuity of credit flows to the broader economy.

This facility supports the stability of the money markets, which, in turn, is essential for the effective implementation of monetary policy. By ensuring financial institutions can secure liquidity as needed, STR operations help maintain orderly market conditions and foster confidence among market participants. The availability of such liquidity provisions acts as a backstop against potential market volatility that could arise from sudden liquidity squeezes, ensuring that short-term funding rates remain aligned with the central bank's policy objectives.

Moreover, the STR operations serve as a conduit for the transmission of monetary policy, as the rates at which the central bank provides liquidity signal its stance to the market. This, in effect, influences the broader interest rate environment, impacting the rates at which financial institutions lend to one another and their clients. In essence, STR operations are a vital component of the central bank's toolkit, upholding the stability and operational efficiency of the money markets, which are the bedrock of the broader financial system.

While the immediate liquidity-providing function of STR operations may be less pronounced in an excess reserves environment with interest paid on those reserves, these operations can still serve strategic purposes within the central bank's broader toolkit for implementing monetary policy and ensuring financial stability. Even with plentiful reserves, STR operations may still hold relevance. They can provide a helpful backstop facility for financial institutions that, due to unexpected outflows or other idiosyncratic reasons, need overnight funds and prefer not to diminish their reserve holdings.

The Asset Purchase Facility (APF) is the BoE's primary vehicle for quantitative easing – a monetary policy instrument involving large-scale acquisition of government and corporate bonds. The rationale behind the APF is to influence long-term interest rates, easing borrowing conditions across the economy. By purchasing these bonds, the Bank injects additional liquidity into the financial system, which, in turn, tends to raise the price of bonds and lower their yield. This reduction in long-term interest rates is intended to stimulate economic activity by encouraging investment and spending. The opposite is true when assets are sold down in the APF, with quantitative tightening influencing long-term rates upward.

Financial Stability Tools

As orchestrated by the BoE, liquidity support operations constitute a fundamental safety net for the banking system. These operations are designed to provide a buffer against systemic liquidity shocks – unexpected and severe disruptions in the availability of funds that can cascade through the financial system, precipitating broader economic distress. Central banks deploy these mechanisms to assure continuous liquidity, thereby pre-empting the kind of cash shortages that can lead to bank runs, a freeze in credit markets, or even the collapse of financial institutions.

These operations typically take the form of short-term loans to banks secured by high-quality collateral. They are intended to ensure that banks have the necessary funds to meet their day-to-day operational needs, even during financial stress. By standing ready to provide liquidity, central banks aim to maintain the smooth functioning of payment systems and interbank lending markets – both critical to the day-to-day operations of the economy.

Moreover, Liquidity Support Operations serve to instil confidence among market participants. Knowing that the central bank stands ready as a lender of last resort can mitigate the risk of a sudden and disorderly deleveraging process, where financial institutions might otherwise rapidly sell off assets to meet their liquidity needs, potentially at fire-sale prices. This can help prevent a downward spiral where falling asset prices erode the value of collateral, further straining the liquidity positions of financial institutions.

In the broader context, these operations help cushion the real economy from the shocks that originate within the financial sector. By averting or alleviating credit squeezes, the central bank's liquidity support helps sustain the flow of credit to businesses and households, supporting investment, consumption, employment, and income. This protective layer is particularly critical during financial turbulence when the risk of contagion from the financial sector to the real economy is most pronounced.

The Discount Window Facility (DWF) is an integral conduit for short-term liquidity insurance within the financial ecosystem. This facility is specifically engineered to enable banks to weather transient episodes of financial strain, thereby mitigating the potential for such stress to metastasise into systemic instability. By providing banks with the means to borrow money against a wide range of collateral, the DWF offers a flexible lifeline that can be activated to address liquidity pressures.

The strategic value of the DWF lies in its capacity to reassure market participants of the availability of liquidity even in the face of adverse conditions. This assurance is crucial because it reduces the likelihood of individual banks engaging in precipitous asset liquidation to meet short-term obligations. This process could otherwise lead to broader market dislocations and a tightening of credit conditions.

In practice, the DWF enables financial institutions to discreetly access central bank funds, thus circumventing the stigma associated with emergency borrowing and the potential signalling effect such borrowing might have on market perceptions of a bank's solvency. This discretion helps to maintain market confidence and orderliness, preventing the kind of information-driven panics that have historically characterised banking crises.

Moreover, the DWF acts as a buffer for the banking system, absorbing the shocks of liquidity shortages and allowing banks to continue functioning effectively. This, in turn, preserves the continuity of lending and payment services that banks provide to the real economy. By ensuring that banks can navigate periods of stress without resorting to destabilising measures, the DWF contributes to the overall resilience of the financial system and its economy.

The Indexed Long Term Repo (ILTR) operation is designed to provide medium-term liquidity. By offering repos (repurchase agreements) that are indexed to the Bank Rate, the BoE ensures that the cost of this liquidity is coherent with its broader monetary policy objectives. The ILTR operations help smooth market liquidity fluctuations over a longer horizon than overnight facilities, allowing banks to plan their liquidity management more accurately. By calibrating the cost of these repos to the central bank's policy rate, the ILTR reinforces the transmission of monetary policy into banking and lending rates, thus permeating the broader economy.

In contrast to the regular and pre-scheduled ILTR operations, the Contingent Term Repo Facility (CTRF) is a responsive measure activated during acute stress. The CTRF is designed to provide an additional layer of liquidity insurance when markets are roiled by unforeseen events, offering banks access to funds against a wide array of collateral. The broad eligibility criteria for collateral under the CTRF ensures that liquidity support is available even when marketable securities become illiquid, safeguarding against the risk of contagion and the seizing up of credit markets.

Finally, the Alternative Liquidity Facility (ALF) is an example of the BoE's expansion of scope in catering to the liquidity needs of diverse banking operations, including those that do not engage in interest-based transactions. This facility reflects a nuanced understanding that financial stability is not just about the conventional banking sector but also about accommodating different business models, such as Islamic finance, which requires Sharia-compliant instruments. Through the ALF, the BoE provides non-interest-based liquidity support, ensuring that all segments of the banking system have access to necessary funds while adhering to their specific operational principles.

These facilities – each tailored to address distinct aspects of liquidity risk – collectively demonstrate the BoE's comprehensive approach to maintaining financial stability. They provide banks access to funds under various conditions and ensure that the Bank's monetary policy stance is effectively communicated and implemented across the financial system.

Monetary Policy Transmission Mechanism

The desired outcome is not immediately realised when the BoE raises interest rates to counter inflation. The transmission mechanism is non-linear and works through multiple channels. Monetary policy targets the demand for credit, adjusting the price of borrowing to influence the quantity of money issued by banks. It also influences government budgets, which have to offset escalating interest costs with cuts to other expenditures. In foreign trade, policy rates can influence the exchange rate in a free-floating currency, affecting imported inflation or deflation.

The wealth effect encapsulates the economic phenomenon where changes in the value of financial assets influence consumer spending and investment decisions. A key driver of this effect is the movement in risk-adjusted interest rates, which are instrumental in the valuation of future cash flows. When central banks adjust policy rates, there is a corresponding shift in these risk-adjusted rates, affecting the present value of future cash flows across various financial assets.

Bond prices, particularly those with longer durations, are immediately and acutely sensitive to changes in interest rates. This is because the fixed cash flows of bonds are discounted at the new, higher rates, which reduces their present value and, consequently, their market price. The impact on bond prices is thus direct and quantifiable, with the magnitude of price change inversely proportional to the change in interest rates – longer-duration bonds will experience more significant price fluctuations than those with shorter durations.

However, equities and real estate valuations tend to respond to interest rate changes with less certain temporal lags. For equities, the discount rate applied to expected future earnings adjusts as risk perceptions change, reflecting the higher cost of capital. As the market gradually integrates these revised risk-adjusted earnings expectations, equity valuations may adapt accordingly. However, this process is often less immediate in equities than bonds, as it is predicated on a complex set of expectations about future earnings growth, which may take time to recalibrate.

Similarly, real estate valuations respond to interest rate changes with a lag, but the transmission mechanism is more indirect and can be protracted. Higher interest rates can lead to increased borrowing costs for property purchases, potentially cooling demand in the real estate market. Yet, the effect on real estate values may be tempered or delayed due to factors such as the inelastic supply of property, location-specific demand pressures, and the time it takes for changes in borrowing costs to permeate the housing market. The duration and maturity profile of the outstanding mortgages play a crucial role in the effectiveness of interest rate policy on real estate prices. In countries like the US, where fixed 30-year mortgages are common, increases in interest rates may have the unintended consequence of reducing the supply of housing on the market as moving costs escalate for those facing a mortgage rate reset. In effect, the market value of a 30-year mortgage loan goes down as interest rates rise, which is a net wealth gain to the borrower. In countries where shorter maturities and floating rates dominate the mortgage market, rising mortgage service payments will reduce prices as distressed sales increase the housing supply.

Figure 9: Market Value of Pensions Decline as Interest Rates Rise[7]

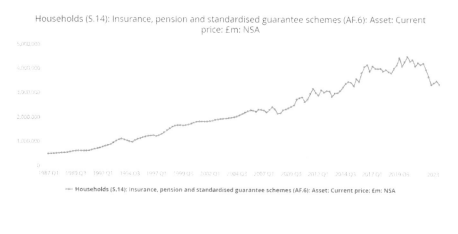

Households (S.14): Insurance, pension and standardised guarantee schemes (AF.6): Asset: Current price: £m: NSA

—▸— Households (S.14): Insurance, pension and standardised guarantee schemes (AF.6): Asset: Current price: £m: NSA

---

7 Office for National Statistics, "Households (S.14): Insurance, pension and standardised guarantee schemes (AF.6):

Asset: Current price: £m: NSA," September 29, 2023,

https://www.ons.gov.uk/economy/grossdomesticproductgdp/timeseries/npxp/ukea.

Figure 9 illustrates the impact of rising interest rates on the largest long-term financial asset for the *Households* sector, insurance and pension schemes. The effect of rising interest rates on pension wealth is immediate because fixed income's relationship with interest rates is a mathematical certainty. Equities' valuation also declined in 2023 as markets began to absorb the impact of the new rate regime on risk-adjusted returns. This decrease in pension wealth may not be apparent to its owners as the majority are defined benefit pensions, with very little adjusted for inflation. The wealth effect in this category may be more pertinent to those already in retirement.

Another intended consequence of monetary policy works through the interest expense channel, wherein adjustments to the policy interest rate by the central bank affect the cost of borrowing across the economy. If all loans and bonds in the financial system were subject to floating interest rates, then policy rate changes would immediately affect the interest expenses incurred by borrowers. This would swiftly influence consumer behaviour and business investment decisions, as the cost of servicing debt would rise or fall concurrently with the central bank's policy adjustments.

However, the reality is that the financial landscape is composed of a mix of fixed and variable-rate financial instruments, and not all debt is subject to immediate interest rate resets. This results in a lagged effect of monetary policy changes on the economy. The lag reflects the duration and distribution of maturing loans and debt securities due to be rolled over or refinanced. When these financial instruments reach their reset or maturity date, borrowers begin to feel the impact of the central bank's policy rate adjustments.

For monetary policy to achieve its desired effect on the economy through the interest expense channel, the scale of the interest rate resets on the horizon must be significant enough to overshadow the interest income channel. In other words, the alteration in borrowers' interest expenses must be substantial enough to alter net interest cash flows in the economy meaningfully. This dynamic underlines why changes in monetary policy often take time to percolate through the economy and why the central bank must carefully consider the timing and anticipated impact of policy moves. The effect on net interest cash flows is critical in determining how monetary policy can stimulate economic activity or cool down inflationary pressures.

Figure 10: Lagging Effects of Monetary Policy on Cash Flows[8]

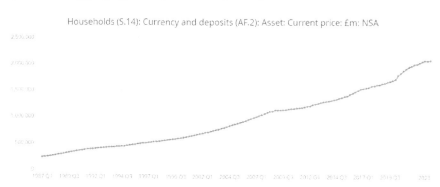

Households (S.14): Currency and deposits (AF.2): Asset: Current price: £m: NSA

— Households (S.14): Currency and deposits (AF.2): Asset: Current price: £m: NSA

Figure 10 illustrates the lagged effect of monetary policy on the quantity of Household currency and deposits. A significant portion of deposits in the banking system is characterised by zero maturity or short duration, which means they can be withdrawn without notice or mature in a short period. When the central bank raised interest rates in 2023, these deposits tended to benefit almost instantaneously from increased interest income. Savers holding these deposits received more income from their bank holdings, which offset any rise in interest rate expenses.

Linked to the cost of funding, the investment component of GDP is its most volatile component and is highly sensitive to interest rate changes. The demand for new investment is intrinsically linked to the cost of funding, which is directly influenced by the central bank's base rate. When the base rate increases, it translates into higher funding costs for borrowing, which, in turn, compels commercial banks to escalate the interest rates charged to

---

8 Office for National Statistics, "Households (S.14): Currency and deposits (AF.2): Asset: Current price: £m: NSA,"

September 29, 2023, https://www.ons.gov.uk/economy/grossdomesticproductgdp/timeseries/nirv/ukea.

their customers. This increment in the cost of borrowing is a critical factor that businesses must consider when evaluating new investments.

In an environment where the base rate is on the rise, companies that lack robust pricing power – that is, the ability to pass on increased costs to consumers through higher prices – may find themselves at a crossroads. Their profit margins are squeezed, making new investments less attractive or financially unviable. The higher interest rates affect the cost-benefit analysis of potential projects and increase the hurdle rates that investments must overcome to be considered worthwhile. This dynamic can lead to a contraction in demand for credit as businesses shelve expansion plans or delay capital expenditures due to the higher cost of capital. Such a pullback in investment activity can dampen GDP growth, as investment is a critical component of aggregate demand. Additionally, innovation and productivity growth will slow down and dampen the economy's potential output if businesses curtail investment.

Moreover, the ripple effects of reduced investment do not stop at GDP growth; they also extend to prices. With businesses investing less in capacity expansion and efficiency improvements, the economy's supply side can become constrained, potentially leading to higher prices in the long term. However, in the short term, the reduced demand for credit and investment can have a disinflationary or deflationary effect as less spending circulates within the economy.

Lastly, the monetary transmission mechanism operates through foreign exchange by impacting interest rates on international capital flows and the subsequent effect on the exchange rate in a regime where the currency is allowed to float freely. Interest rates are a pivotal determinant of investment attractiveness; higher rates in a country typically lure foreign capital seeking higher returns, while lower rates might deter such inflows. This dynamic becomes particularly pronounced in a globalised financial environment where capital can move swiftly across borders in response to changes in the yield potential.

When a central bank raises interest rates, it can strengthen the country's currency relative to others by attracting foreign investors looking for higher yields on investments such as government bonds. As these investors convert their currencies into another country's currency with higher rates, they increase the demand for that currency, thereby driving up its value. Conversely, when the central bank lowers interest rates, the relative attractiveness of assets denominated in that currency diminishes, potentially prompting investors to seek higher returns elsewhere and exerting downward pressure on the currency as capital outflows ensue.

The adjustments in exchange rates resulting from these shifts in capital flows have profound implications for the economy. A stronger currency can make imports cheaper and exports more expensive, affecting the balance of trade, while a weaker currency can boost export competitiveness but increase the cost of imports. These changes in the cost of cross-border trade can influence inflation, domestic production, and overall economic growth. However, the extent and nature of these impacts are not uniform across different economies, largely due to variances in their economic structures and reliance on international trade. For instance, the US economy, where net trade constitutes a relatively minor component of GDP, experiences a different degree of susceptibility to currency valuation changes compared to the United Kingdom, where trade represents a more significant segment of the GDP. Consequently, fluctuations in currency value tend to exert a more pronounced effect on the UK economy than the US.

Chapter *four*

System Control

Plato's Allegory of the Cave, presented in his work *The Republic*, remains one of Western philosophy's most compelling metaphysical and epistemological narratives. It describes prisoners who are eternally chained in a cave, only able to see shadows cast on the wall from objects passing in front of a fire behind them, and it profoundly illustrates the difference between the appearance of things and their reality. Between the prisoners and the fire is a walkway along which figures pass, casting shadows on the wall that the prisoners face. These shadows form the entirety of the prisoners' perceptual universe; they have no concept of the objects or the world outside the cave that casts these shadows.

One prisoner is freed and compelled to turn and face the fire, a painful and disorienting process. This initial exposure to the fire's light represents the first step towards a deeper understanding of reality. The prisoner is then dragged out of the cave into the sunlight, a complex and bewildering journey. Once outside, the prisoner is initially blinded by the sun's brightness but gradually adapts and begins to perceive and understand the real world – a stark contrast to the shadows on the cave wall.

The allegory concludes with the now-enlightened prisoner contemplating a return to the cave to free the others. However, having been accustomed to the brightness of the natural world, the cave is now blindingly dark to the prisoner. Upon return, the prisoner tries to share the newfound knowledge with the others. Still accustomed to the shadows, they reject and ridicule these revelations, unable to comprehend or accept a reality beyond their immediate perception.

This allegory is a profound metaphor for enlightenment and the journey from ignorance to knowledge, from illusion to truth. It speaks to the human condition — our quest for understanding and challenges in comprehending realities beyond our immediate perception. In the realm of economics, considering the cave metaphor can be helpful to understanding the complexities and often hidden nature of the monetary system and the behaviours of its participants.

As interpreted in this context, Plato's philosophy suggests that our understanding of money, much like his allegory of the cave, is a mere reflection of a deeper, more abstract reality. In this context, the physical existence of money is only the shadow on the wall, while the true essence of money lies in the collective belief and trust placed in it by society. This perspective is used to explore the idea that the perceived need of the Government to borrow money from the non-government sector is part of this shadow, an arguably necessary illusion within the broader economic system.

Money as a Social Construct

Chapter One examined the common perception that bank deposits are tantamount to physical currency, such as coins or state-issued cash. This view, however, overlooks the more substantive essence of money as a form of debt or a manifestation of trust. From an accounting standpoint, money is indeed categorised as another variety of debt — a liability counterbalanced by a financial asset on the financial sector's balance sheet. This treatment underscores the fundamental nature of money as an instrument of credit within the economy.

The unique position of the Government in the monetary system is particularly noteworthy in this context. Unlike other economic sectors, the Government does not balance its currency issuance in the conventional sense. This distinctive role stems from the sovereign's inherent legal authority, which includes the power to withdraw money from circulation via taxation. In the context of the British economy, this authority is exercised under the stipulation that only pound sterling is accepted for the settlement of tax liabilities. The government does not accept gold, foreign currencies, or any alternative forms of payment for taxes. This policy effectively reinforces the status of the pound sterling as the sovereign currency of the land. It underscores the Government's singular role in the monetary system, highlighting its capacity to regulate and control the nation's money supply.

The BoE's literature does acknowledge the mechanism by which loans create deposits in the system. In the accompanying Figure 11, the bank's 2014 Q1 Quarterly Bulletin depicts hypothetical proportions of different types of money in the balance sheets of the central bank, commercial banks and consumers. The figure is non-proportional to actual balances in the real world, only to illustrate the effects of creating new loans in the banking system. As denoted by (b), the central bank's balance sheet is simplified to include only base money liabilities and the corresponding assets on a consolidated level. In part (c) of the figure, commercial banks are assumed to have no previous liabilities before these new loans are made. All other economic sectors are denoted by (d) and labelled "Consumers."

Figure 11: Loans Create Deposits[9]

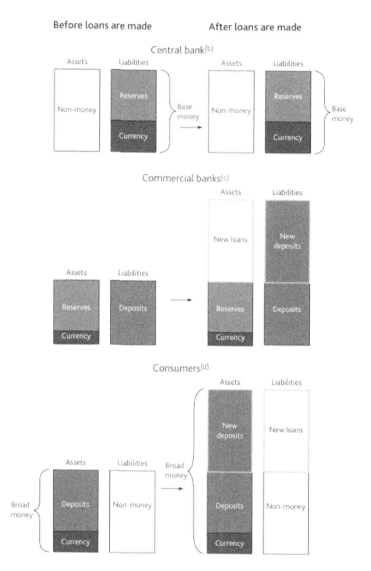

The prevailing official delineation of money notably excludes various forms of currency directly issued by the *Central Government*. This exclusion encompasses a range of instruments such as coins, national savings certificates, income bonds, deposit bonds, premium savings bonds, national savings stamps, and deposits held at the National Savings and Trustee Savings Banks. These instruments represent direct issuances by the Treasury, yet they are omitted from the conventional definition of money. Furthermore, this definition does not account for government bonds (gilts) held by the general public. While gilts held by the BoE are indirectly included, as they are used to counterbalance the zero-maturity bank reserves and currency issued by the BoE, the official stance categorises these gilts as "non-money," perpetuating a mindset rooted in the constraints of the gold-standard era, which views currency as an external commodity to be acquired.

While illuminating the debt-based nature of bank money, this depiction subtly implies that the Government's fiscal position is analogous to that of consumers or other economic sectors. However, within the discourse of MMT, government-issued debt instruments like gilts are conceptualised as a form of money. The differentiation based on the maturity profiles of bank deposits does not diminish their classification as money within this framework. In contrast, gilts, which essentially extend the maturity of state-issued money, are inconsistently disregarded as a form of money.

This book proposes a redefinition of money in a manner that aligns with MMT principles with a strategic intent. The reform plans advocated by the UK and US Green Parties aim to discontinue the issuance of treasuries and gilts, transitioning instead to direct money issuance by the Treasury. This approach diverges from MMT on the aspect of necessity, where MMT economists argue that the current system works and does not need reform. However, the Greens point out that the system has adapted additional layers of controls based on this erroneous premise, controls that work to constrain governments from implementing policies serving the public interest. The Green Parties only see gilts and treasuries as being recognised

---

9 Michael McLeay, Amar Radia, and Ryland Thomas, "Money creation in the modern economy," Bank of England Quarterly Bulletin 2014 Q1, https://www.bankofengland.co.uk/-/media/boe/files/quarterly-bulletin/2014/money-creation-in-the-modern-economy.pdf.

as forms of money by policymakers if there is a fundamental restructuring of the monetary system to make this fact self-evident. Advocates of MMT would stand to gain from a formalisation of the money issuance process, underscoring that this is a prerogative of the legislative bodies - Parliament in the UK and Congress in the US. This formalisation would clarify the role and authority of these institutions in creating and managing national currencies, aligning monetary policy more closely with public welfare objectives.

Consider the typical objections raised against financing social or environmental initiatives. The discourse often justifies inaction, citing concerns about "unfunded liabilities" or reckless fiscal borrowing. This framing of the debate is intrinsically linked to the prevailing conceptualisation of treasuries and gilts as "non-money." Such a perspective poses a significant impediment to mobilising funds for essential projects, such as those crucial for the green transition. The prevailing perception of money as an asset of the non-government sector, which the Government must ostensibly borrow, has been perpetuated as a "necessary lie." This social construct is deeply embedded in our economic functioning, but its necessity warrants scrutiny. This lie serves a critical purpose: it maintains the illusion of scarcity and restraint as a control system within the world of infinite money creation. Applying this perspective to the notion that governments issuing their currencies need to borrow to spend, we can view this belief as a control mechanism – perceived by many to be a vital part of the checks and balances within the monetary system.

From a philosophical standpoint, this is no different than Plato's Allegory of the Cave. This functional fiction can be viewed as a mechanism to safeguard against the potential abuse of monetary sovereignty. The belief in the need to borrow to spend imposes a self-regulating constraint on government actions, ensuring that fiscal policy decisions are made with a semblance of prudence and accountability. It creates a psychological and political barrier to unrestrained spending, which, if unchecked, could lead to inflation, currency devaluation, or a loss of market confidence.

This social construct also serves to depoliticise monetary policy to a certain extent. Framing government spending within the context of borrowing and debt repayment provides a narrative that is more easily digestible and less contentious for the public and politicians. It simplifies the complex dynamics of government finance, making it more analogous to personal or corporate finance, with which people are more familiar. It upholds an illusion of scarcity and fiscal restraint, acting as a control mechanism in an environment theoretically capable of infinite money creation. When viewed through this lens, the widespread belief that governments issuing their own currencies need to borrow in order to spend is revealed as a foundational element of system control. While ostensibly a safeguard, this control mechanism also constrains the Government's capacity to address pressing societal and environmental needs through direct fiscal interventions. Understanding and challenging this conceptual framework is thus essential for reorienting fiscal policy towards more progressive and transformative objectives.

Systems Theory and Feedback Loops

In the context of systems theory, the monetary system can be viewed as a complex, adaptive system with various interacting components and feedback mechanisms. Systems theory emphasises the importance of understanding how these components work together as a whole rather than in isolation. In a scenario where a government can spend without the constraint of borrowing, there may be a temptation to use this power for short-term political gains, potentially leading to long-term economic imbalances. Such a development could precipitate long-term economic distortions. Political actors, driven by the imperative of electoral survival, may eschew the essential yet politically unpalatable task of raising taxes to regulate the money supply. This tendency, rooted in pursuing political self-preservation, may supersede the broader public interest.

Within the context of systems theory, feedback mechanisms are integral to the preservation of a system's equilibrium and operational efficacy. The stipulation that governments must borrow to facilitate spending acts as a critical negative feedback loop within the monetary schema. This stipulation serves to temper governmental fiscal behaviour, ensuring that spending decisions are judiciously weighed against the potential ramifications of accruing debt and aligned with fiscal prudence and sustainability principles. Such a mechanism is instrumental in averting unchecked governmental expenditure, scenarios that could culminate in inflationary spirals or a deterioration of confidence in the national currency, thereby preserving the system's stability.

Furthermore, from a systems standpoint, the concentration of power is a risk that can lead to systemic failures. In this case, the centralisation of fiscal authority is identified as a potential point of systemic risk. The requirement for governmental borrowing inherently diffuses fiscal authority, incorporating an array of stakeholders, including legislative entities, financial markets, and international investors, into the fiscal decision-making process. This dispersion of fiscal power is perceived as a more accountable and transparent approach to government spending. It mandates that fiscal decisions undergo a process of justification and ratification, a process that is broader in scope and participation, thereby aiming to enhance the legitimacy and soundness of these decisions within the fiscal landscape.

This is how the monetary system's controls have been constructed, on the premise that gilts and treasuries do not constitute money. While MMT is correct on an operational level in describing the mechanics of money creation, the Green Party is right to critique the very tangible constraints imposed by these system controls. If a sufficient number of people accept them as reality – aided by academia, the media, and political discourse – they assume the force of truth. In this play, the Government is like a magician with the power to conjure money at will. Yet, there is a persisting fear that if this power were widely acknowledged and used without restraint, it could lead to an economic narrative fraught with hyperinflation and a loss of confidence in the currency. The "lie" of borrowing becomes a self-imposed constraint – a narrative device to keep the magician's power in check, ensuring the audience remains engaged, and the story of money in the economy being something outside government control remains believable.

Now, let's consider the impact of this narrative on the audience – the public. It shapes their understanding of government spending and debt, framing discussions around fiscal responsibility and national debt ceilings. It's as if the audience is watching a thriller where the stakes are high, and the tension is palpable, not realising that the script could be rewritten at any moment.

But this story has its plot holes. The necessary lie can lead to policy decisions that prioritise maintaining the narrative over addressing societal needs. Austerity measures, for instance, can be seen as the tragic consequences of adhering too strictly to this script, even when the scene calls for a more compassionate approach. One of the hallmarks of a sound system is its adaptive capacity and resilience. The constraint on government spending through borrowing requirements adds a layer of resilience to the monetary system to resist the politicisation of spending powers. Still, it obstructs the system's ability to adapt to changes in the economic environment, such as financial crises, which can lead to suboptimal decisions.

Behind the Shadow

So, what can we take away from this philosophical exploration of the monetary system? Perhaps it is that while this necessary lie serves to maintain economic stability and prevent the abuse of fiscal power, it also constrains our collective imagination and our capacity to address societal challenges creatively. It reminds us that the structures we navigate daily are not immovable truths but are, in fact, stories we have collectively agreed to tell. In this light, the monetary system – our stage – becomes a space where economic narratives are performed and where the lines between reality and fiction, truth and lie, are as fluid as the money that flows through it. And just like any good play, it invites us to question, critique, and imagine what other stories might be possible if we dare to rewrite the script.

Envision a hypothetical scenario wherein the BoE does not exist, where its operations and functions are subsumed into another government department and consolidated in the *Central Government*'s balance sheet. This is a reality in which the Government issues currency at varying maturities as the market demands, much like the service currently provided by the Debt Management Account Deposit Facility (DMADF). As a proof of concept that this more direct exercise of *Central Government* power to issue money at various maturities already exists today in the United Kingdom, the DMADF offers interest-bearing, fixed-term deposits to local authorities, and it is accounted for as liability on the balance sheet of the *Central Government*.

In this imagined scenario, bank reserve balances would be reclassified and appear as liabilities on the *Central Government*'s ledger, attracting interest at the policy rate determined by the Government. By dispelling the layers of complexity and recognising that a government bond (gilt) is fundamentally a government liability, just as a fixed-term deposit issued by the Government is a form of debt obligation, we gain clarity in our understanding of what state-issued money is. Despite their differing structures and purposes, both gilts and government-issued deposits serve as forms of money in their respective rights.

This conceptual exercise underscores the inherent similarities between various forms of government liabilities and the artificial distinctions often drawn between them. By simplifying and unifying these concepts under the umbrella of government-issued liabilities, we remove the veil of obfuscations and demystify monetary and fiscal policy operations. To proceed, let us look at what happens when consolidating the *Central Government*'s balance sheet with the BoE's assets and liabilities.

The bulk of assets on the BoE's balance sheet is composed of a loan to another entity called the BoE's Asset Purchase Facility Fund Ltd (APF). The central bank also holds gilts outside the APF and other minor assets in money market instruments, listed foreign government securities, loans and advances to banks and other financial institutions, and cash balances with other central banks. The government authorises the BoE to use the loan to the APF to buy high-quality assets issued by the Treasury. The APF also holds cash and a small allocation to investment-grade corporate bonds purchased to ease credit conditions in the aftermath of the 2008 financial crisis. The gilt assets in the APF are used to implement monetary policy objectives by buying and selling debt instruments on the open market financed by the creation of bank reserves in the system, a process central to setting the policy rates as described in Chapter Three.

The APF also makes gilts available for repo operations by the Debt Management Office's (DMO) cash management operations. This may sometimes involve the temporary creation of the specified gilt to meet the demand for a specific maturity, akin to providing a fixed-term deposit for a particular maturity. Without these operations, the banking system's capacity to offer bid and ask prices for gilts in the secondary market becomes impaired as dealers may be unable to deliver the maturities demanded by the savers in pounds sterling.

Any adverse market movement impairing the market valuation of the APF's assets is covered by a debt payable by the Government under the "HM Treasury under Indemnity" account. This guarantee to make the APF's balance sheet whole is another accounting obfuscation that hides the ultimate issuer of the currency liabilities. The bank reserves and notes in circulation on the liability side of the BoE's balance sheet appear to be backed by diverse financial assets, including the APF. In reality, the Central Bank can never be insolvent because the *Central Government* covers any negative capital by issuing more debt.

Certain debt perceptions are significantly altered in a hypothetical consolidated balance sheet, which aggregates the *Central Government* and the BoE. This consolidation diminishes the apparent volume of debt attributed to the *Central Government* while concurrently augmenting its asset base through claims on non-government sectors. However, it adds the reserve balances and notes in circulation as new liabilities.

As of the first quarter of 2023, the Asset Purchase Facility (APF) was valued at £843,736 million, comprising £7,067 million in corporate bonds, with the remainder distributed among gilts, cash holdings, and an indemnity provided by the Treasury. Additionally, the BoE's assets external to the APF included £17,739 million in other bond holdings and £175,925 million in the Term Funding Scheme for SMEs (TFSME). The foreign currency reserve assets, amounting to £11,578 million, were counterbalanced by £11,594 million in foreign currency public securities. The liabilities of the BoE comprised reserve balances and notes outstanding, totalling £908,804 million and £86,006 million, respectively.

A series of accounting operations are executed to merge the Central Government Balance Sheet with that of the BoE, as illustrated in Figure 12. This consolidation process results in a substantial contraction of the *MFI* sector's balance sheet, with a reduction exceeding £1 trillion in assets and liabilities.

Figure 12: Consolidation of Central Government and BoE

Central Government Balance sheet

Figures in £ millions: 2023 Q1

Assets	Liabilities
Debt Securities	**Debt Securities**
+ 7,067	- 836,669
+ 17,739	+ 11,594
+ 175,925	
	Currency and deposits
Currency and deposits	+ 908,804
+ 11,578	+ 86,006

Monetary Financial Institutions Balance Sheet

Figures in £ millions: 2023 Q1

Assets	Liabilities
Debt securities	**Debt Securities**
- 836,669	- 11,594
- 7,067	
- 17,739	**Currency and deposits**
- 175,925	- 908,804
	- 86,006
Currency and deposits	
-11,578	

In this consolidated view, the illusion that £836,669 million represents something other than money is dispelled, as the *Central Government* balance sheet now incorporates the increase in currency and deposit liabilities previously recorded on the BoE's ledger. Moreover, the Government's holdings in debt securities and foreign currency deposits experienced an uptick due to this consolidation.

The consolidation of the *Central Government* and BoE balance sheets sheds light on a pivotal aspect of monetary theory: the often-obscured true nature of money within the United Kingdom's monetary framework. This accounting "trick" – the consolidation of balance sheets – reveals a fundamental but frequently overlooked reality: money, in the context of a sovereign state, does not necessarily originate from external sources, contrary to popular belief. This understanding is particularly relevant for countries that operate with their currency, and it is the crux of the MMT argument: the consolidation of the Government and central bank balance sheets reveals the true nature of government debt as interchangeable with money. Both are the ultimate liabilities of the *Central Government*, and the choice of mix in maturities is a political choice that has more to do with setting rates along the yield curve than with debt management.

However apt this model may seem to be, it is crucial to note that the situation may differ for nations choosing to peg their exchange rates to an external currency or fund themselves in a currency other than their own – a decision that also stems from political choice rather than economic necessity. This distinction is crucial as it underlines sovereign states' flexibility and autonomy in their monetary policy, primarily when they issue and control their currency in a floating foreign exchange regime. The United Kingdom's failed attempts to maintain a peg in the European Exchange Rate Mechanism and subsequent abandonment of that policy in October 1990 is a case in point, where a fixed exchange rate regime turns the issuer of a sovereign into a user of a foreign currency. Similarly, the Eurozone countries' relinquishment of individual state currencies in favour of a shared supranational currency disrupts this model at the state level. In the context of the Eurozone, both MMT and the UK and US Green Parties' proposals for direct currency issuance would necessitate a comprehensive reform of their collective fiscal capabilities, specifically the establishment of a fiscal union empowered to engage in federal-level spending.

This discourse unravels the "functional lie" deeply entrenched in economic thought and public perception – that money must emanate from a source outside the Government. Traditionally, money is perceived as a resource that governments must gather through taxation, borrowing, or other means. However, this perspective overlooks that, in a sovereign currency system operating under a free-floating foreign exchange regime, the Government can issue the sovereign currency to achieve policy objectives as long as the economy has excess capacity to absorb the increased spending. The government, therefore, does not operate under the same financial constraints as a household or business; it does not need to "find" money, but rather, it creates it. When examining the *Central Government*'s liabilities, it becomes evident that what is often classified as debt or external obligation is, in fact, an issuance of financial assets for the non-government sector with a counterbalancing liability for the government sector. It comes into existence as the Government spends and is extinguished as the Government taxes. In this broader perspective, government debt can be seen less as an accumulation of external liabilities and more as a byproduct of the Government's role as the primary issuer of currency in the economy.

The Keynesian Perspective

The illusion that money is a private sector creation that the Government must borrow is also inconsistent with the later work of John Maynard Keynes. At the heart of this social construct is the evolution of central bank independence. In his seminal work *The General Theory of Employment, Interest, and Money*, John Maynard Keynes delved into the economy's dynamics and the state's role in monetary creation. Keynes laid the foundational ideas about government intervention in the economy, particularly in managing aggregate demand. This necessitated government deficit spending as a tool for demand management.

Keynes argued that when private sector demand is insufficient to achieve full employment during economic downturns, the state can and should intervene to stimulate demand. This can be achieved by increasing government spending, which, in essence, introduces new money into the economy. He theorised that such expenditures could have a multiplier effect, where an initial injection of spending by the Government leads to increased income and consumption, further stimulating economic activity. Keynes believed government spending needed to exceed its income, particularly during recessions. This notion implicitly involves the state creating new money or borrowing money to finance this spending, underscoring the government's unique position in influencing the economy's money supply.

However, Keynes also recognised the central bank's role as an arm of the state in managing the economy's interest rates. By adjusting interest rates, the central bank can influence the cost of borrowing and, thus, the level of investment and consumption. This is the primary tool through which the state can impact economic activity more immediately than waiting for the effects of fiscal policy to pass through to the economy. Throughout *The General Theory*, Keynes demonstrated a supportive approach to monetary policy, advocating for state intervention to correct market failures and stabilise the economy. This perspective acknowledges the state's significant role in shaping the monetary environment, though it stops short of explicitly framing the state as a creator of money.

Although Keynes's economic thinking evolved since his earlier work, and given his transformation by his experiences of the post-WWI period and the Great Depression, he did advocate for some forms of central bank independence in an essay titled "The monetary policy of the Labour Party," published in *The New Statesman and Nation* in 1932. He was motivated by concerns that the Labour Party's view on integrating central bank functions with the Government's would expose the management of money supply to political influences. The separation was intended to enhance the monetary system's controls over reckless spending, but this would soon become an undesired constraint as WWII demanded that these institutions be aligned.

Keynes always stopped short of directly conceptualising the state as a creator of money, but he exhibited an understanding of the state's role in creating demand by spending. Long gone were the days of the gold standard, where the Government constrained its capacity to spend to the supply of precious metals. His ideas about government intervention, deficit financing, and interest rate management all underscore the state's pivotal role in influencing the money supply and overall economic activity. His later writings also reveal his more profound understanding of the role of this fiscal power in creating inflation or deflation. In *The General Theory*, his primary motivation was fighting deflation by using the state's power to deficit-spend. As mobilisation for WWII took root, Keynes's concerns shifted from worrying about a shortage of demand to dealing with its excess.

In his 1940 policy pamphlet *How to Pay for the War: A Radical Plan for the Chancellor of the Exchequer*, John Maynard Keynes presented a fiscal strategy aimed at curbing inflation by augmenting the desire to save among the wealthier demographics, thereby reducing aggregate demand. Keynes wanted to avoid disrupting the economic mechanisms by immediately targeting tax increases during and after the war. In WWI, for instance, the US would eventually tax the highest income groups 94% to pay for the war effort. This approach bears relevance to contemporary economic challenges, where managing inflationary pressures remains a critical policy objective. However, challenges that can only be met with a greater government role in the economy demand either an increase in deficit spending or a rise in taxes. In modern times, the political discourse appears to overlook the potential of utilising fiscal policy to tackle the challenges by encouraging private-sector savings to dampen aggregate demand. This is especially useful in today's environment, where the state is withdrawing from the responsibility of providing the same generous pensions at old age for future generations.

Keynes argued that the accumulation of additional private sector savings would not precipitate an inflationary surge when released during periods of excess aggregate demand if incentives were given to save. He argued for government policies to provide incentives for the deferral of spending until the economy was no longer constrained by resource and labour scarcity. This perspective aligns with the cyclical nature of economic pressures; there have been phases where stimulating consumer spending was paramount to counter deflationary trends, and such phases will likely recur.

Keynes underscored that an excess stock of savings within the economic system does not inherently fuel inflation, barring their active circulation through expenditure. Suppose spending is postponed, particularly during high unemployment. In that case, these savings can serve as a counter-cyclical fiscal tool, with the additional income encouraging higher labour participation and increased productive capacity. In *How to Pay for the War*, Keynes elaborates on page 46:

> If the deposits are released in these circumstances, the system will be self-liquidating both in terms of real resources and of finance. In terms of real resources it will be self-liquidating because the consumption will be met out of labour and productive capacity which would otherwise run to waste. In terms of finance it will be self-liquidating because it will avoid the necessity of raising other loans to pay for unemployment or the public works and the like as a means of preventing unemployment.

This statement encapsulates the dual efficacy of this approach: utilising latent labour and productive resources while simultaneously obviating the need for additional borrowing to finance unemployment mitigation measures. More importantly, the Keynesian era displayed a pragmatic treatment of fiscal policy aligned with the real capacity for output in the economy. The language and terminology used to describe the monetary constraints for funding wartime efforts eschewed rhetoric about unsustainable debt or questioning the origins of funding. Instead, it focused on managing supply and demand to prevent inflationary pressures while operating the economy at full capacity.

Keynes, with his astute understanding of macroeconomic dynamics, would likely find the contemporary approach of austerity measures to address debt somewhat perplexing. From his perspective, such measures would be akin to squandering a nation's genuine wealth –

the idle capacity and potential of its workforce and resources. In his view, enforcing austerity is not just an economic misstep but also a neglect of a country's real wealth, favouring imaginary monetary constraints over the tangible, productive capabilities that truly underpin a nation's prosperity. For Keynes, the focus should always be on harnessing and maximising these real resources rather than fixating on the illusory constructs of monetary wealth. On this front, both MMT economists and the Greens are aligned.

Chapter Five

Unelected Technocrats

Central bank independence is justified as a mechanism for checks and balances of fiscal power. The established line of thinking emphasises that this independence cultivates a more democratically accountable and transparent approach to government spending. It mandates that fiscal decisions undergo a process of justification and ratification by trained economists. However, there are several issues with this line of thinking. 1) The process of selecting policymakers at the central bank is not democratic, 2) the monetary framework withholds resources from the Government to deal with an existential crisis like climate change, and 3) the fiscal power is diffused more broadly in scope than central bank decisionmakers, incorporating an array of self-interested non-government special interests such as banks, investors, and foreign governments.

Central Bank Power over Fiscal Policy

When Keynes argued for central bank independence, the BoE was a privately-held bank owned by private shareholders[10]. This independence ended after WWII in 1946 when the UK Government nationalised it. The debt accumulated during the war meant a permanent change in the money

---

10 Bank of England, "Who Owns the Bank of England?," May 19, 2020,

https://www.bankofengland.co.uk/explainers/who-owns-the-bank-of-england.

system, with a return to the gold standard becoming increasingly impossible. The BoE's role in issuing money by buying government debt became too important for the functioning of the state to leave it in private hands.

In May of 1997, independence was granted and enshrined in law as Parliament passed the BoE Act 1998.[11] Since then, the bank has set interest rates at what it deems to be the most appropriate level to realise its inflation target. It has specific legal responsibilities for setting interest rate policy, financial stability, and regulation of banks and insurance companies. The UK Government still owns it, but it carries out its responsibilities independently of the Treasury within a framework set by the Government, free from day-to-day political influence.

In the era following the re-establishment of central bank independence, there has been a noticeable reversion to a gold-standard mentality among politicians regarding deficit spending. This shift signifies a departure from Keynesian principles, where government spending was primarily viewed as a tool for regulating aggregate demand. Under this renewed gold-standard paradigm, money is perceived as a resource that must be obtained from the private sector before the Government can deploy it. This perspective fundamentally misconstrues the nature of money in a sovereign currency system and overlooks the state's inherent capacity for money creation.

The occurrence of major economic crises, such as the 2008 Global Financial Crisis and the COVID-19 Pandemic, has intermittently peeled back the curtain on the inner workings of the monetary system. These events have laid bare that when necessity dictates, the reality that the Government's capacity to create money is unfettered by the constraints of a gold standard or by the available stock of private-sector savings. In these instances, the necessity and ability of governments to engage in expansive fiscal policy, funded not by accumulated savings but through money creation, become starkly evident.

---

11 "Bank of England Act 1998," legislation.gov.uk, https://www.legislation.gov.uk/ukpga/1998/11/contents.

The BoE's mandate to maintain its monetary policy interest rate at its target necessitates intervention in the government debt market. When the private sector cannot absorb excess government debt issuance, the BoE must step in to purchase these securities. Failure to do so would lead to a problematic escalation in interest rates, undermining its policy objectives. This is the operational reality of how the BoE sets rates; it is not merely a matter of preference but a fundamental requirement to ensure the stability of interest rates and, by extension, the stability of the broader economy.

This is a critical aspect of modern monetary systems; central banks indirectly underwrite government spending in managing the policy rate, particularly during economic stress. This reality challenges the common view on government borrowing and spending, highlighting monetary and fiscal policy's interconnectedness in ways often obscured in more stable economic times. This power to print money becomes apparent only during severe crises that force the BoE to work with the fiscal authority to support spending at any level required to stabilise the system.

The capacity of central banks to influence interest rates across the maturity spectrum has been further evidenced through the implementation of quantitative easing (QE). This monetary policy tool, widely employed in response to financial crises and economic downturns, entails the central bank's large-scale purchasing of government securities, such as bonds. This action decreases interest rates in the short-term market and across various maturities, thereby influencing the broader cost of borrowing and investment in the economy.

The BoE's engagement in QE, while not as overtly targeted across specific maturities as some other central banks' policies, nevertheless demonstrates its substantial influence over the yield curve. For instance, the US, in the aftermath of World War II, and Japan, through its ongoing yield curve control operations, have more explicitly manipulated interest rates across different maturities. However, the underlying principle remains consistent with the BoE's approach: as the currency issuer, a central bank possesses the inherent ability to purchase government securities, including gilts, at any maturity. The central bank can influence supply and demand for these securities such that their prices and yields are at whatever level the bank chooses for them to be.

This capability is a crucial aspect of the central bank's monetary toolkit. By intervening in the market for long-term government debt, the central bank can effectively lower long-term interest rates, which are pivotal for business investment decisions and long-term financial planning by households. This broader control over the yield curve extends the central bank's traditional role in setting short-term interest rates and represents a more comprehensive approach to steering economic activity.

However, within its operational mandate, the BoE is responsible for addressing the inflationary consequences that may arise from excessive fiscal spending, particularly when such spending surpasses the absorptive capacity of the real economy. Should deficit spending foster an environment of overly robust demand, especially when the economy is already operating at full capacity and achieving full employment, inflationary pressures are expected.

In the framework of what has been termed the "functional lie," this scenario endows the BoE with a unique and indirect influence over fiscal policy. This influence is exerted through the central bank's control over interest rates, which, in turn, affects the cost of government debt financing. As the BoE raises interest rates, the incumbent political leaders are confronted with an escalating proportion of the national budget allocated to servicing new debt. This phenomenon is not immediate; an inherent lag exists before such interest rate hikes begin to impact government cash flows materially. However, once they do, they substantially influence fiscal policy decisions.

In this respect, monetary policy serves as a lever through which the central bank can indirectly prompt the Government to reassess and curtail other forms of spending. Political leaders become overwhelmed with a drive to reduce deficit levels to avoid appearing profligate and irresponsible spenders at a time of runaway inflation. The rising cost of servicing debt is a deterrence against additional discretionary fiscal expansion and necessitates more prudent spending decisions.

This interplay between monetary policy and fiscal spending highlights a complex dynamic where the central bank can indirectly steer fiscal policy through its interest rate policy. It underscores the delicate balance that needs to be maintained between stimulating economic growth and controlling inflation and between the role of the central bank in influencing the monetary environment and its duty to issue currency backed by the purchase of government debt. While ostensibly focused on managing inflation and maintaining monetary stability, the BoE wields significant power over fiscal policy outcomes. This power, exercised through interest rate adjustments, is a critical factor in the broader economic policy landscape, shaping the contours of government spending and influencing the trajectory of national economic policy.

The implication here is that this indirect power and influence of the BoE over fiscal policy, as delineated through its control over interest rates, raises critical questions about the democratic nature of economic governance. The core of the issue lies in the fact that the decision-makers within the BoE, who are unelected, wield considerable influence over the fiscal realm, a domain typically reserved for elected government officials. While not direct, this influence bestows significant power upon the central bank in determining the fiscal landscape, particularly in relation to aggregate government spending.

Given the relationship between interest rates and government debt servicing costs, adjustments made by the BoE can effectively dictate the fiscal budget available to the Government. When the central bank raises interest rates, the increase in the cost of debt can constrain government spending, acting as a de facto limitation on fiscal expansion. Conversely, in a low-interest-rate environment, the Government may find more room to manoeuvre, with lower debt servicing costs allowing for increased spending or investment.

This control system positions the BoE as a critical arbiter of fiscal policy, albeit indirectly. Such a role, however, conflicts with traditional democratic principles where fiscal decision-making is the purview of elected representatives and subject to public debate and scrutiny. Therefore, the central bank's influence over fiscal matters introduces technocratic oversight into a democratic process, raising concerns about the balance of power between elected government officials and unelected monetary policymakers.

Moreover, this situation underscores the interdependence of monetary and fiscal policy, challenging traditional notions of the benefits of central bank independence. While central bank independence is often advocated to insulate monetary policy from short-term political pressures, it also creates a scenario where critical aspects of economic policy are shaped outside the direct democratic process.

Private Money's Power over Central Bank

One school of thought among post-Keynesians explains the delineation of money from a transactional viewpoint as two separate circuits: one within the banking system and another for the general public. In his paper on "Split-circuit reserve banking – functioning, dysfunctions and future perspectives," Joseph Huber explains why the central bank must accommodate the banking system's needs for reserves to facilitate transactions between banks. For the most part, the general public pays and gets paid in privately created bank money – the exception being payments made with money issued by the central government, like coins and notes in circulation. Figure 13 illustrates Huber's split-circuit model of the modern monetary system.

Figure 13: Joseph Huber's Model of Split Circuit Theory of Money

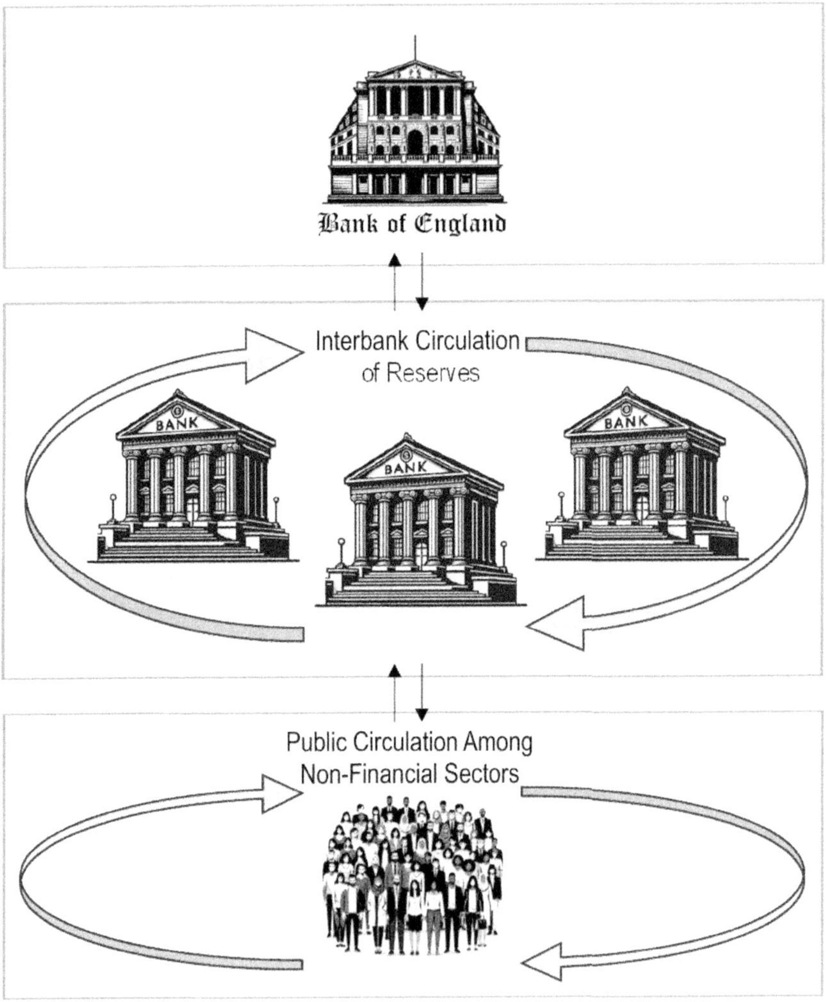

Firstly, it's essential to outline the traditional framework of monetary and banking systems, which includes the creation, circulation, deactivation, and deletion of money. Traditionally, it has been perceived that banks act as mere intermediaries in the financial system, gathering deposits to lend out as loans. This perception is rooted in theories like financial intermediation, loanable funds, and the credit multiplier. These theories suggest a simplistic view where banks gather deposits, which are multiplied through lending under the regulatory auspices of the central bank's reserve requirements (the reserve position doctrine).

However, advanced approaches to understanding monetary systems, such as chartalism, which emphasises the state's role in designating legal tender, and the concepts of endogenous and exogenous money, have somewhat disoriented this orthodox view, as described in Chapters Two and Three. These theories challenge the false identity of money and credit and the vague notions of where money originates. Bank reserves represent money issued by the state, but they do not influence the level of bank money issuance because the level of reserves is a monetary policy choice. The central bank has to accommodate the banking system's reserve requirements to successfully reach its interest rate target.

In the two-tier system formed by the central bank and the banking sector, a fundamental aspect often misrepresented is the split-circuit structure of reserve banking. This structure encompasses the public bank-issued money (bank money) circuit versus the interbank reserve circulation. Bank money consists of deposits in commercial banks, and reserves are part of a separate money circuit held at the central bank, which are non-exchangeable classes of money. In this modern economy, non-cash bank money dominates, with cash playing a residual role. The emergence of digital cash and blockchain technology further complicates this model as a modern equivalent to traditional cash, but their role remains small and can be ignored.

Since the general public does not use bank reserves for transactions, they are segregated as a separate circuit to settle transactions between banks. This is why the Green Parties often emphasise that bank money constitutes approximately 97% of the total money supply in modern economies. This conceptualisation of money diverges from the MMT terminology we have used in this book, yet it underscores the significance of the public money circuit as delineated by economists like Huber. To illustrate, in the first quarter of 2023, the total value of notes in circulation was approximately £86,006 million, accounting for a mere 1% of the currency and deposit liabilities on the *MFI* balance sheet. Including an additional £244,749 million of currency and deposits directly issued by the

Central Government, the aggregate of state-issued money accessible to the general public constitutes about 3% of the total bank money reflected on *MFI* balance sheets. It is important to recognise that the primary medium for everyday transactions in the general public domain is bank money, which originates as a byproduct of the credit creation process within commercial banks. This reality highlights the significant role that private banking institutions have over payment systems and monetary bookkeeping for people and businesses alike.

The creation of bank money is a joint process of crediting an account and extending credit. Here, it's crucial to note that the banks, not their customers, initiate this money-creation process by extending credit. This observation leads to a critical insight: banks, to a large extent, determine the money supply, and the central bank largely accommodates these decisions. This contradicts the traditional view that money creation is a linear process emanating from the central bank's money, which is then multiplied through banking activities.

In this framework, endogenous money is created within the economy by the banking sector, marking a departure from the traditional view of money as something external or exogenous. Both the banks and the central bank emerge as primary money creators, blurring the lines between endogenous and exogenous money. The money system is bank-led, with the central bank playing a supporting role by refinancing banks by providing the necessary liquidity.

The cooperative nature of bank money creation and mutual acceptance in the banking sector underscores a collaborative environment in the financial system. The process of account crediting and debiting for money transfers involves deleting and creating money, moving away from the straightforward intermediation model. Transactions are facilitated in real-time, and there is never an issue with insufficient reserves because the central bank must supply any requirement for reserves as a consequence of these transactions.

Payment systems are differentiated based on whether transactions occur within a single bank, requiring mere rebooking, or between banks, necessitating the use of reserves. The payment systems used by the general public are largely independent of central bank reserves, and they concentrate power to create money in the banking sector. Despite this, state-issued money cash transactions are still a necessary component in the system, but they constitute an increasingly smaller proportion of payments as bank money remains an extensive and largely independent privilege of banks.

Huber deliberately excludes government debt from his definition of money, focusing primarily on the role of money in facilitating payments. This role is dual: first, in transactions between banks, and second, in transactions between members of the public. Within this paradigm, the central government is effectively relegated to a mere user of bank money and a price-taker when issuing currency linked to sovereign debt. This is contrary to MMT's broader definition of money, but it is not the Greens' primary motivation for ridding the Government of indirect currency issuance. A further discussion on this point will follow in Part II of this book.

Huber's perspective portrays the central government not as a sovereign issuer of money but as an entity operating within the constraints set by the banking system. While it is acknowledged that the central government can generate reserves through spending and destroy reserves via taxation, Huber attributes it to a process of creation or deletion of bank reserves through the critical role played by the central bank. The central bank actively manages its portfolio of government bonds, adjusting it to align reserves with its target interest rate or by aligning with interest rates shaped by market forces. This alignment is a political choice, as the market-driven nature of interest rates is the outcome of central bank independence.

The rationale behind this market-driven approach is rooted in the interaction between the central bank and market expectations of future interest rates. Financial markets can significantly influence the Government's fiscal position by dictating the interest rates demanded on new debt issuance. This dynamic bestows a considerable amount of influence on private-sector money creation. For instance, expanding credit within the private sector can increase the money supply. This, in turn, can initiate a feedback loop where increased credit availability boosts profits, leading to improved credit ratings and further credit expansion, eventually leading to an overheated economy and higher interest rates. The reverse is true when a negative feedback loop precipitates contraction of credit, lower credit ratings leading to unemployment and excess capacity to push the economy further into contraction.

An overheating economy is characterised by escalating interest rates. Long-term rates ascend in response to anticipated policy rate hikes aligned with rising inflation, while base rates increase as a direct consequence of the central bank's efforts to rein in the burgeoning credit expansion. In this scenario, the central bank's intervention is not merely a monetary policy adjustment but also a strategic move to temper fiscal policy. The overarching implication of this model is the substantial influence wielded by private sector money creation. It suggests that while the central government and the central bank are significant players in the monetary system, their roles are primarily reactive to the conditions set by the dynamics of private money creation and market expectations.

A Case Study: The Fall of Liz Truss's Government

The fall of Liz Truss's government in the United Kingdom serves as a poignant example of the interplay between fiscal policy and the indirect influence of monetary institutions like the BoE and the broader financial sector. Following the announcement of Truss's government's budget, which included significant tax cuts and increased spending without clear indications of how this generosity would be financed, financial markets reacted negatively. This reaction was characterised by a sharp sell-off in gilts, leading to a rapid rise in yields and an increase in the cost of government borrowing.

This episode involving the BoE coincided with a brewing crisis in the Liability-Driven Investment (LDI) sector that was already under stress from rising policy rates. As interest rates increased across the yield curve, a situation exacerbated by market reactions to the fiscal policy announcements of Truss's government, the LDI sector faced panic liquidations in financial markets.

LDIs, often used by pension funds to match their long-term pension liabilities with long-term cash flows, were under pressure because rising rates prompted their counterparties to demand more eligible collateral to be posted for these contracts. Some market participants also misused these instruments to increase leverage because these derivative instruments allowed these managers to free up cash that would have been otherwise tied up in fully funded purchases of bonds. As interest rates rose, the valuations of these fixed cash flow obligations were repriced to much lower levels, and the collateral requirements to maintain these contracts overwhelmed the ability of these pension funds to raise liquid assets to post as collateral quickly. Margin calls ensued, and the selloff of these derivative positions threatened to turn a liquidity issue into a solvency crisis.

As interest rates rise, the valuations of pension liabilities decrease because most obligations are in the form of fixed defined benefit pensions. Simply stated, it takes much less capital to guarantee the same defined benefit cash flows promised to pensioners. Despite matching future liabilities with future cash inflows, the demand for liquid assets for collateral threatened to turn the panic liquidation of these positions into a solvency issue for pensions using LDIs as a cash flow management tool. These constraints did not arise from insolvency risks but from the immediate need for additional cash to meet margin requirements. In response, the BoE initially opted to provide time-limited liquidity support to the LDI market, with a clear deadline for withdrawing this support. This approach effectively compelled LDI participants to begin liquidating their positions, selling off bonds where they could, which exacerbated the uncontrolled selloff in the broader bond market.

The BoE's response to the LDI crisis illustrates the indirect influence that the market has over the central bank and the influence a central bank can exert over fiscal policy as a response to market-driven dynamics. The central bank indirectly influenced the broader fiscal and political environment by choosing not to address the LDI crisis primarily as a liquidity issue and by setting a firm deadline for its liquidity facility withdrawal. This action placed additional pressure on the Government's fiscal policy, as the market instability fed back into the cost of government borrowing and the overall financial stability, which are essential underpinnings of any fiscal strategy.

Consequently, the fiscal plans laid out by Liz Truss's government were destabilised by these monetary and market dynamics. The combination of a market-adverse fiscal announcement and the BoE's handling of the LDI crisis contributed to a loss of confidence in financial markets, triggering a political backlash that led to the eventual downfall of her government. The BoE found itself in an integral position in the unfolding political situation by influencing the actions of these institutions and using its monetary policy as a tool to coerce politicians to change course. The market's response to the fiscal measures introduced by Truss's government effectively tightened financial conditions, indirectly influencing the Government's fiscal policy. The increased cost of borrowing for the Government, driven by market reactions and the BoE's response, underscored the constraints imposed by the central bank's policy and market perceptions of fiscal sustainability.

The BoE, while not directly intervening in the Government's fiscal decisions, was nevertheless a central figure in the economic narrative that unfolded. The market reaction to the fiscal policy announcement and the subsequent limited actions by the BoE to stabilise the bond market highlighted the delicate balance between fiscal policy decisions made by the Government and the broader economic environment shaped by the central bank. This episode illustrates how fiscal policy does not operate in a vacuum, particularly in the context of significant changes or announcements. Instead, it is deeply interconnected with the monetary environment and the perceptions and reactions of financial markets, over which institutions like the BoE hold considerable sway.

Chapter Six

System Malfunction and Unintended Consequences

The argument for central bank independence often hinges on the premise that it provides a necessary check against the tendencies of governments to engage in excessive spending, thereby mitigating inflationary pressures. Yet, a historical examination reveals that the effective containment of inflation, particularly during the turbulent economic period of the 1970s, was achieved under a regime before the BoE attained independence. This observation suggests that stabilising inflationary trends cannot be solely attributed to this cause. Arguably, its independence has made it more susceptible to influence by the private banking system's interests at the expense of the general public.

Moreover, the political consequences of the existing structures, which integrate central bank autonomy with governmental fiscal policy, warrant a deeper analysis. There is growing evidence that the austerity measures, often advocated by independent central banks as a means to control inflation and stabilise economies, can inadvertently contribute to socio-political unrest. Austerity, while ostensibly a tool for economic stabilisation, can engender conditions of desperation and helplessness among the populace. These conditions, in turn, may foster the emergence of extreme political movements, as history has periodically demonstrated. The relationship between stringent fiscal policies, often influenced by the directives of independent central banks, and the rise of political extremism underscores the complex interplay between economic policy and social stability.

This advocacy for central bank independence, a cornerstone of modern economic policy, gained traction parallel to the rise of Neoliberalism within academic circles. This period marked a significant shift in the field of economics, which began to reinterpret Keynesian theory through the classical lens of Adam Smith. Under this new paradigm, money was conceptualised not as a fiscal policy tool but as a traded commodity independent of the state, a financial asset ideally backed by assets of intrinsic value, such as gold. This conceptual shift was a departure from Keynesian views of money as primarily a tool for managing aggregate demand.

This chapter delves deeper into the historical record and the consequences of undermining the state's fiscal power to address the needs of its citizens. The policy failures of the Neoliberal movement suggest that markets cannot solve every problem, and the state's fiscal powers must be restored to contribute to challenging economic, social and environmental goals that would otherwise be impossible to achieve in the current system. In reassessing the role of markets, it is crucial to adopt a broader perspective beyond maximising profits for the few at the expense of the many. Neoliberal policies have failed, and their impact on the wider socio-political landscape must be carefully reconsidered.

Neoliberal Takeover and Market Fundamentalism

The Cold War era provided fertile ground for Neoliberalism to flourish and eventually become the dominant economic ideology within academic circles. Its ascendancy was marked by a growing preference for market mechanisms and scepticism towards state intervention in the economy. This ideological shift gained momentum in the academic world and subsequently permeated political discourse and public policy. The rebellion against the Keynesian school of thought grew from a few literary critics to an avalanche of politically motivated purge that characterised the polarised world of that era. Academics were judged along a simplistic binary classification: they were classified as either pro-Communism or pro-Liberalism. There was little room for discussing the nuances of the state's role in ensuring social justice under a capitalist system.

Initially seeded in academic discourse, this ideological transformation gradually diffused into the broader realm of political rhetoric and policy formulation. A pivotal moment in this transformation was the widespread adoption in school curricula of Paul Samuelson's textbook, *Economics: An Introductory Analysis*, first published in 1948. Samuelson's work filled a critical gap in economic education by offering an interpretation of Keynesian economics more acceptable to the anti-Communist sentiment prevalent during the McCarthy era. The text sought to align Keynesian ideas with a market-oriented framework, emphasising the efficiency of markets and relegating Keynesian fiscal intervention to a special-case scenario within a self-correcting market-driven framework rather than a standard policy tool.

This shift was not merely an academic realignment but was deeply intertwined with the political dynamics of the Cold War. Samuelson's approach effectively compartmentalised Keynes's broader economic theories and took over the economic and political discourse on conducting fiscal and monetary policies. As Neoliberal thought gained traction, it manifested in a burgeoning chorus of academic critics who increasingly challenged Keynesian principles, advocating for greater reliance on market autonomy and reduced state influence in economic matters. For Samuelson, supply created its own demand, a notion that formed the basis of supply-side economics that underpinned Reaganomics in the 1980s. This perspective championed the power of markets and minimised the role of the state in economic management, a viewpoint that contrasted sharply with Keynes's understanding of the limitations of markets and advocacy for active government intervention to stabilise and stimulate economies.

The economic turmoil of the 1970s stagflation provided more ammunition for the political backlash against the state's involvement in economic affairs. However, as many of today's post-Keynesians would point out, this breakdown was the result of the US dollar's peg to the value of gold, a condition under which the MMT model fails because the state's debt is denominated in an external currency. This inflationary episode can also be traced back to the Arab oil embargo that fuelled cost-push inflation, which followed the breakdown of the Bretton Woods system.

Under the Bretton Woods international exchange system, established in the aftermath of World War II, the value of the US Dollar was pegged to gold, and other currencies were pegged to the dollar. This arrangement reflected a classical economic mindset that conflated money with a physical commodity rather than viewing it as an abstract unit of account or a tool for managing debt and economic activity. The Bretton Woods system was a hybrid one, attempting to combine the stability of the gold standard with the flexibility of fiat currency. By pegging the dollar to gold, the system ascribed a fixed physical value to the currency, thereby constraining the US's ability to respond to changing economic conditions or continue to fund its war in Vietnam without eventually devaluing its currency. The dollar's value was not merely a reflection of economic policies or market conditions but was tethered to the physical and finite resource of gold. This linkage imposed significant limitations on the capacity of the US and other countries within the Bretton Woods framework to manage their economies effectively under a Keynesian paradigm.

The collapse of the Bretton Woods system in the early 1970s, marked by President Nixon's decision to end the dollar's convertibility into gold in 1971, was a turning point. This decision effectively transitioned the global financial system to a regime of floating exchange rates, where the currency values were determined by market forces rather than their peg to gold. However, the transition was not smooth. The end of the gold peg unleashed significant volatility and uncertainty in currency and commodity markets, contributing to the self-reinforcing economic challenges of the 1970s, including high inflation and stagnant growth.

In academic circles, the experience of the 1970s was blamed on Keynesian economics instead of the US government's ill-conceived policy of pegging to gold at highly inflated levels. With its emphasis on demand-side management, Keynesian economics appeared to have caused the inflationary spiral with policies that advocated the reckless creation of money in excess of gold reserves available to back the new currency. The simultaneous occurrence of high inflation and economic stagnation strengthened the Neoliberal school of thought, which emerged as a seemingly potent antidote to the economic ailments of the 1970s. These policies, in stark contrast to the interventionist and regulatory stance of Keynesianism, advocated for a laissez-faire approach characterised by deregulation, the promotion of free markets, and a strong emphasis on monetarism. The latter, particularly the concept of controlling the money supply as a means to combat inflation, gained prominence as an alternative strategy for economic management. This shift was part of a broader ideological realignment favouring market solutions over state interventions.

Two schools of thought gained prominence during this period. Friedman's monetarism and Friedrich Hayek's Austrian economics offered distinct critiques of Keynesian economics and significantly influenced economic policy in the subsequent decades. Milton Friedman, a leading figure in the Chicago School of Economics, championed monetary policy over fiscal policy to regulate demand in the economy. He was critical of discretionary fiscal policy and advocated for a rule-based approach to monetary policy, contending that central banks should focus on maintaining a steady rate of money supply growth. Friedrich Hayek, a prominent figure in Austrian economics who had opposed Keynes for decades prior, was celebrated among the libertarian class for emphasising the importance of individual choice, market signals, and the limitations of government intervention.

Austrian economics, rooted in the work of economists such as Ludwig von Mises, blamed economic cycles on misguided government policies. Hayek criticised Keynesian economics for its focus on aggregate demand and government spending, arguing that such policies led to distortions in the market, misallocation of resources, and economic instability. Hayek's emphasis on free markets and scepticism of government intervention resonated with the growing Neoliberal sentiment of the time.

The geopolitical landscape further cemented this ideological shift. The fall of the Berlin Wall in 1989 and the subsequent collapse of the Soviet Union were interpreted as the definitive victory of market capitalism over the socialist economic model, which solidified the opposition against Keynesian economics as a wider and more general opposition to the power of the state as being incompatible with the empowerment of the individual. This event had profound symbolic significance, reinforcing the perception of Neoliberalism as the superior economic doctrine. In the context of this global realignment, Keynesian economics was increasingly portrayed as an outdated and ineffective approach, unjustly conflated with the failed economic system of the Soviet bloc.

The association of Keynesianism with the socialist policies of the Soviet economic model, although a misrepresentation of Keynes's theories, contributed to its decline in influence. This association overlooked the fundamental differences between Keynes's advocacy for government intervention to stabilise capitalist economies and the centrally planned economies of the Soviet bloc. Nevertheless, the prevailing narrative of the time underscored the perceived superiority of market mechanisms and a minimal role for the state in economic affairs.

In retrospect, had the US Dollar not been pegged to gold under the Bretton Woods system, the economic landscape of the 1970s might have been markedly different. Without the constraints of a gold peg, the US might have had greater flexibility to employ fiscal policy to address economic challenges more effectively. The classical thinking underpinning the Bretton Woods system – viewing money as a physical commodity rather than a flexible tool for economic management – limited the ability of countries to respond to the dynamic and complex economic realities of the post-war world.

The transition towards Neoliberalism and the embrace of market fundamentalism in academic and political circles had profound implications for economic policy and theory. It paved the way for the push towards central bank independence, reflecting a broader shift from Keynesian interventionism towards a more market-centric economic ideology. This transition marked a significant realignment in the understanding and application of economic principles, shaping the trajectory of monetary and fiscal policy for decades to come.

From Primacy of Markets to Central Bank Independence

The political successes of leaders like Margaret Thatcher in the United Kingdom and Ronald Reagan in the US during the late 1970s and early 1980s solidified Neoliberalism's political influence. Their platforms successfully tapped into dissatisfaction with the status quo and won public support for Neoliberal reforms, such as reducing the size of government and lowering taxes. Their political triumphs symbolised the consolidation of Neoliberalism's influence and set in motion a series of policy shifts that had far-reaching implications. The 1980s witnessed the implementation of extensive deregulation, privatisation of state-owned enterprises, and a focus on monetary policy as the primary tool for managing the economy. These policies were underpinned by a conviction in the efficiency of markets and a scepticism towards state intervention, reflecting a fundamental realignment in the philosophy guiding economic policy.

The trend continued in the 1990s and 2000s, regardless of which party was in power. The shift in economic thought permeated subsequent governments that traditionally had not aligned with such ideologies. Notably, this included the Democratic Party in the US under President Bill Clinton and the Labour Party in the United Kingdom under Prime Minister Tony Blair. The adoption of Neoliberal policies by these traditionally left-leaning parties marked a significant ideological shift and underscored the pervasiveness of Neoliberal thought in the late 20th century.

In the US, under the Clinton administration, Neoliberal policies were manifested through a series of economic and regulatory reforms. This period saw the continuation and expansion of deregulation, most notably in the financial sector, with the repeal of the Glass-Steagall Act, which had previously separated commercial and investment banking. This repeal was a quintessential example of the ideology's emphasis on market freedom and deregulation. The Clinton administration also embraced free trade agreements, such as the North American Free Trade Agreement (NAFTA), promoting globalisation and the reduction of trade barriers, in line with Neoliberal principles.

Similarly, in the United Kingdom, Tony Blair's Labour government, which came into power in 1997, marked a departure from the party's traditional socialist roots, embracing what Blair termed the "Third Way." This approach sought to reconcile left-wing social policies with right-wing economic policies. Under Blair, the Labour government continued several Neoliberal reforms initiated by the Thatcher government, particularly in market liberalisation and privatisation. The government maintained a strong commitment to fiscal discipline, emphasising the importance of controlling public spending and promoting private sector involvement in areas traditionally operated by the state.

Today, the British electorate is cynically pushed into a choice of conservative extremes, with little choice for those on the left. Arguably, the ascendance of the Green Party of England and Wales in recent years can be partly attributed to the perceptible drift of traditional left-wing parties, notably the Labour Party in the United Kingdom, towards the political centre, with the Starmer-led Labour acting increasingly like the old conservatives. This shift, often characterised by a departure from core left principles and a movement towards more market-friendly policies, has created a void on the political left. Consequently, a segment of the electorate without a political home, particularly those committed to progressive, socio-environmental agendas, has become increasingly disenchanted with this traditional bastion of left-wing politics. This disaffection has catalysed the search for alternatives that more authentically represent their values and aspirations, leading to a surge in the popularity of the Green Party. With their strong emphasis on environmental issues, social justice, and anti-austerity measures, the Greens have effectively captured the imagination and support of those who perceive the mainstream left as having forsaken its foundational ideals in pursuit of broader electoral appeal. This phenomenon underscores a significant realignment within the political left, signalling a profound shift in favour of the Greens for their unambiguous and unwavering commitment to progressive policies.

The Green Party of England and Wales has achieved significant electoral success in recent local elections, marking a notable expansion of its political influence across numerous local authorities. The party now boasts 547 councillors across 167 local councils, reflecting a substantial net gain of 124 seats, including 78 seats previously held by Labour, Conservative, Liberal Democrat, and Independent representatives. Notably, the Green Party outperformed Labour with seat gains in England and exhibited the highest percentage increase in seats among all parties in England and Wales. In Wales, the party also witnessed historic victories, securing eight seats in councils including Newport, Monmouthshire, and Neath Port Talbot, among others. These results have positioned the Greens as the second-largest party in several councils, including Exeter, South Tyneside, Reading, St Helens, and Reigate & Banstead.[12]

The electoral advancements of the Green Party signal a shift in the political landscape, reflecting a growing public demand for alternative approaches to governance and policy-making. This change in political support is particularly stark when contrasted with the entrenched Neoliberal ideologies that have dominated the economic and political spheres for decades. This trend may culminate in revisiting some sacrosanct tenants of the monetary system, including central bank independence. Central bank independence, granted under the Tony Blaire government in 1997, was pivotal in embracing these Neoliberal principles. The belief in the efficiency of markets, a cornerstone of Neoliberal ideology, played a crucial role in this decision, and it was emblematic of a broader trend towards depoliticising monetary policy and reinforcing the primacy of market mechanisms in economic governance.

The rationale for central bank independence is deeply rooted in Neoliberal economic thought, which argues that monetary policy should be insulated from political influence to ensure its sole focus on controlling

---

12 Green Party, "Greens celebrate record breaking results as party breaks 500 councillors mark across England and Wales," press release, 6 May 2022, accessed 2 December 2023,

https://www.greenparty.org.uk/news/2022/05/06/greens-celebrate-record-breaking-results.

inflation and maintaining price stability. Monetary policy was no longer a state policy tool and was to be subservient to markets. The argument follows a belief that political actors, driven by electoral cycles and short-term objectives, might be inclined to pursue expansionary monetary policies that could lead to long-term economic instability. Therefore, by granting independence to the central bank, the decision-making process concerning monetary policy could be entrusted to technocratic experts who are ostensibly free from political pressures and who would base their decisions on economic data and market signals.

The move to grant the BoE operational independence allowed it to set interest rates without direct political interference, marking a significant shift in the UK's approach to monetary policy. It reflected a broader confidence in the ability of markets, and by extension, market-oriented institutions like independent central banks, to efficiently allocate resources and manage economic cycles. This decision was influenced by the perceived success of other independent central banks, notably the Federal Reserve in the US, in managing inflation and contributing to economic stability.

However, this shift also raised questions about democratic accountability and transparency in economic policymaking. While central bank independence was seen as a means to shield monetary policy from short-term political considerations, it also distanced the process of critical economic decision-making from democratic oversight. Critics argued that such a move could lead to a disproportionate focus on inflation control at the expense of other economic objectives, such as employment, growth, and reducing inequality. Independence to the BoE represented a significant realignment in economic governance, positioning the central bank as a quasi-autonomous entity guided by market principles and expert judgement rather than the political objectives of elected officials.

Throughout the 1980s and 1990s, the so-called "Washington Consensus" emerged as a standard policy advice for crisis-wracked developing countries, prescribing privatisation, deregulation, and trade liberalisation, further entrenching Neoliberalism. The apparent early success of Neoliberal policies – rapid growth in global GDP and financial valuations, the initial revival of economies that implemented substantial reforms, and the creation of new markets – added to its allure and reinforced its dominance as the go-to economic strategy. By the 1990s, the principle of central bank independence had become a global policy trend, endorsed by international institutions such as the IMF and the World Bank. Countries worldwide reformed their monetary institutions to align with this Neoliberal policy prescription, viewing it as a necessary step for integration into the global financial system and attracting foreign investment.

This combination of academic dominance, political momentum, and institutional push made Neoliberalism the compelling and oft-unchallenged paradigm for economic and social policy during the latter part of the 20th century. Its initial success and the fervour with which it was promoted effectively sidelined other economic philosophies for a significant time until the Global Financial Crisis of 2008 (GFC) exposed the fallacies of its resistance to demand-side intervention.

Failure of Monetarism

In the decades preceding the GFC, there was a concerted effort to reduce what was termed "Fiscal Dominance," a concept premised on the notion that fiscal policy should not exert undue influence over monetary policy. Central banks were charged with maintaining this regulatory role at a distance from direct political influence, ostensibly to ensure objectivity and effectiveness in monetary policy. However, the practical outcome of this approach was a policy mix that often skewed towards austerity measures, disproportionately impacting those least able to bear such burdens.

Implementing these policies frequently resulted in a concentration of financial resources to systemically important institutions, notably the banks, while neglecting the needs of individuals most affected by economic crises. Subprime borrowers during the GFC are a case in point; these homeowners paid the price for the irresponsible lending practices of the financial sector. The increase in government debt in the aftermath of financial sector bailouts triggered a political drive to re-establish government debt-to-GDP ratios to the levels prevailing before the GFC. This approach tolerated high levels of unemployment and maintained a fixation on fiscal prudence at the expense of broader economic and social well-being.

One of the most striking consequences of this policy mix was the exacerbation of income and wealth inequality. The steadfast commitment to Neoliberal principles, including the prioritisation of monetary policy over fiscal interventions and the reluctance to engage in substantial demand-side stimulus, contributed to a widening economic divide. This situation was further compounded by the bailout of financial institutions during the GFC, which contrasted sharply with the lack of substantial support for those directly affected by the housing market collapse. Could governments have bailed out the banks by assisting homeowners in making their mortgage payments instead of providing direct central bank funding to the banks? As the Greens rightly explain, a failure to regulate the private credit expansion caused the problem in the first place.

Fast forward to 2020, and the COVID-19 pandemic further exposes the fallacies and limitations inherent in Neoliberal economics. The pandemic, escalating into a global crisis, further underscored the critical need for robust government intervention. This was a challenge to core Neoliberal tenets, and it witnessed the rise of MMT as an alternative model for managing the state's role in economic affairs. Despite MMT's successes in guiding US policy, conservative voices continue to dominate the UK media and control the political narrative to restore minimal state involvement, market self-regulation, and fiscal austerity.

The pandemic highlighted the indispensable role of government in managing public health emergencies. Neoliberal economics, with its emphasis on reduced government spending and privatisation, has often led to under-investment in public health infrastructure and services. The COVID-19 crisis demonstrated the necessity of a well-funded and efficient public health system, which many countries found lacking due to years of adherence to small-state policies. The economic shutdowns implemented to contain the spread of the virus resulted in a massive and sudden contraction in economic activity. In this scenario, traditional Neoliberal approaches proved inadequate, such as tight fiscal policy and reliance on the private sector to drive recovery. Governments worldwide were compelled to enact large-scale fiscal stimulus measures, including direct financial support to businesses and individuals, to mitigate the economic fallout. This intervention was antithetical to Neoliberal prescriptions but proved essential in stabilising economies and providing a lifeline to millions affected by the pandemic.

The fiscal response and Russia's invasion of Ukraine put Monetarism's doctrines to the test. The monetary tightening that followed did not target the economy most equitably. What effectively happened is that the burden of interest rate hikes fell on the poorer and younger households. Those who could take advantage of lower rates would typically lock them in for several years, insulating them from rate shocks. Floating-rate mortgages, ostensibly cheaper for the younger and poorer households, expose these classes to interest rate risk. The government policy of "Right to Buy" is partly to blame for increasing the debt burden for the fundamental right to shelter, as the least privileged segments of society barely squeeze through the minimum thresholds needed to make the initial purchase, accepting variable rates to reduce their initial costs. Looking at the interest rate channel in isolation, more affluent households benefit from rising rates because it bolsters their interest income. Those who could not afford the fixed rates bear a disproportionate share of the pain.

The pandemic also laid bare the deep inequalities and vulnerabilities within societies, which Neoliberal policies had often exacerbated. The crisis disproportionately affected lower-income groups and highlighted the fragility of many individuals and families who lacked adequate social safety nets, a direct consequence of years of austerity and welfare retrenchment. This realisation prompted a re-evaluation of social spending and the state's role in providing social security. The experience with this extensive governmental response to the pandemic prompted a rethinking of the state's role in the economy. The rapid and effective deployment of fiscal resources to support healthcare systems, businesses, and individuals underscored the capacity and responsibility of the state to manage large-scale crises. This experience contrasted sharply with the

Neoliberal advocacy for a reduced state role. It prompted discussions about the need for a more balanced approach to the relationship between the state, markets, and society.

Wealth and Income Inequality

In a profound shift from previous optimism, very few people today are confident that their lives – or those of their children or grandchildren – will be better than their own. In *False Dawn: The Delusions of Global Capitalism*, John Gray criticises both extremes of Marxist and modern Neoliberal ideologies for disregarding the casualties of their versions of progress. In post-WWII Britain and other Western countries where social democracy reigned, there was a time when capitalism was restrained, and the state played a role in moderating inequality and reinforcing social cohesion. This approach was informed by direct experiences of the 1930s and the war, leading to a political consensus that unchecked capitalism can lead to severe societal and political consequences, including the rise of fascism and other forms of right-wing extremism.

By the late 1970s, the global environment of capitalism shifted, leading to a loss of this moderation. Notable figures like Margaret Thatcher had a vision of the traditional British society they wanted to rebuild – primarily based on a pre-existing national culture – but paradoxically, the economic policies they implemented dismantled the very societal structures they aimed to preserve. The wholesale privatisation of iconic British institutions and assets only eroded their British identity as they were absorbed into global multinationals and came under the ownership of international shareholders. Today's right-wing backlash is a response to this erosion of national identity that became prevalent in the Neoliberal internationalist order.

The postwar consensus, rooted in Keynesian economics, advocated for a regulated capitalist economy buttressed by social safety nets to mitigate the extremes of poverty and prevent economic crises. This framework assumed that government intervention was essential in managing economic cycles and safeguarding social welfare. However, the ascent of Neoliberal thought gradually eroded this consensus, championing an unrestrained capitalist model where market forces, purported to be self-regulating, would ostensibly lead to optimal outcomes for society. Far from leading to optimal outcomes, the dismantling of the welfare state and financial safety nets led to social inequities that were further exacerbated by financial deregulation and market liberalisation.

The Keynesian approach was characterised by a belief in the positive role of state intervention, fiscal policies to stimulate demand, and regulatory oversight of financial markets. It reflected a world recovering from the economic calamities of the 1920s and 1930s, aiming to prevent the recurrence of such disasters. As detailed in earlier sections of this book, the Neoliberal transformation, rooted in the writings of figures like Friedrich Hayek and Milton Friedman and actualised by political leaders such as Margaret Thatcher and Ronald Reagan, presented a radically different notion. They argued that economic activities should be liberated from state-centric constraints to unleash innovation and drive growth.

The transformation of global economic policy and practice under the influence of Neoliberalism unfolded through a multifaceted and gradual process, reshaping the landscape of international finance, market operations, and state involvement in the economy. Central to this transformation was the sweeping deregulation of financial markets. This movement is premised on the belief that unrestricted capital flows would be a universal boon, facilitating a global integration of financial systems. However, it also introduced heightened volatility and vulnerability to financial crises, as witnessed in the late 20th and early 21st centuries.

Simultaneously, Neoliberalism championed the liberalisation of markets, extending the reach of globalisation. Sectors previously operated under national protections were exposed to international competition, ostensibly to foster efficiency and consumer choice. While this process did integrate global markets and economies, it also had significant repercussions for domestic industries. In many cases, the opening of markets led to the disruption of traditional manufacturing bases and the rise of precarious employment conditions as firms sought to maximise profits in an increasingly competitive and globalised marketplace.

The privatisation of state assets was another hallmark of the Neoliberal era. Driven by the argument that the private sector was more efficient than the public sector, this policy saw the transfer of ownership of various state enterprises and services to private entities. While aimed at reducing public expenditure and ostensibly improving service quality, privatisation often led to increased costs for essential services like utilities, education, healthcare, and housing. This shift not only commodified public goods but also contributed to widening socio-economic disparities, as the benefits of market operations increasingly favoured capital owners and high-income earners, leaving behind the majority for whom real wage growth stagnated.

These Neoliberal policies collectively contributed to the erosion of social safety nets and a weakening of mechanisms designed to ensure economic stability and equitable growth. Reduced state intervention in labour markets and social services and a diminished focus on industrial policy often failed to mitigate negative externalities such as job insecurity, loss of traditional industries, and inadequate social protection. Globalisation, as pursued under Neoliberal policies, often disproportionately benefited a narrow segment of society, contributing to growing inequality and a sense of disenfranchisement among large swathes of the population. This sentiment, in turn, has fuelled populist backlashes in various countries as people reacted against what they perceived as an economic order that favoured the elite at the expense of the broader populace.

Furthermore, the inclination towards fiscal austerity, a core aspect of Neoliberal reform, reduced public investment in critical areas such as infrastructure, education, and research. This retrenchment potentially stifled innovation and long-term economic growth, as under-investment in these critical areas can have far-reaching impacts on a nation's economic potential.

A case in point is Norway, a country that has a long tradition of democratic socialism, which has proven to be far superior to the Neoliberal dystopia that many Western nations find themselves grappling with. After discovering oil in the North Sea, Norway enjoyed decades of boom as it pursued a different strategy of subsidising and protecting its local industries. Under Thatcher, market forces were let loose on the industrial North, embracing globalisation and the financialisation of the economy. The financial sector grew at the expense of manufacturing output. An analysis of the Organisation for Economic Co-operation and Development (OECD) data positioned the United Kingdom at a modest 20th place in terms of real GDP per capita, descending from 10th place in 1979. Income inequality was visibly worse and ranked in 9th place. This ranking situates Britain as a nation grappling with relatively pronounced economic disparities and declining per capita output, starkly contrasting Norway's success during the same period.

In a detailed examination by John Burn-Murdoch, a journalist for the Financial Times, evidence is presented that the affluent segments of British society continue to prosper while lower-income groups continue to languish. For instance, in the pre-COVID-19 era of 2019, the income levels of the top 10% of households in the UK and Germany were comparable, each exceeding $120,000 when measured in US dollars at 2020 purchasing power parity. However, a stark contrast emerges at the lower end of the income spectrum. In the UK, the bottom 5% of the population had incomes averaging around $15,900, which was over 20% lower than their counterparts in Germany.

The implications of these findings are significant, underscoring the challenges faced by policymakers in addressing the widening economic divide. It is not enough to pursue headline GDP growth and make the Government subservient to financial interests at every opportunity. The persistence of such inequality poses profound questions about the sustainability of the current economic model and the efficacy of existing policies in promoting equitable growth and prosperity, arguably providing a more lasting basis for a nation's overall economic health.

Privatising Profits and Socialising Losses

The irony of the Neoliberal approach is that market solutions are championed until they go awry, externalising costs to society and the environment. Unfettered market fundamentalism, where profits are privatised and the risks of market activities are socialised, does not increase wealth at the national level. It results in a skewed economic system that exacerbates inequality and undermines the social fabric; it results in damage to the ecosystem and an unquantifiable cost to future generations. The general public bears the costs of environmental damage, bailouts and economic downturns, while the profits from these market activities are privatised, accruing predominantly to a wealthy minority.

One of the most significant manifestations of this policy is the operation of public services such as railways, electricity, sewage, and water as private enterprises. This privatisation masks the true costs borne by the general public. While priding itself on fiscal discipline, Neoliberalism often places the balancing of the Government's financial books above all other considerations. This has led to wholesale liquidation of the state's real assets to create over-leveraged, profit-seeking private and foreign-owned companies. It is an incongruity of the system that ownership of public infrastructure by limited-liability debt-ridden private entities, often based in tax havens, is considered more efficient than state ownership aimed at the public interest. It is a recipe for disaster to place the profit motive of these increasingly international entities above all considerations for the nation's public health, well-being, and social justice.

The argument for privatisation rests on a seemingly straightforward premise: that markets, driven by profit motives and disciplined by competition, achieve greater efficiency and innovation than state-run entities. However, the empirical evidence from the British privatisation experience presents contrary evidence of unintended consequences and the persistence of market failures that challenge the neat boundaries of economic theory.

In implementing this vision, both Tory and Labour governments had to rely heavily on regulatory frameworks to manage market failures. For instance, OFGEM's mandate was to husband energy market competition as a bulwark against the dominance of any single player. However, the pursuit of competition occasionally came at the expense of other goals, such as supplier resilience, leading to situations where, in the wake of the Russo-Ukraine conflict's energy price spikes, the market saw a swathe of bankruptcies amongst smaller energy firms, like the emblematic collapse of Bulb, with taxpayers shouldering the staggering £6.5 billion exodus. The regulators can barely catch their breath with numerous acts of energy price manipulation, overcharging, fraud, and profiteering from the plight of the poorest segments of society. The question for Neoliberal thinkers should be: what makes you sure that privatisation of public infrastructure will work to reduce costs in the future when it has had such a dismal record in the past? A quick scan of the headlines in 2023 reveals many nefarious actors in the energy sector:

- 14 August 2023: "Rogue energy brokers spark £2.5 billion worth of compensation claims"[13]

- 25 July 2023: "Liars and manipulators: the energy dealmakers overcharging small firms, charities, care homes and others"[14]

- 8 April 2023: "The scandal of UK prepayment gas and electricity meters"[15]

---

13 Chris Choi, "'Rogue' energy brokers spark £2.5 billion worth of compensation claims," *ITV News*, 14 August 2023, accessed 16 December 2023, https://www.itv.com/news/2023-08-14/energy-scandal-fears-as-brokers-accused-of-inflated-charges-and-secrecy.

14 Jillian Ambrose, "'Liars and manipulators': the energy dealmakers overcharging small firms," *The Guardian*, 25 July 2023, accessed 16 December 2023, https://www.theguardian.com/business/2023/jul/25/energy-brokers-small-firms-commissions.

15 Eric Albert, "The scandal of UK prepayment gas and electricity meters," *Le Monde*, 8 April 2023, accessed 16 December 2023, https://www.lemonde.fr/en/united-kingdom/article/2023/04/08/the-scandal-of-uk-prepayment-gas-and-electricity-meters_6022121_135.html.

- 23 March 2023: "Consumers Foot the Bill for Traders 'Manipulating' UK Power Market"[16]

These are only those caught in the acts of wrongdoing, with many corporations getting away with activities that can only harm the national interest. The brazen, nefarious activities in this sector warrant a critical societal conversation about the private operation of our energy infrastructure. Individuals can be banned from working in a profession on ethical grounds or even go to jail, but the limited liability structure of corporations has allowed them to evade similar accountability, allowing them to siphon off billions from consumers and taxpayers without facing a ban on operating in the same markets. The advertised market efficiencies that Neoliberals sold to the public have yet to materialise in any benefit to society. In many ways, the energy sector has been plagued by anti-competitive practices, as one Bloomberg investigation reveals:

> *Traders at firms* including Vitol's VPI, Uniper SE and SSE Plc have frequently announced they would cut off electricity capacity — sometimes with just a few hours' notice – ahead of the busiest evening periods. At the same time, they offered power from their plants in a special side market *where they charged higher prices to meet the shortfalls they helped create.*[17]

The 2021-2022 energy crisis epitomises the perils of privatising the UK energy sector, exposing the vulnerabilities and drawing parallels between this crisis and the GFC, particularly with the lapses in regulatory oversights and systemic fragility. The crisis, marked by unprecedented gas price hikes, exposed the UK's over-reliance on profit-maximising just-in-time gas supplies and inadequate storage capacities, leaving it susceptible

---

16 Gavin Finch, Jason Grotto, and Todd Gillespie, "Consumers Foot the Bill for Traders 'Manipulating' UK Power Market," *Bloomberg*, 23 March 2023, accessed 16 December 2023, https://www.bloomberg.com/graphics/2023-uk-power-electricity-market-manipulating/?sref=qvMYxUts.

17 Gavin Finch, Jason Grotto, and Todd Gillespie, "Consumers Foot the Bill for Traders 'Manipulating' UK Power Market," Bloomberg, 23 March 2023, accessed 16 December 2023, https://www.bloomberg.com/graphics/2023-uk-power-electricity-market-manipulating/?sref=qvMYxUts.

to volatile market prices. This situation, combined with a consumer retail market directly tied to fluctuating prices, resulted in significant economic stress, echoing the preludes of the financial crash in 2008. The soaring energy costs strained household budgets, reducing consumer spending and raising concerns about the socialisation of these costs. The significant financial burden borne by taxpayers to mitigate this crisis prompted debates on equitable policy approaches and targeted protections for the most vulnerable. The retail energy market's struggles, both pre and post the price cap introduction, and Ofgem's questioned regulatory efficacy mirror the financial market's pre-crisis oversight failures.

This latest energy crisis underscores the urgent need to re-evaluate the Neoliberal hypothesis about market efficiency in delivering vital energy services. The costly regulatory infrastructure, increased complexities of global energy trading, and slow response time of regulators call for a complete overhaul of the private model for managing the nation's energy needs. In the same way banks undertook significant systemic risks during the GFC to make a profit at the taxpayer's expense, energy companies continue to undertake risks without setting aside a sufficient capital buffer to protect against failures. After all, if the Government is letting limited liability companies continue to extract value under the guise of market efficiency, why will these energy companies ever stop abusing this privilege? As Chris Giles of the Financial Times describes it:

> *Before the energy price cap, companies used every tactic to reel people in with teaser rates and then exploit their inertia, generating high margins. After the price cap was introduced to solve that problem, companies tied themselves to the spot market to offer the cheapest deals. They knew that if things went well, they would make good money and if prices rose, they would go bust with the rest of the sector – or the government would pick up the tab. Heads, we win; tails, you lose.*[18]

---

18 Chris Giles, "The rotten UK energy market is expensive and difficult to fix," *Financial Times*, 6 January 2022, accessed 16 December 2023, https://www.ft.com/content/0dc34e5c-1471-4227-9db2-582aa5aa6f96.

The phenomenon of financialisation has further complicated the privatisation discourse, characterised by a relentless emphasis on profit maximisation, often myopic in perspective and detrimental to other considerations such as competition, long-term planning, and environmental protection. The UK's Energy Security Strategy epitomises this shortsightedness – fixated on immediate gas crisis mitigation while eschewing substantial commitments to reduce greenhouse emissions. The nation's infrastructure has become mere chips in a cynical game to gain votes.

The UK railway system's privatisation exemplifies the inherent challenges of this approach. It led to an industry fragmented with high transaction costs and declining service quality, where achieving economies of scale became increasingly elusive. The railways faced mounting debts and fare hikes, ultimately leading to the renationalisation of Railtrack into Network Rail. Against this backdrop of unreliability, the railway industry's penchant for masking cancellations with pre-emptive measures further eroded trust, leading to a disjunction between reported performance figures and passenger experience, as evidenced by controversies surrounding operators like TransPennine Express. Market policies did not improve railway infrastructure; they made it worse. The pandemic was a clear reminder of how critical infrastructure in private hands does not save the taxpayers money. The bailout for railway companies cost taxpayers £3.5 billion during the COVID-19 pandemic.

In the water industry, the regulatory body Ofwat has struggled to balance consumer protection with fostering competition and ensuring efficiency in a sector naturally inclined towards monopoly. Its privatisation has been criticised for lack of transparency, regulatory evasion, and under-investment, particularly in sewage control infrastructure. Private equity's involvement in water utilities has heightened these concerns, with increased debt levels and a focus on financial engineering overshadowing the primary goal of service provision, infrastructure maintenance, and environmental protection. The actions in this sector warrant immediate nationalisation on health and safety grounds. Externalising costs by dumping sewage into the waterways should provide sufficient grounds to take legal action and put them out of business, but the current government does nothing.

The financial sector could also be seen as an extension of this problem. Commercial banks acting as depository institutions have a semi-public role in providing money. As Chapter Two describes, banks are guaranteed convertibility into state money for the private money created in their lending operations. As the Government withdrew from the provision of public services in favour of privatisation, it also abdicated its role as the primary currency issuer, with banks dominating credit creation and payment systems. This phase of financialisation allowed the banks to increase their share of the economy at the expense of all other economic sectors. This power is not unlimited, and regulatory oversight is essential for protecting taxpayers in the event of default.

However, even in the most heavily regulated markets like the UK, the complexity of the banking system leads to inadvertent outcomes like the GFC. The edifice of Monetarism, rising to special prominence during the latter half of the 20th century, held its ground on the principle that control over the money supply is pivotal in managing economic activity. Yet, it was put to the test by the cataclysmic events of 2008, in a spectacle of systemic failure draped in the paradoxes of bank deregulation and financialisation. As we survey the landscape of the GFC, a conspicuous pattern emerges: profits were privatised during the ascendant phases of economic cycles, and losses were egregiously socialised when the markets tumbled.

At this juncture, one cannot overlook how legal constructs, particularly the one of limited liability, have been co-opted in this grand financial charade. This legal mechanism, designed in its benignity to protect individual investors from the tribulations of bankruptcy by severing personal wealth from corporate risk, was exploited profoundly by financial institutions. Bonuses paid in the years prior were not subject to clawback, and shareholders were asymmetrically rewarded for excessive risk-taking. Citigroup CEO's now-infamous metaphor of "dancing as long as the music is playing" is an apt personification of the prevailing attitude among banking elites during the pre-crisis era. Despite the increasingly risky manoeuvre, the music played on, and the dance of deregulation, subprime mortgages, and securitisation reached a crescendo.

In the aftermath, we witnessed how major US banks, such as Citigroup, were effectively incentivised to endorse the Government's interventionist policies during the crisis. These measures included the Troubled Asset Relief Program (TARP), ostensibly aimed at ensuring the financial system's stability. Yet, these institutions brazenly continued to distribute dividends, underwritten by the taxpayer's purse, despite teetering on the edge of solvency. The collapse of Lehman Brothers, a once-staid partnership transformed into a public leviathan, provides a textbook case of financial engineering and legal asset partitioning. Lehman's ambition led to the creation of 209 subsidiaries and the adroit use of the favourable laws of Delaware for distributing profits while simultaneously partitioning risk. Yet, this partitioning went further with Lehman's deployment of the RASCALS (Remove Assets Subject to Capital Levies) scheme – an appellation almost comically belied by the gravity of its implications. This scheme was designed post-bankruptcy to ring-fence choice assets from creditors, in an epitome of legal manoeuvring within the permissive embrace of the Chancery Court's tradition of leniency, even at the expense of systemic risk.

Fast forward to 2023, and we are confronted with yet another déjà vu, embodied by the Silicon Valley Bank (SVB) collapse. A bank that had previously lobbied against stringent regulatory oversight finds itself and its affiliates precipitously endorsing government bailouts. The tech libertarians and venture capitalists, who once championed the sanctity of market forces and minimal state intervention, now paradoxically stood in the queue for public aid. The venture capital sector's response to the SVB collapse is eloquent in its hypocrisy, as the erstwhile proponents of rugged individualism now clamour for the socialisation of losses. The financial architecture had allowed for the thriving of an environment where profits are zealously guarded private reserves, and losses become democratised burdens, exposing the Achilles heel of Neoliberalism.

Education for the Privileged

The push for market-driven solutions and budget cuts under austerity measures often left public education systems underfunded, affecting the quality of education and widening the gap between public and private schooling. The Neoliberal critique of state-funded education, particularly when juxtaposed with the freedom of parents to opt for independent schooling, raises a series of engaging questions on the role of public policy in education. This discussion leads us to the heart of debates over the provision of "public goods" – a term often misused by economists because it typically applies to goods such as national defence, which cannot easily, if at all, be subdivided and made exclusive. Is schooling rightly classified amongst these goods? Neoliberals often argue for the divisibility of educational services and, thus, the applicability of market principles.

Elite independent schools are a poignant example of social exclusivity and bespoke parental influence over the educational process. In acknowledgement of this issue, Julian Le Grand – a notable connoisseur of social policy – articulated the concept of a "quasi-market" in education. Under this model, public funds, perhaps in the form of vouchers, follow the parental choice, directly incentivising schools to compete for pupils. The model envisions a system where autonomy is granted, and funding correlates with pupil numbers, inspiring innovation and responsiveness in educational institutions. Moreover, Le Grand argued for additional funding premiums to be allotted to schools that take on more challenging pupils, thus introducing a potential corrective measure to issues of educational equity.

The enactment of the Education Reform Act in 1988 in the United Kingdom marked a turning point by implementing elements of this quasi-market concept, shifting the locus of control from local authorities to central regulation. The establishment of the National Curriculum and standardised testing was intended to inform parental choice and apply a universal metric to assess and compare schools, subsequently leading to the creation of league tables.

The funding formula in England for 2023-2024 incorporates an intricate calibration that considers pupil factors, reflecting the sophisticated mechanisms seen in the healthcare sector to align funding with needs. Nevertheless, the crux of the challenge lies in calibrating this funding – a task of significant complexity, as evidenced by the limitations of using free school meal eligibility as a sole indicator of poverty. Advocates for a competition policy in schools, in which parental choice directs funds – bolstered by enhanced autonomy for school heads and supply-side flexibility – induced the prevalence of failed schools burdened with difficult-to-teach students. This system eroded genuine competition because it favoured those with the economic capacity to afford housing near high-performing schools. Evidently, geographic location continues to dictate educational outcomes, a fact underscored by proposals for a lottery system designed to distribute school places equitably.

Before the Neoliberal takeover of education policy, the Attlee settlement played a transformative role in university funding, significantly broadening access for the working class. Yet, in subsequent years, both Neoliberals and the New Labour movement have come to endorse tuition fees for university education. The Blair government was at the helm of this shift, instituting tiered tuition fees funded through loans. In 2003, further liberalisation occurred when elite Russell Group universities successfully negotiated a higher tuition fee ceiling. This pivot to an income-contingent loan system translated to increased financial burdens on students and diluted standards, as the phenomenon of grade inflation suggested.

The coalition government's decision in 2010 to permit the tripling of tuition fees resulted in considerable political backlash, particularly for the Liberal Democrats. This change reportedly led universities to display opportunistic behaviours aligned with marketisation, yet innovation within the sector remained stifled. Presently, concerns regarding a marketised university system persist, notably its implications for financial strain and the accessibility to high-quality education.

Further criticisms have surfaced regarding the removal of policies designed to support the educational attainment of disadvantaged students. The responses from academic institutions to the quasi-market in education have led to market impacts extending to housing, with parents often relocating to areas associated with prestigious schools. Concurrently, the Institute for Fiscal Studies (IFS) has reported stagnation in literacy and numeracy skills amongst England's youth, suggesting that the marketised system has failed to deliver the improvement in educational outcomes it promised. England ranked 25th out of 32 countries in literacy skills for the 16-24 age group. Literacy amongst those aged 55-65 in England performed relatively well, which suggests that the old system had more desirable outcomes.[19]

Neoliberal policies wanted market-driven solutions: tuition fees should fluctuate based on the quality of a university and its courses. The expectation was that readily available information on quality and costs would be accessible to students and their parents. Competition was thought to increase the quality of education and eliminate weaker degree programs. Additionally, the policies aimed to foster innovation without causing unplanned government debt.

In practice, universities began charging the maximum fee the Government allowed them to charge. This is exemplified by the identical tuition fees for a diverse set of degrees from several universities, irrespective of their economic value or societal benefit. Despite the availability of university rankings in regulators' league tables and various private sector guides, these resources do not leave students with many choices about future tuition fees or inform students about potential income. With respect to unplanned government debt, this turned out to be another fantasy as the Government now projects that it expects only 25% of loans to be fully repaid.

In constructing this narrative, we find that the representation of educational policy debates benefits from broader considerations, including social equity, resource allocation efficiency, and the underlying moral imperatives that govern public goods. While seductive in its simplicity, the

---

19 Christine Farquharson, Sandra McNally, and Imran Tahir, "Education Inequalities," in *IFS Deaton Review of Inequalities* (2022), https://ifs.org.uk/inequality/chapter/education-inequalities.

paradigm of a quasi-market in education must face the granular realities of implementing a policy that affects a diverse spectrum of individuals. Thus, policymakers must weigh these dimensions with a measured approach, ensuring that the pursuit of choice and autonomy does not unduly sacrifice the foundational principle of equality of opportunity upon which any society's educational philosophy should rightly rest.

Populism and Brexit

The contemporary geopolitical landscape, characterised by heightened populism and social unrest, can be partly attributed to the growing inequality and the prevailing perception that governments have increasingly catered to the interests of corporations and the affluent elite. This phenomenon, a byproduct of the Neoliberal policies that dominated the latter part of the 20th century, has led to widespread political instability and has posed significant challenges to the democratic consensus that underpinned the post-war order.

In this context, the United Kingdom's 2016 referendum, resulting in the decision to leave the European Union, is a stark manifestation of these broader socio-economic and political dynamics. The Brexit vote, as it came to be known, reverberated across the international community, signalling a seismic shift in the geopolitical landscape. The decision to withdraw from the EU, a union that represented economic integration and a post-war commitment to collective security and cooperation, marked a significant departure from the established path of European and global politics.

However, it is crucial to recognise that the factors leading to the Brexit decision were multifaceted and cannot be simplified to the UK's membership in the EU alone. A closer analysis reveals a complex web of domestic issues shaped by decades of adherence to Neoliberal principles, which contributed to disenfranchisement and disillusionment among many British citizens. A confluence of economic frustrations, concerns over national sovereignty, immigration, and a profound sense of alienation from the political establishment influenced the referendum outcome.

The Neoliberal era, with its emphasis on market liberalisation, deregulation, and globalisation, while contributing to economic growth in some sectors, also led to widening income disparities, deindustrialisation, and a perceived erosion of national autonomy. These factors, coupled with the aftershocks of the 2008 financial crisis and austerity measures, fostered a fertile ground for populist rhetoric. Populist leaders tapped into these sentiments, framing the EU as a scapegoat for a range of domestic issues and positioning Brexit as a panacea for the UK's complex socio-economic challenges.

The United Kingdom's decision to leave the European Union is a symptom rather than the origin of Britain's deeper socioeconomic challenges. The blame is misdirected, and Brexit can only solve these problems by reversing decades of Neoliberal policies. Before leaving the EU, policy failures were frequently blamed on Brussels. After leaving the EU, the same policy failures continue to be championed by political leaders, and Brexit is blamed for Britain's misfortune. The arguments for and against EU membership oversimplify Britain's complex tapestry of issues. British Remainers often romanticise the EU as a beacon of stability in which nothing wrong can happen – despite evidence to the contrary, such as the crisis in Ukraine, the rise of far-right parties across Europe, and its championing of Neoliberal policies that prioritised markets over democratic institutions. Political discourse amongst the Brexiteers was based on the oversimplified association of immigration challenges with EU membership.

Britain's erstwhile industrial prowess gave way to deindustrialisation well before thoughts of an EU referendum crystallised. The decline of manufacturing, partly due to globalisation, impacted Northern England, the Midlands, Wales, and Scotland, leading to job losses and community degradation. The resulting economic disillusionment created a fertile ground for anti-EU sentiments, which erroneously became attributed to the EU's freedom of movement policies rather than domestic policy failures.

Among developed nations, the UK exhibits substantial levels of socioeconomic inequality, with stark disparities in income, health, education, and life expectancy. Austerity measures and public sector cutbacks have exacerbated the uneven distribution of socioeconomic privileges. These inequalities have bred resentment and a sense that the status quo – represented by the EU – was neither working in the interests of all British citizens nor addressing the widening socioeconomic chasm.

The failures of the austerity measures post-GFC also disenfranchised the electorate, who had no choice but to overthrow the system that the establishment had imposed on them. It led to a rise of populist rhetoric that catalysed dissatisfaction with traditional political institutions, many associated with pro-EU stances. The Leave campaign successfully harnessed and amplified discontent with the political establishment, framing Brexit as an opportunity for the UK to "take back control" from Brussels. Nonetheless, this narrative overshadowed the significant domestic policy shortcomings and governance issues, redirecting public frustrations toward the supranational entity of the EU.

The Eurozone crisis also raised critical questions about economic sovereignty and the stability of the EU's financial architecture. Despite not adopting the euro, Britain became wary of the economic ramifications of EU policies, the perceived loss of autonomy over British economic affairs, its financial sector regulations, and its forced contribution to EU bailouts. Nevertheless, these concerns often overlooked the potential economic turbulence tied to an EU departure, with few of its supporters ever suggesting that any benefits from Brexit would take more than a generation to bear fruit; it would only do so if Britain used this autonomy to take bold political action to rewrite the Neoliberal script for nation's economic management. To be clear, this book is neither for nor against Brexit, but it is self-evident that the Green Party's reform plans – described in Part II of this text – are far easier to implement in an autonomous UK than in the EU, where even the prerequisites for a Eurozone fiscal union are yet to be achieved. It is not an accident that monetary reform has been overlooked by the Greens in the EU and the Scottish Green Party, which prioritises Scottish nationalism by advocating to leave the UK to join the EU as a full member.

Predatory Financialisation

While ostensibly championing the cause of competition in the private sector, Neoliberal policies have paradoxically led to a stifling of genuine competitive dynamics. This contradiction is notably evident in the case of Britain's approach to managing vital utilities and infrastructure. The adoption of Neoliberal tenets encouraged the formation of natural monopolies in key sectors and the establishment of simulated market conditions, which, contrary to expectations, have resulted in some of the highest utility costs globally. The facts are indisputable: privatisation of utilities did not yield the anticipated cost reduction or environmental protection benefits, and they have saddled taxpayers with staggering losses from socialised losses. The UK's experience, in particular, underscores several critical issues.

Despite promises of better management, privatisation has led to significant environmental damage. The UK's waterways have been subject to increased pollution, raising questions about the efficacy and priorities of privately managed utility firms. No amount of regulatory oversight will fix this problem because privately run infrastructure companies will prioritise profits at every opportunity and use leverage to maximise risk-adjusted returns. If environmental risks can be externalised, these companies will do it. What else can we expect when the payoffs exhibit such asymmetrical outcomes, where profits are paid to offshore companies in tax-efficient limited liability companies, and losses are borne by the taxpayers?

Privatising the railways has also become prohibitively expensive for the taxpayer and users of public transport alike, as debt-ridden operators fail to maintain a reasonable level of service. These costs disproportionately affect the less affluent segments of society who depend on public transport to commute to their places of work. The entire transportation system contradicts the Government's stated objectives for greening the economy. Green transportation initiatives, essential for sustainable urban development, have become so prohibitively expensive for average citizens that it motivates more polluting forms of transportation.

The energy infrastructure, crucial for meeting future needs, remains underdeveloped and insufficient, reflecting a failure to invest adequately in long-term capacity. It is lost on officials that the excessive financialisation of this sector has only increased costs due to increased requirements for a workforce dedicated to energy trading, marketing, administration, reporting, and regulatory compliance. The added complexity of managing a privately owned energy infrastructure makes it conducive to unethical trade practices by profit-seeking companies with little incentive to reduce consumer prices.

The risk-adjusted returns demanded by private utility companies substantially exceed what it would cost the Government to fund, build, and operate similar public services. The UK Government's funding cost is the interest it pays on gilts. The cost of funding for a private company includes an equity risk premium and a spread over the Government's funding rate to account for credit risk. This financial reality is lost on proponents of privatised infrastructure: it has to cost more to attract investors because there is a risk to the deployed capital. The government has no choice but to provide essential services like electricity and water; a private company can walk away and leave taxpayers to absorb catastrophic losses. This non-symmetrical discrepancy raises questions about the efficiency and public benefit of privatising such essential services. To further exaggerate this payoff asymmetry, privately run infrastructure companies can domicile in tax havens and pay dividends while being highly leveraged. Given this misalignment in financial risk and public interest, it is not surprising that default rates in this sector are unusually high, with taxpayers frequently required to bail out these sham enterprises.

In 2023, the UK's tax burden reached its highest level since 1948. Yet, despite this increased taxation, the Government provides fewer public services than in the immediate post-WWII era. This situation points to a fundamental mismatch between revenue collection and public service delivery, exacerbated by the emphasis on financialisation over direct public sector involvement. Figure 14 highlights the failure of the Neoliberal programme for privatisation to reduce the size of government as measured by the tax burden to maintain current services.

Figure 14: UK 2023 Tax Burden at Highest Level Since 1948[20]

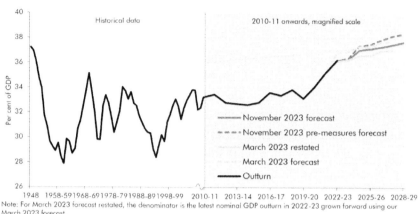

Note: For March 2023 forecast restated, the denominator is the latest nominal GDP outturn in 2022-23 grown forward using our March 2023 forecast.
Source: ONS, OBR

Paradoxically, the financialisation of the economy has profoundly impacted the efficiency of capital markets, diminishing the traditional role of households in participating directly in the economy's productive capacity through share ownership. Thatcher would be horrified to find out that her policies did quite the opposite of what they purported to do. Financialisation has created several layers of abstractions from the operations of a business to the ultimate owners of productive capacity as taxes incentivised the creation of an extractive financial sector to manage the increasingly complicated private pension system. The growth of private equity has further compounded this layer of abstraction from business operation to public share ownership.

Private equity, a symptom of the Neoliberal financialisation era, has been chipping away at publicly listed companies and reducing the choice and diversity in markets for publicly listed shares. The recent move by the Tory party to purportedly promote growth by channelling public pension funds into private equity highlights the insidiousness of this trend.

---

20 Office for Budget Responsibility, *Economic and fiscal outlook*, November 2023,

https://obr.uk/docs/dlm_uploads/E03004355_November-Economic-and-Fiscal-Outlook_Web-Accessible.pdf.

Private equity's business model often involves high leverage, asset stripping, and a disproportionate share of returns to the sponsors, frequently at the expense of long-term business viability and public interest.

Pensions are already an extractive industry, made necessary by the state's withdrawal from responsibility for providing a decent standard of living for its future pensioners. Neoliberal philosophy has transformed the pension system into an extractive industry dominated by financiers and intermediaries. Fees are collected at multiple levels – from pension fund managers to private equity fund managers, brokers, and financial advisors. This structure has led to a significant portion of productive capacity being diverted to serve the financial sector through complex tax incentives and financial products rather than being invested in productive, sustainable, and socially beneficial enterprises.

The Neoliberal embrace of privatisation and financialisation has inadvertently undermined actual competition and market diversity. It has led to environmental neglect, unaffordable public services, and an overemphasis on financial gains for the few at the expense of broader economic and social welfare. It has neither saved the taxpayer money nor made the Government any smaller. While successive UK Governments got praise for reducing the Government's financial debt, they were making the taxpayer poorer by transferring publicly-owned real assets into profit-motivated private-sector hands. What is worse is that these were not competitive enterprises; they were natural monopolies, requiring evermore government expenditures on regulatory oversight and bailouts. The UK's experience serves as a cautionary tale of the potential pitfalls of this economic philosophy, highlighting the need for a reassessment of policy priorities and a reorientation towards sustainable, inclusive, and genuinely competitive economic practices.

The Attack on Public Healthcare

The establishment of the National Health Service (NHS) in the United Kingdom stands as a seminal event in the history of British social policy, emblematic of the post-World War II spirit of reconstruction and progressivism. Founded in an era when the UK's national debt was more than 230% of its Gross Domestic Product (GDP), the NHS represented a bold and ambitious undertaking. It materialised when the country grappled with the war's financial aftermath, yet it demonstrated a remarkable vision and a commitment to social welfare and equity.

The NHS, envisaged by Aneurin Bevan, stands as a monumental social contract – one where citizens are provided medical care for free at the point of need, funded through a system of progressive taxation which sees the public pay according to their financial ability. Rooted in this idea is the Rawlsian ethical view – based on *A Theory of Justice* by philosopher John Rawls – that emphasises empathy to construct a society from behind the "veil of ignorance" of one's luck of the draw. In the absence of certainty about one's chance of falling ill without the ability to afford treatment, Rawls argued that humans would not demand total equality due to the insecurity of the unfettered liberty of laissez-faire capitalism. Faced with this risk, rational actors would opt for a society where the basics, such as healthcare, are guaranteed. Intriguingly, Rawls' secular perspective on justice strikes a chord with the religious ethos embedded within Western cultures – most notably, the "golden rule" found within Christian and other religious and moral teachings. The ethical imperatives of mutual respect and equality before the law reverberate with the idea that one should treat others as one would wish to be treated. Therefore, if one had the misfortune of needing healthcare without the ability to afford it, one would choose as a matter of justice that society absorb the cost of care. This tool of justice underpins the NHS model, justifying it on the grounds that ignorance of one's own future needs engenders the desirability of a collectively assured healthcare safety net.

In the contemporary context, the UK Government's efforts to reduce its fiscal burden by cutting NHS funding can be seen as deeply problematic, especially when viewed against the backdrop of historical debt levels. Figure 15 illustrates the absurd notion that the NHS is unaffordable because of a high public debt-to-GDP ratio. Even before removing all the biases in that headline figure, the Government's debt-to-

GDP ratio over time highlights that current debt levels are relatively low compared to the historical peak of 230% in the post-WWII era. This comparison is instructive; it demonstrates that high debt levels did not preclude the Government from undertaking significant social investments in the progressive era of British history, including the creation of the NHS at the heights of its indebtedness.

Figure 15: The NHS Established When Public Debt/GDP was Over 230%

Public sector net debt excluding public sector banks, percentage of GDP, UK, financial year ending (FYE) 1921 to September 2023

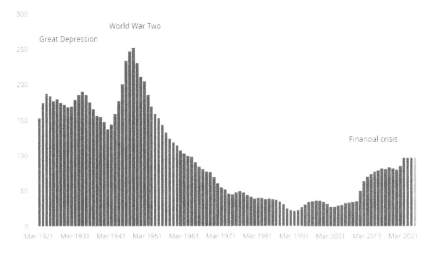

Source: Public sector finances from the Office for Budget Responsibility and the Office for National Statistics

In 2021, the total expenditure on healthcare in the United Kingdom amounted to £280.7 billion, representing 12.4% of the nation's GDP. A significant portion of this expenditure, totalling £233.1 billion, was financed by the Government, encompassing spending by the NHS, local authorities, and other public entities involved in healthcare provision. This government-financed segment constituted 83.0% of the overall healthcare expenditure. While there was a notable increase in spending by 9.7% in real terms from 2020 to 2021, the Office for National Statistics (ONS) acknowledges the complexities in interpreting this growth due to the impact of the COVID-19 pandemic.

Nonetheless, the UK has witnessed a continued push by the Conservative government to constrain the NHS budget in subsequent years. The latest government budget outlines nominal increases in NHS funding, projecting an annual real-term rise of merely 0.1% from 2022/23 to 2024/25. Such constrained budgetary allocations have led to a diminishing capacity within the healthcare sector, exemplified by the exodus of medical professionals driven primarily by economic factors. This reduction in workforce participation is not confined to the healthcare sector alone; burgeoning NHS waiting lists further exacerbate productivity challenges across the economy.

A comprehensive study conducted by Carnall Farrar for the NHS Confederation sheds light on the intrinsic link between healthcare investment and economic growth. The analysis undertaken by the NHS Confederation reveals a statistically significant correlation between increased NHS spending and growth in Gross Value Added (GVA). The study concludes that for every £1 invested in the NHS, there is an approximate economic benefit of £4, underscoring the substantial impact of healthcare spending on the broader economy. Investment in community and primary care is particularly potent, with every £1 spent in these areas yielding an impressive £14 in economic growth. The economic contribution of NHS spending is multifaceted and contributes to enhancing economic activity not only through improved health outcomes – which foster a more productive workforce – but also through the direct stimulation of local economies. This stimulation is facilitated by increased employment within the NHS, higher spending by the healthcare workforce, and augmented tax revenues. Furthermore, judicious investment in healthcare holds the potential to mitigate long-term healthcare costs, offering a prudent fiscal strategy for sustainable economic growth.

The gradual embrace of Neoliberal ideologies advocating for privatisation is steadily eroding the foundations of what has long been considered a social contract in healthcare. This ideological shift poses a significant risk of transforming a fundamental public good into a commoditised insurance product, akin to the highly financialised insurance models prevalent in the automobile and housing sectors, often characterised by extensive exclusions and a propensity to disadvantage those least capable of challenging such practices. The encroachment of American-style medical care, increasingly observed in London, represents a concerning trend. In this model, NHS doctors frequently straddle the divide between private and public healthcare sectors. It is imperative, however, to recognise that the American healthcare system, often idolised by Neoliberal proponents, had a pre-pandemic life expectancy of 77 years – markedly lower than the 81 years observed in the United Kingdom. Emulating market-based healthcare systems, which evidently do not align with the public interest, seems to be a misguided venture. The NHS should be the healthcare system for the US to emulate, not vice versa.

Under Neoliberal governance, market-based solutions to public healthcare invariably exacerbate disparities in access to medical services, culminating in inferior health outcomes, particularly for those in lower-income brackets or without insurance coverage. As individuals, we are confronted with an uncertain future regarding our healthcare needs. At the same time, societies grapple with the challenge of designing healthcare systems that mitigate these uncertainties, balancing financial viability with ethical imperatives.

Moreover, the private sector's inherent limitations in managing systemic risks, such as those associated with ageing populations or pandemic crises, must be considered. Comparative studies, including the "natural experiment" observed in the healthcare frameworks of Canada and the US, provide compelling evidence supporting models like the NHS. The Canadian healthcare system, despite its challenges, generally delivers a more equitable distribution of care at a lower cost to society than the US healthcare system.

One frequently proposed approach to navigating the healthcare cost dilemma involves the adoption of Health Maintenance Organizations (HMOs) and the utilisation of gatekeeper general practitioners (GPs). These models endeavour to offer cost-effective care by directing patients through a primary care provider responsible for managing necessary resources.

However, the US's experience is a cautionary example, where market-driven motives often result in inequities, substandard outcomes, and escalating costs. This experience underscores the complex nature of healthcare system reform and the need for a thoughtful approach prioritising equitable access and quality care over market efficiency.

The conundrum of healthcare reform is deeply intertwined with the issue of costs. In this area, the US endures exceptionally high medical staffing expenses while the UK grapples with its NHS political gridlock and ill-reasoned austerity measures. In the absence of augmented funding, efforts to stimulate NHS improvements have often hinged on bureaucratic and administrative tweaks, such as public reporting mechanisms, predicated on the belief that reputation is a significant catalyst for elevating the standard of care. However, this increased reliance on reporting and its attendant rise in administrative responsibilities has inadvertently escalated administrative costs and diminished doctors' time with their patients.

The pursuit of market efficiencies in the NHS, particularly through the new economic model of contracting with hospitals, has not yielded the desired outcomes in terms of efficiency gains or cost reductions. This disjunction between policy objectives and their practical realisations is indicative of a recurring discord within healthcare reform efforts, with the Government increasingly abdicating its responsibility for providing the necessary funding directly to the NHS. Furthermore, the inherent motivations of public service professionals, who are not driven exclusively by financial rewards, introduce an added layer of complexity. Consequently, the healthcare sector has struggled with overutilisation of resources and chronic underinvestment.

In this context, the Government's choice to scale back public funding for the NHS warrants a critical examination of its commitment to social welfare and its prioritisation of governmental resources. As elucidated by the analysis from Carnall Farrar, there is a compelling economic rationale underscoring public healthcare expenditure; investment in the NHS is not a mere cost but a catalyst for enhanced economic activity, yielding increased tax revenues. This effect is particularly pronounced at the margins, where every additional pound invested in the

NHS generates disproportionately more positive economic impacts than the perpetual cycle of austerity measures that keeps people ill and out of the workforce.

The irony lies in the views of many politicians who are critical of the austerity policies prevalent during Cameron's tenure but often fail to directly correlate these policies and their detrimental effects on the NHS and the subsequent stagnation in productivity. Such fiscal contraction poses substantial risks, threatening to erode the quality and accessibility of healthcare services. This concern is heightened by the NHS's integral role in the UK's social equity, where it stands as an essential healthcare provider to a significant segment of the population who do not have the same income levels as their US counterparts to pay for private healthcare.

The implications of reduced NHS funding extend beyond the immediate realm of healthcare. Adequate healthcare investment is not merely a social justice issue but an economic necessity. A healthy populace is fundamental to maintaining a productive workforce and ensuring societal stability. Therefore, while austerity measures targeting the NHS might yield short-term fiscal relief, they will likely incur substantial long-term costs. These costs manifest in various forms, including public health deterioration, decreased workforce productivity, and eroded social cohesion, underscoring the multifaceted impact of healthcare funding decisions on the broader fabric of society. The US and UK Green Parties understand the importance of public healthcare, and on this aspect, it is the US Greens who want to emulate the UK for the provision of publicly funded healthcare.

Financialisation of Housing

The historical trajectory of housing development in Britain, particularly from the interwar period up to the early 1970s, reveals a complex interplay of policy, planning, and political will in addressing housing needs. During the interwar years, Britain experienced an unprecedented boom in housebuilding, primarily in response to the burgeoning demand fostered by the proliferation of suburbs. This period was marked by a significant expansion in residential development, laying the foundations for the modern suburban landscape.

However, concerns over unchecked urban sprawl led to the introduction of a more controlled planning system. Influential entities such as the Royal Institute of British Architects (RIBA) and the Town and Country Planning Association (TCPCA) advocated for a more regulated and thoughtfully shaped development approach. This shift towards controlled planning aimed to balance housing needs with environmental sustainability considerations and urban design.

The landmark Town and Country Planning Act of 1947 marked a pivotal moment in this regard. The legislation empowered local authorities with considerable control over housebuilding, a significant departure from previous laissez-faire approaches. Despite the entrenchment of these planning controls, Britain continued to build at rates far higher than those observed today. This was partly a response to the acute housing shortage that emerged following the Second World War and the need for rapid reconstruction and development.

The 1950s, under a Conservative government, saw a brief interlude of conservative policy in housing, driven by the exigency of the ongoing housing shortages. The government at the time bolstered housebuilding efforts without imposing the stringent licensing and controls of the previous administration. This period witnessed a peak in housing construction in 1954, a development that was not solely attributable to policy shifts but was also facilitated by the groundwork laid by influential urban planner Patrick Abercrombie. Abercrombie's legacy, particularly his advocacy for planned New Towns and the restriction of urban sprawl, stood as a testament to the era's commitment to rational suburban and rural growth, balancing developmental needs with environmental and urban planning considerations.

However, with the rise of Neoliberalism as a dominant force in shaping economic and social policy, there was a notable shift in the approach to housing development. The advent of Thatcherism marked a departure from the more interventionist policies of previous decades. Under Margaret Thatcher, the solution to the housing shortage was sought through market mechanisms, with a significant reduction in the role of state and local authorities in housing provision. This approach, however, was not accompanied by serious reforms in planning laws, which could have addressed some of the systemic issues in housing supply.

The rise of homeownership in Britain, particularly among former council tenants, is a tale of market ideology, social aspiration, and unintended consequences. With its penchant for market-driven solutions, the Thatcher administration introduced the "Right to Buy" scheme – a policy that has arguably reshaped the nation's socio-economic fabric. Under this scheme, the duration of tenancy was instrumental in determining the discount levels offered to council tenants eager to own their homes. This, in theory, was a potent incentive intertwining with the intrinsic desire for homeownership, and it indeed engendered a substantial shift from public to private ownership. However, with the Right to Buy, tenants were not only enabled to become homeowners but also granted the liberty to profit from subsequent property sales, creating a quasi-speculative fervour that had previously been absent from the council housing realm.

Amidst this homeownership revolution, a less conspicuous yet equally significant narrative was unfolding: the dramatic ebb in the construction of council houses during the Thatcher era. This phenomenon contributed to a precipitous decline in the social housing stock, arguably contributing to an imbalance in the housing market that echoes into the present day. The zenith of this ownership shift materialised in 2001 when homeownership peaked, and the stock of social housing plunged, revealing a stark policy trade-off between the promotion of ownership and the preservation of public housing.

The tenure of Prime Ministers Blair and Brown witnessed the persistence of the Right to Buy policy. Their administrations, encumbered by the hiatus in council house construction, bolstered private renting as an interim measure against the backdrop of a squeezed public housing sector. As the Global Financial Crisis unfolded, with it came a profound impact on housebuilding. Despite being criticised by many as a questionable subsidy that potentially inflated house prices beyond what was reasonable, the policy continued in one form or another.

Figure 16: New-build dwellings completed in England, 1969-2022

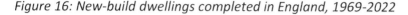

Sources:
1969-70 – 2005-06:
Building control reported new build dwellings, Live Table 213
2006-07 – 2021-22:
Total New Build: Housing supply: net additional dwellings, Live Table 120
Housing Association and Local Authority New Build: Affordable housing supply, Open Data
Private Enterprise New Build: Modelled as Total New Build - Housing Associations - Local Authorities

A notable shift during this period, as seen in Figure 16, was the drastic reduction in the construction of new council houses in England. From the substantial figures between 75,000 and 130,000 units in the 1970s, the number plummeted to a mere 8,000 by 1991. This trend of diminishing public housing provision continued under subsequent Conservative and Labour governments, leading to a significant contraction in the stock of council and socially rented homes.

The policy shift under the Thatcher government also profoundly impacted the UK's homeownership landscape. Owner-occupation reached its zenith at about 72% in 2001. However, by 2006, the stock of council and socially rented homes had nearly halved, a stark indicator of the diminishing role of the state in housing provision. This decline in public housing was coupled with a push towards privatisation and market-based solutions, a hallmark of the Thatcher government's approach to social policy.

The Right to Buy scheme encouraged a growing involvement of financial markets and institutions in housing and real estate. Therefore, the housing market became excessively financialised, driven by a self-reinforcing feeding frenzy on mortgage debt that was only temporarily interrupted in the 2008 market collapse. The continuation of this policy following the crisis has exacerbated the socioeconomic disparities, especially in terms of intergenerational wealth and opportunity in education and job opportunities. Access to homeownership became increasingly contingent on familial wealth, as the "bank of mum and dad" became a crucial factor in enabling the children of affluent families to afford housing, particularly in high-demand areas. This dynamic contributed to the entrenchment of geographical inequalities, with certain regions, particularly England's "golden triangle," becoming increasingly inaccessible to those without substantial financial backing.

Housing continues to be at the mercy of financialisation, wherein the industry's high profits are juxtaposed against limited supply and demand dynamics. Traditionally reflecting the interplay between supply and demand, markets have seemingly been overridden by speculative interests that engender profit at the expense of broader societal needs. Increasing the cost of shelter was viewed less in terms of its inflationary impact and more as a measure of financial wealth. Resistance to planning reform materialises not from a concern for the national interest or the environment but from a fear of facing catastrophic losses by those who have already committed much of their wealth to housing.

Financialisation changed the price mechanism with which house prices are determined in a normal market, in which price increases reduce demand. It became a speculative market in which increased prices fuelled demand from home and abroad. This has been accompanied by the emergence of a high-end property market underpinned by the "plutonomy" concept, with luxury sales predominantly driven by wealth concentration rather than general consumer demand. In 2008, a global collapse in this model ensued when people with subprime mortgages could not make their monthly payments, and the house of cards of financial derivatives progressively collapsed. The authorities opted to fix the problems with more Neoliberal policies: drive interest rates lower and encourage leverage to buy houses that were disproportionately priced relative to household income. The mantra continues to be that the market knows best.

One emblematic case of market forces not working for the public interest is that of Persimmon, a housebuilding company whose executive rewards drew public ire, particularly given their disconnect with customer satisfaction ratings. A subsequent review illuminated negligence within the industry, highlighting the schism between profit maximisation and product quality – a schism that may indicate broader sectoral trends.

Arguably, the evolution of homeownership policy in Britain, from the heyday of the Right to Buy to the present climate of financialised housing markets, presents a public policy paradox. It is an interplay of the pursuit of individual property ownership and the erosion of collective housing provision, spanning generations and transcending party lines. As policymakers grapple with the ramifications of past decisions, the quest for a balanced and equitable housing strategy persists and raises profound questions about the right to shelter within a society's social and economic priorities.

Environmental Degradation

The trajectory of Neoliberal policies in the UK has led to a complex interplay of market-driven economic strategies and environmental concerns, culminating in a disconcerting state of affairs. Neoliberalism, with its emphasis on deregulation, privatisation, and market empowerment, while ostensibly championing efficiency and consumer sovereignty, often finds itself at odds with the essential task of environmental safeguarding.

One observes a range of administrative and regulatory challenges that highlight this tension. Within the UK energy industry, there are apprehensions about the future supply of clean energy owing to regulatory lapses. Similarly, the water industry oversight displays systemic deficiencies in managing ecological damage. In his critical observations, Dieter Helm points to the "light-touch" regulations that have plagued the UK's environmental domain, allowing unchecked corporate behaviours with little regard for ecological responsibility. This theme mirrors the financial sector's challenges, as noted by Oliver Bullough, where the enforcement of regulation is sporadic and inadequate and only enforced after a catastrophic loss mobilises public opinion against the bad actors.

The situation of the UK's water industry, regulated primarily by Ofwat and the Environment Agency, epitomises these tensions. Ofwat's mandate, which includes consumer protection, competition promotion, and ensuring resilient water and sewage services, is often undermined by the conflicting pressure to maintain low prices. As the House of Lords indicated, this has led to insignificant price reductions and a significant shortfall in infrastructure investment. Having warned the general public about the water industry for years, the Greens are finally gaining traction with voters who are slowly realising that Labour or Tories will do nothing to change this destructive privatisation of an industry with such an extensive environmental impact.

Further complicating this landscape is the role confusion within the Environment Agency, torn between its commitment to sustainability and its fundamental environmental protection duties. The lack of effective coordination and information sharing between Ofwat and the Environment Agency has led to missed opportunities and contradictory decisions, such as rejecting developments approved by one but not the other. The failure to regulate the water industry is witnessed in many environmental violations, including dumping untreated water into the nation's waterways.

Governmental cutbacks in the era of austerity have exacerbated these issues, diminishing the Environment Agency's capacity for monitoring and enforcement. This has resulted in an over-reliance on self-monitoring by water companies, a process fraught with conflicts of interest and criticised for its inefficacy. Cases of regulatory action, such as Ofwat's fines on Southern Water for infrastructural and operational failures and the Environment Agency's prosecutions for permit violations, underscore the severity of corporate non-compliance with environmental standards. Paying fines is treated as a cost of doing business, escalating the recently announced fee increases. Ultimately, the customers will end up paying higher prices without guarantees of environmental protection.

The Environment Agency's 2021 report, which sharply criticised the environmental performance of water and sewerage companies, coupled with media exposés on widespread sewage dumping, has intensified calls for more vigorous enforcement and regulatory oversight. The case of Thames Water, burdened with significant debt and operational issues, is emblematic of the broader systemic problems within the sector. This scenario presents a stark illustration of environmental policy ensnared by Neoliberal ideology, where the pursuit of market incentives has led to the neglect of environmental stewardship. The ecological domain, treated with the same market-centric approach that failed elsewhere, faces potentially catastrophic and intergenerational consequences.

PART II

The Green Party's Reform Plan

P art II of this book delves into potential resolutions for the economic dilemmas detailed in Part I, focusing on the reformist proposals of the Green Party of England and Wales. It argues that a fundamental transformation of the monetary system is essential to overcome the current paralysis in addressing the dual crises of climate change and social dysfunction. This segment of the book makes the case that the monetary reform advocated by the Green Party could unlock the fiscal barriers impeding significant governmental action in these critical areas.

In Chapters Seven and Eight, we investigate the structural contours of the monetary system as envisaged by the Green Party of England and Wales, noting its conceptual alignment with the monetary reform strategy of the Green Party of the US. A historical case study of Colonial America is presented, where a similar monetary system operated successfully for nearly a century, contributing to the nascent emergence of the US as an economic powerhouse. Chapter Eight delves into the expected changes in liquidity, credit, and interest rate risks within the banking sector under this new monetary regime, and it also argues that reclaiming public ownership of certain assets can mitigate societal risks.

Chapter Nine traverses the intricate path of transitioning to this innovative monetary system. It examines the operational and regulatory challenges inherent in shifting from the current framework to one dominated by a central Monetary Authority. This chapter also delves into the operational and technological implications of this transition, offering a pragmatic strategy for implementation. Additionally, the potential role and design of a Central Bank Digital Currency (CBDC) within this new monetary landscape are thoroughly explored.

In Chapter Ten, the focus shifts to the denominator of the national debt-to-GDP ratio, critiquing the shortcomings and inaccuracies of the GDP metric itself. Previous chapters focused on how to pay for the transition by addressing the debt component of this feared metric. The chapter advocates for reducing GDP's dominance in policy formulation, highlighting its failure to measure economic and societal well-being accurately.

Chapter Eleven introduces an array of alternative economic indicators that could supplement GDP in guiding policy decisions. The chapter emphasises the Green Party's commitment to addressing the climate crisis and enhancing the population's living standards rather than maximising the financial wealth of the few. It explores various metrics, including the Genuine Progress Indicator, the Happy Planet Index, the Green Gross Domestic Product, and the Environmental Performance Index, which collectively provide a more holistic view of societal well-being, including environmental considerations often neglected by GDP. Additionally, it examines the Social Progress Index, the Gini Coefficient, the Multidimensional Poverty Index, and the Human Development Index, offering these as supplementary tools for Green Parties globally in their pursuit of socially responsible progress.

Chapter Seven

New Monetary Framework

The necessity for Green Parties globally to prioritise the reform of the monetary system stems from a fundamental realisation: the architecture of our current financial system is intricately tied to the environmental and social challenges we face. To change the narrative around how society will pay for the green transition and maintain social cohesion, the Green Party of England and Wales and the Green Party of the US have made significant contributions to developing the discourse on an alternative monetary framework. Their propositions for monetary reforms address many of the failures of market-driven strategies that have led to minimal government action to tackle the existential climate crisis. We must move beyond the short-term profiteering and self-imposed fiscal prudence and change the mindset that obstructs any serious action by the fiscal authorities. In the following sections, we explore the structure of these proposed monetary reforms by using the national accounts of the United Kingdom as an example.

The chapter develops a new monetary framework that explores how banks will function under a system without the ability to create money independently. Far from being radical, the approach redefines the existing liabilities of the Government and financial sector to create a new monetary policy tool for credit creation. Banks will continue to provide loans, but they will be required to borrow from a central Monetary Authority established by the Government. This shift represents the primary departure from the current system, where commercial banks play a significant role in money creation through lending. The proposed model places the Government at the helm of money supply control, turning bank borrowing into a powerful policy tool for regulating the economy.

The proposed banking and money supply model brings with it profound policy implications. It allows the Government to regain control over the quantity and price of money in circulation, aligning it more closely with broader economic goals such as full employment, inflation control, environmental protection, and sustainable growth. This approach contrasts starkly with the prevailing system, where private banking activities largely dictate the money supply. Monetary policy aimed at expanding and contracting private credit by aggressive changes in interest rates will no longer be necessary as the fiscal authority becomes the dominant force for currency issuance in the economy. The monetary reforms reduce the costs associated with the current system, leading to better decisions and policy actions to achieve environmental and social objectives.

To provide historical context to this discussion, the chapter includes an in-depth case study of the Colonial Scrip system used in Colonial America. This exploration is crucial as it offers practical insights into a similar state-issued fiat money system with a successful historical record. The chapter examines how the American Colonies managed their currency for nearly a century, maintaining economic stability and growth despite British attempts to curtail their monetary sovereignty. The British eventually moved to ban the Colonies' power to issue their currency, significantly contributing to the growing tensions leading up to the Revolutionary War. The Colonial Scrip system serves as a historical precedent and proof of concept, demonstrating a state-controlled money system's viability and offering valuable lessons for contemporary monetary reform.

Explorative Exercise in Accounting

In Chapter Two, we delineated the separation of money creation into two classifications: exogenous and endogenous money. Entities such as the *Central Government* and the BoE are delineated as creators of exogenous money. Conversely, the banking sector is responsible for issuing endogenous money, which emerges as a corollary of its credit extension activities. The financial flows from this prevailing monetary framework are encapsulated in Figure 17.

Figure 17: Financial Flows Under Old Regime

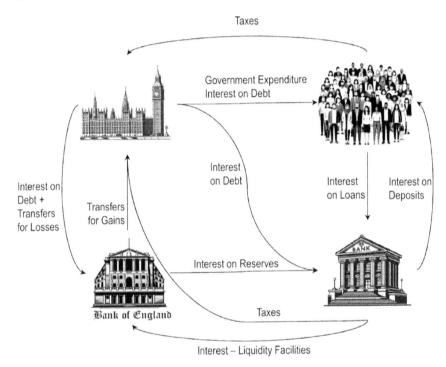

Within the same context, we expounded on how the aggregate balance sheets of the UK *Central Government* and *Monetary Financial Institutions* (*MFI*) are aggregated quarterly by the Office for National Statistics in the Flow of Funds Report. These balance sheets serve as a tableau reflecting the creation of money within the economy, which we defined as IOUs or liabilities with specific attributes of convertibility into the sovereign's currency of account. For example, *Households* would pay taxes to the Government using privately-created money without worrying about the convertibility of bank deposits into physical notes and coins. This guarantee of 1:1 convertibility with the sovereign's currency makes the bank money circuit the dominant payment system.

Progressing further, we re-conceptualised the perspective on *Central Government* debt. This re-conceptualisation was predicated on a hypothetical consolidation of the *Central Government* and the Bank of England (BoE) into a singular entity by combining their respective assets and liabilities. The resulting accounting transactions for the 2023 Q1 data are depicted in Figure 18:

Figure 18: Transactions for Consolidation of Government and BoE

Central Government Balance sheet

Figures in £ millions: 2023 Q1

Assets	Liabilities
Debt Securities	Debt Securities
+ 7,067	- 836,669
+ 17,739	+ 11,594
+ 175,925	
	Currency and deposits
Currency and deposits	+ 908,804
+ 11,578	+ 86,006

Monetary Financial Institutions Balance Sheet

Figures in £ millions: 2023 Q1

Assets	Liabilities
Debt securities	Debt Securities
- 836,669	- 11,594
- 7,067	
- 17,739	Currency and deposits
- 175,925	- 908,804
	- 86,006
Currency and deposits	
-11,578	

Before executing these consolidating transactions, the cumulative *MFI* balance sheet indicated a net worth of £64,623 million, computed as the residual of assets over liabilities. Excluding the BoE from this aggregate net worth, the remaining equity of the monetary financial sector at large is reduced to £22,049 million.

Figure 19: Aggregate Balance Sheet of MFIs ex BoE

MFIs ex BoE Balance Sheet
Figures in £ millions: 2023 Q1

Assets	Liabilities
Currency and deposits 4,678,442	Currency and deposits 8,704,413
Debt securities 509,974	Debt securities 917,954
Loans 4,462,715	Loans 3,369
Equity and investment fund shares/units 217,501	Equity and investment fund shares/units 265,393
Insurance, pension and standardised guarantee schemes 12,565	Insurance, pension and standardised guarantee schemes 8,676
Financial derivatives and employee stock options 3,524,900	Financial derivatives and employee stock options 3,479,102
Other accounts receivable/payable 665	Other accounts receivable/payable 5,806

Notwithstanding the exclusion of the BoE from this aggregate balance, the privately created money, leveraging this £22 billion in equity, amounts to £8.7 trillion in currency and deposits. A further refinement, accounting for the inter-sectoral holdings by deducting £4.7 trillion of money from the asset side of the balance sheet, leaves an astonishing £4 trillion of currency and deposit obligations. These are predicated on a relatively meagre margin of equity left to absorb any misjudgements concerning capital adequacy or the integrity of assets underpinning these liabilities. The loan portfolio alone, amounting to £4.5 trillion, could precipitate a fiscal burden should this delicate equilibrium falter, as evidenced by the financial crisis in 2008 that was triggered by the subprime mortgage collapse.

After consolidating the balance sheet of the *Central Government* and BoE, we witness a transmutation in characterising what is conventionally recognised as government debt. The gilts held by the BoE are netted against the liabilities of the *Central Government*, reclassifying the money previously categorised under *MFI* issuance into state-sanctioned currency. This approach aligns with the legal constructs insofar as the liabilities of the BoE are, in essence, liabilities of the *Central Government*. Notably, the BoE is indemnified against potential losses from its monetary policy undertakings, with taxpayers absorbing any such losses.

Figure 20: Aggregate Balance Sheet of Government and BoE

Combined Government & BoE Balance sheet
Figures in £ millions: 2023 Q1

Assets	Liabilities
Monetary gold and special drawing rights 49,332	Monetary gold and special drawing rights 32,014
Currency and deposits 75,420	Currency and deposits 1,239,559
Debt securities 284,628	Debt securities 1,245,356
Loans 226,880	Loans 36,401
Equity and investment fund shares/units 53,630	Insurance, pension and standardised guarantee schemes 686
Financial derivatives and employee stock options 2,464	Financial derivatives and employee stock options 2,167
Other accounts receivable/payable 146,497	Other accounts receivable/payable 45,752

The combined balance sheet of the *Central Government* and BoE underscores its pivotal role as the counterbalance to the owners of financial assets within the economy. The aggregate of financial assets throughout the economy must equate to the aggregate of financial liabilities, a balance that solely the *Central Government* sector can achieve in creating net financial assets for the private sector because the Government has no solvency constraints in carrying such a significant net financial liability.

Expanding our inquiry, let us hypothesise a paradigm where banks are not assured of 1:1 convertibility between state and private money. In such a framework, banks would be relegated to the status of money users, procuring funds from the sovereign currency issuer. Deposits owed to the private sector would be held at accounts with a government-owned bank or the BoE. The ensuing accounting transactions would reflect this shift, with a novel entry for a Revolving Loan Facility that underwrites the banks' lending operations through an adjustable overdraft mechanism.

Figure 21: Transactions for State Currency Regime

Combined Government & BoE Balance sheet
Figures in £ millions: 2023 Q1

Assets	Liabilities
Revolving Loan Facility + 8,704,413	Currency and deposits + 8,704,413

MFIs ex BoE Balance Sheet
Figures in £ millions: 2023 Q1

Assets	Liabilities
	Currency and deposits - 8,704,413
	Revolving Loan Facility + 8,704,413

The accounting illustrations elucidate the repercussions on the *Central Government* and BoE's combined balance sheets and how this recalibration affects the *MFIs ex BoE*. What alterations ensue? The aggregate balance sheet size for the *MFIs ex BoE* remains intact (Figure 23); the sole difference is that its currency and deposit liabilities are now liabilities for the *Central Government,* where deposits for all other economic sectors are held (Figure 22). Under this new regime, the joint balance sheet of the Government and BoE now encompasses the totality of money outstanding in the economy as a liability.

Figure 22: Balance Sheet of Government and BoE Under New Regime

Combined Government & BoE Balance sheet

Figures in £ millions: 2023 Q1

Assets	Liabilities
Monetary gold and special drawing rights 49,332	Monetary gold and special drawing rights 32,014
Currency and deposits 75,420	Currency and deposits 9,943,972
Debt securities 284,628	Debt securities 1,245,356
Loans 226,880	Loans 36,401
Equity and investment fund shares/units 53,630	Insurance, pension and standardised guarantee schemes 686
Financial derivatives and employee stock options 2,464	Financial derivatives and employee stock options 2,167
Other accounts receivable/payable 146,497	Other accounts receivable/payable 45,752
Revolving Loan Facility 8,704,413	

Figure 23: Balance Sheet of MFIs Ex BoE Under New Regime

MFIs ex BoE Balance Sheet
Figures in £ millions: 2023 Q1

Assets	Liabilities
Currency and deposits 4,678,442	Revolving Loan Facility 8,704,413
Debt securities 509,974	Debt securities 917,954
Loans 4,462,715	Loans 3,369
Equity and investment fund shares/units 217,501	Equity and investment fund shares/units 265,393
Insurance, pension and standardised guarantee schemes 12,565	Insurance, pension and standardised guarantee schemes 8,676
Financial derivatives and employee stock options 3,524,900	Financial derivatives and employee stock options 3,479,102
Other accounts receivable/payable 665	Other accounts receivable/payable 5,806

Furthermore, considering all government-issued debt securities as a variant of money analogous to longer-term deposits held by the non-government sectors as financial assets, we can now reclassify these debt securities as fixed-term deposits. We observe that these securities occupy an identical position within the combined government balance sheet as other forms and maturities of currency and deposits, the distinction being largely semantic.

This exercise leads us to a few conclusions. The ensuing figures illustrate an alternative configuration wherein depositors accrue interest on deposits held at the BoE instead of a commercial bank. Under such a scenario, any remaining deposits held at banks would no longer benefit from deposit insurance and should attract a higher interest rate for being a riskier form of lending to the financial sector. Significantly, privately-owned banks would no longer capitalise on money creation as this prerogative would shift to the sovereign, who is expected to benefit from seigniorage as the sole issuer of money in the economy. As mere users of state-issued currency, banks must remunerate the interest determined by the BoE for the Revolving Loan Facility that supports their lending ventures. Interest on deposits would become a fairer and more uniform policy rate instead of being captive to the transactional arrangements that force depositors to fund banks at rates far lower than the BoE's base rate.

Figure 24: Financial Flows Under New Regime

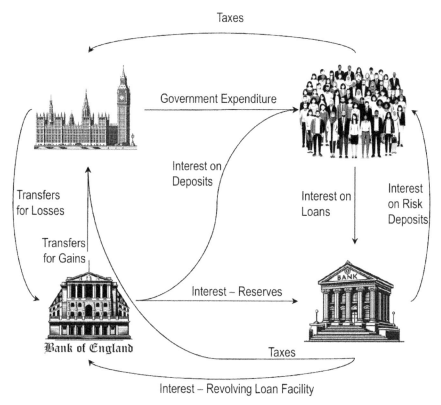

A monetary system under this revised regime could be actualised through a simple legislative enactment. Should the Government elect to do so, it could be implemented with minimal disruption to existing operations. Existing capital adequacy regulations and requirements can be used to set the initial limits for each bank's utilisation of the Revolving Loan Facility. The BoE would continue to hold currency and deposits for the banking sector in the form of reserve balances while developing the infrastructure to extend deposit account services to the broader populace. In this reimagined fiscal landscape, banks would be compelled to offer deposit rates at or above the base rate stipulated by the BoE, concurrent with the additional risk they carry as a form of funding for banking activities. Thus, banks are positioned as users rather than issuers of money.

A Case Study: Colonial America

The state-money framework in the previous is more than merely theoretical. History is replete with examples where such state-issued currencies replaced private money when privately created notes became either too contractionary or too inflationary. Two historical precedents for a state money system were seen notably under the Song dynasty in China and separately in the American Colonies in the century leading up to the American Revolution.

During the Song dynasty, private promissory notes known as "Jiaozi," issued by merchants, initially functioned as a supplement to coin-based money. These notes, exchangeable among individuals, gradually became an abstraction of money in themselves, leading to inflationary pressures as they proliferated beyond their backing in coinage. In response, the Chinese government introduced a state-money system known as "Huizi," establishing a government monopoly on money issuance and a unified tax regime to stabilise the monetary system.

A similar experiment of money was the development of Colonial Scrip as a form of state-issued money in the American Colonies in the 17th and 18th centuries, with the first colonial currency issued in 1690 by the Massachusetts Bay Colony. The system of Colonial Scrip presents us with a more direct evolution of the monetary system from the one imposed by the British Government on the Colonies, as it allowed the Colonies to facilitate commerce and overcome the perennial shortage of official British currency. In that period, colonial governments issued money rather than banks. The system could have been better; the value of Colonial Scrip varied between different Colonies, and it was subject to depreciation and counterfeiting. Moreover, the British Parliament viewed the unregulated issuance of currency as a potential problem, particularly as it could affect trade between the Colonies and Britain.

In Franklin's time, the monetary system of the Colonies was inherently different from England's, primarily because the Colonies were not allowed to mint their own coin. To tackle the currency scarcity, the Colonies started to issue paper money. Colonial scrip was typically backed by the promise of future tax revenues or specific goods, such as land or silver, depending on the colony that issued it. Colonial Scrip served as a common payment method in the day-to-day colonial economy. It was standard for transactions such as land purchases, payment of wages, and the buying of goods. The control and distribution of Colonial Scrip were managed by the Colonial Governments, who determined the amount to be issued, thus enabling them to influence their local economies directly. With a sufficient supply of money to represent goods and services, each person in the colony could trade labour or goods for scrip and then use it to purchase other services or goods, creating a more self-sustaining and prosperous economy.

The system worked effectively because it provided the liquidity needed to develop commerce in the Colonies. By controlling the issuance of Colonial Scrip, the Colonial Governments could avoid the deflationary pressure that a shortage of currency could have created. Reduced dependency on British currency and the increased local control of the money supply had allowed the colonial economy to prosper amid a shortage of money in its mother country because the Colonial Governments had more direct local economic control and reduced reliance on Britain, subsequently influencing colonial attitudes towards British monetary policies.

Different Colonies had their own practices and laws governing the issuance of scrip, but they honoured each other's money in inter-colony trade. Colonies closer to the frontiers exhibited higher inflation due to higher spending on military expeditions in native lands, but even in frontier economies like colonial New England between 1711 and 1749, peacetime inflation was only about 5% per annum. To put this in perspective, inflation reached 35% during King George's War. Each issuing authority had strict control over the newly printed money by accompanying each issuance with taxes and customs duties to redeem them.

Initially, the British government tolerated Colonial Scrip but eventually attempted to restrict and even prohibit its issuance. Several laws and acts attempted to regulate currency in the Colonies, such as the Currency Acts of 1751 and 1764, which restricted the issuance of paper money in New England and later in all colonies. This reduced the amount of currency available, creating financial difficulties for many colonists and adding to the tensions that would eventually lead to the American Revolution.

The conflict over monetary control was witnessed in Benjamin Franklin's testimony to the House of Commons, in which he highlighted the growing resentment towards the British crown that ultimately played a role in the Colonies' quest for independence. In the Parliamentary examination of Benjamin Franklin in 1766, before an August Assembly, relating to the Repeal of the Stamp Act, Franklin attributes deteriorating colonial attitudes towards the British Parliament to the series of laws that prevented the Colonies from issuing their Colonial Scrip and an increase in taxes that severely restricted a sufficient provision of gold and silver in the Colonies as means of exchange. In the pamphlet documenting this testimony, Benjamin Franklin explains:

> To a concurrence of causes; the restraints lately laid on their trade, by which the bringing of foreign gold and silver into the Colonies was prevented; the prohibition of making paper money among themselves; and then demanding a new and heavy tax by stamps; taking away, at the same time, trials by juries, and refusing to receive and hear their humble petitions.[21]

---

21 The Examination of Doctor Benjamin Franklin, before an August Assembly, relating to the Repeal of the Stamp-Act (Boston: Edes and Gill, 1766), image, Massachusetts Historical Society,

https://www.masshist.org/database/viewer.php?item_id=251&mode=large&img_step=7&pid=2#page7

It is crucial to note that private enterprise thrived under the colonial money system, indicating that the modern criticism of state money as an anti-capitalist, socialist ideal misses the point of unbiased inquiry. Reducing the debate to an ideological and binary choice between capitalism and socialism ignores the anti-capitalist tendencies that develop when extreme concentrations of financial wealth exist. History is rife with examples of private money creation bringing about such concentration of wealth and capital in a few hands, stifling competition and creating new modes of oppression. The colonial system of currency issuance, managed by publicly owned entities rather than private banks, contrasts the later development of private banking institutions that dominate the world today.

In Colonial America, banks as we know them today were not widespread. The BoE had been established in 1694, but in the Colonies, private banks that could issue currency were a later development. Early colonial "banks" were more likely to be individual merchants or groups of merchants who would issue promissory notes or credit. Over time, some Colonies began to establish banks that could issue currency. Interest rates have traditionally been central to economies by influencing governments' borrowing costs. Colonial Scrip presented an alternative approach by minimising reliance on interest-bearing loans from British bankers for running government operations, which can be seen as an early instance of American financial innovation.

In the Memoirs of Benjamin Franklin, a collection that includes a series of his correspondences, Franklin offers a detailed and insightful account of the workings of the American paper money system during the Revolutionary War. Despite a scarcity of gold and silver, Franklin, in one of his letters, elucidates how the American Colonies were able to sustain and ultimately triumph in their conflict against Great Britain using a currency system that was largely reliant on paper money:

> *The whole is mystery even to the politicians, how we have been able to continue a war four years without money, and how we could pay with paper, that had no previously fixed fund appropriated specifically to redeem it. This currency as we manage it, is a wonderful machine. It*

performs its office when we issue it; it pays and clothes troops, and provides victuals and ammunition; and when we are obliged to issue a quantity excessive, it pays itself off by depreciation.[22]

In the same correspondence, Franklin recognised that the only feasible means to restore the value of the depreciated currency would be through vigorous taxation, an option he deemed impractical and unnecessary. He reasoned that the populace had already indirectly paid through the diminished value of the currency. Furthermore, he astutely observed that this depreciation effectively reduced the public debt proportionally, a point often overlooked in modern political discourse. Contemporary politicians seem too eager to impose additional financial burdens on a strained citizenry through increased taxation or reduced government spending on public services, infrastructure, and initiatives to advance the green transition.

---

22 Benjamin Franklin, William Temple Franklin, and William Duane, *Memoirs of Benjamin Franklin* (United States: Derby & Jackson, 1859), 325.

Chapter Eight

A Green Perspective on
Monetary Reform

The Global Greens' advocacy for a successful green transition is anchored in upholding democratic principles and fostering respect for diversity, equity, and social justice. At the heart of its longstanding commitment to the environment is an understanding that people cannot be motivated to look to the planet's future when they are grappling with questions of fairness, equity, and well-being. To achieve these lofty goals, an often-overlooked aspect in these discussions is the reform of the monetary system. The Green Party of the US and the Green Party of England and Wales have made notable strides in this area, developing principles for democratising money that resonate with the monetary framework discussed earlier in Chapter Seven.

These parties converge on the belief that money should be managed democratically and in the public interest, advocating for a publicly owned monetary system. This perspective challenges a prevalent but rarely contested truth: that the majority of money in circulation is created not by government mints but by private banks through loan issuance. This process, inherently undemocratic, vests significant power in private institutions at the expense of public control. The primary reform these parties advocate involves transferring the power of money creation from private entities back to democratically accountable bodies. They propose that a government department, answerable to the elected legislature, should issue debt-free currency, ensuring that the generation and distribution of money align with democratically established principles.

The Greens in both countries recognise that private banks create most of the money used for payments in the economy when they make loans. Bank reserves and government debt constitute a form of money under the MMT model, but they are not part of the money circuit used by the general public for transacting with one another. Payment systems are effectively in private hands because of the way bank money comes into existence. The Greens argue that this credit creation process has profound implications for the economy and society; it is designed to optimise for maximising profit, not the well-being of society or the environment.

There is a shared understanding among these parties that to truly protect the environment, a fundamental rethinking of the sustainability of the current banking system is necessary. The existing banking system, as per their critique, is undemocratic, unfair, and environmentally destructive. Banks exacerbate inequality and contribute to economic instability by deciding the initial allocation of the money they create – often favouring financial speculation and reckless mortgage lending over investments in productive and socially responsible businesses. The reliance on debt-creation through loans, coupled with the interest charged, perpetuates inequality and frequently precipitates economic crises. The cycle of boom and bust, where banks extend increasing amounts of credit until the debt levels become unsustainable, often results in taxpayer-funded bailouts of institutions deemed "too big to fail."

Furthermore, the need to service the growing mountain of debt that underpins the banking system is identified as a driving force behind unsustainable economic growth, poverty, and inequality, which further exacerbate environmental degradation. The average person has no time or agency to confront the existential crisis facing humanity when there is an immediate threat of homelessness for not meeting debt obligations. At the heart of Rawlsian ethics is the principle that a just society should ensure that every individual is afforded the bare necessities – such as healthcare, education, and a minimum standard of living – that secure a baseline quality of life while maintaining the prospects of ascending the socioeconomic ladder. This dual focus on welfare provision and equal opportunity is a foundation for mobilising society to act beyond its immediate needs to meet environmental challenges. The Greens' monetary reform plans oppose the establishment's tolerance for extremes of destitution and fixed hierarchy that bestows disproportionate political power onto private financial wealth.

The UK and US Green Parties contend that the power to create money must be wrested from private banks and restored to democratic and public control. They argue that the national currency supply should be issued free of debt and directed towards environmentally and socially beneficial initiatives, such as renewable energy, social housing, and community business development. This reformed approach to monetary policy is seen as vital not only for achieving a more equitable and democratic economic system but also for facilitating a transition to sustainable, environmentally conscious development.

Green Monetary Reform Proposals in the UK and the US

The Green Party of England and Wales proposes monetary and banking reform that includes the establishment of a National Monetary Authority. The planned reforms mark a significant shift from the current private money system towards a more public-oriented approach. The core of this proposal is that all national currency, both physical and electronic, would be created debt-free by the Monetary Authority, which is accountable to Parliament. This shift entails updating the 1844 Bank Charter Act to prohibit banks from creating national currency in the form of credit, thereby compelling banks to source national currency from savers and investors for their lending and investment activities. The Monetary Authority would be legally mandated to manage the national currency stock to support full employment and price stability while considering the development of local currencies.

The creation of new money by the Monetary Authority would directly benefit government revenue, allowing its expenditure to complement its parliamentary budget without the turbulence of interest rate variability. The members of the Monetary Authority would be appointed by a Parliamentary Select Committee for fixed terms, ensuring independence and transparency. The Monetary Authority's operations would be safeguarded against conflicts of interest and undue influence from any private interests, taking measures to guard against conflicts of interest and prohibiting undue influence.

In parallel, a structural separation of retail and commercial banking from investment banking is proposed to protect borrowed funds from being deployed to high-risk investment strategies. In the New Monetary Framework, government policy will determine the rate at which deposits in the system grow by setting usage limits on the Revolving Loan Facility, which is fully funded with deposits held at the Treasury's Revolving Loan Fund. In Chapter Seven, we illustrated how the accounting treatment would work: the Revolving Loan Facility is an asset on the *Central Government*'s balance sheet and a liability on the balance sheet of *MFIs ex BoE*. The offsetting liability on the *Central Government*'s balance sheet is a larger stock of currency and deposits owed to the non-government sector. This ensures that the volume of currency issuance created in the process of banking credit expansion is managed as a matter of public policy.

Additionally, the UK Greens argue for a structural separation of retail and commercial banks from investment banks to protect against high-risk activities and ensure stability. The separation is tied to a broader plan to remove the limited liability investment banks enjoy, moving towards a partnership model to protect taxpayers from extreme losses. Further bank reforms include a proposal to create a national People's Bank to guarantee access to banking services and non-profit, community-based banks with the authority to issue local currencies. This specific provision might be beneficial in uniting the Green Parties in Scotland and Ireland with the cause of the Green Party of England and Wales. Any devolved tax authority should technically be able to issue a local currency accepted in payment for local taxes. This is not as radical as it appears to be, and the concept has been tested twice in California when it issued IOUs redeemable as tax credits.[23] Complementing these measures are size restrictions on banks to dismantle their "too big to fail" status, limitations on interbank lending and speculative trading, and a focus on stabilising the financial system.

In the US, similar proposals have been put forward by the Greens, advocating for the establishment of a Monetary Authority to oversee all deposits. The US Greens proposed a complete restructuring of the monetary system in a bill before the House in the 112th Congress. The US Greens plan for a phased implementation, where the replacement of Federal Reserve Notes with currency issued by the US Treasury will take place over time, with convertibility guaranteed until all the old currency is retired. The operations for the US payment system will be transferred from the Federal Reserve to the new Monetary Authority, and the Federal Reserve will be subsequently dissolved. Monetary policy control will immediately transfer from the Federal Reserve to the new Monetary Authority, including setting interest rates and bank lending limits. The prohibition of government borrowing ensures that any future spending will result in directly-issued US Treasury money; existing government debt will be retired and replaced by Treasury-issued currency at multiple maturities as directed by the Treasury. This is similar to the operation of the UK Government's current Debt Management Account Deposit Facility, which offers interest-bearing, fixed-term deposits at multiple maturities to local authorities.

The US Greens also outline specific regulatory changes and operational controls, including the establishment of independent accounting and audit control for public oversight of currency issuance, the establishment of procedures for the exercise of new Monetary Authority powers to act as a lender of last resort, and the prohibition of interest on certain deposits and limitations on financing fees and rates charged by banks. A key difference between the UK and the US Greens is how local governments are funded. The UK Greens, including the Scottish Greens,

---

23 Jennifer Steinhauer, "Coffers Empty, California Pays with I.O.U.'s," *New York Times*, July 2, 2009, https://www.nytimes.com/2009/07/03/us/03calif.html.

advocate for a devolved power to issue local currencies. For the Scottish Greens, this paves the path to independence, but a broader perspective views the project for monetary reform as international in scale. The UK model is proposed as an example of a workable solution for all countries looking to make optimal fiscal decisions on a local level, irrespective of the size or complexity of their financial systems. On this point, the US Greens propose a more centralised approach that uses grants and interest-free lending to states and local government bodies, with limits set on a per capita basis or to prioritise particular policy objectives.

The UK and US Greens aim to restore public and democratic control over the money supply. By shifting the power of money creation from private banks to publicly accountable bodies, these reforms seek to align monetary policy with broader environmental and social objectives. The expected outcomes of these reforms are significant. Direct government funding would become available for crucial public services and infrastructure, including modernising education and healthcare systems, promoting welfare, and investing in green energy and environmental protection. As envisioned by these proposals, the transformation of the monetary system represents a profound shift towards a more equitable, sustainable, and democratically accountable economic framework.

The End of Funding Liquidity Risk

Under the proposed monetary system reforms advocated by the Green Parties in the United Kingdom and the US, the fundamental dynamics of bank funding and liquidity management would undergo significant transformation. The shift towards a system where banks no longer create money but instead rely on sourcing national currency from investors and the Monetary Authority presents a paradigm shift in the banking sector's operational framework.

Traditionally, banks manage liquidity risk – the risk of being unable to meet their short-term financial obligations – through careful asset and liability matching. They ensure that the maturities of their assets (loans and investments) are aligned with their liabilities (primarily deposits). This matching is crucial to prevent liquidity crises, where banks may not have sufficient liquid assets to cover sudden withdrawals or obligations.

Asset and liability matching is a strictly regulated and heavily monitored activity at bank treasuries. It involves reporting cash inflows and outflows over time horizons to mitigate the risk of sudden funding withdrawals, such as in a run on the bank. In the current system, banks rely on a mix of customer deposits at varying maturities and other funding sources to finance their lending and investment activities. Since deposits can be withdrawn at short notice if depositors lose confidence, banks are susceptible to an unexpected fire-sale liquidation that turns a liquidity crisis into a solvency problem. Banks mitigate this risk by maintaining sufficient liquid assets and utilising interbank lending markets for short-term borrowing to meet immediate cash needs. As a last resort, the central bank steps in as the ultimate lender in a liquidity crunch, which the taxpayer ultimately backs should such bailouts result in a capital loss.

Under the reformed monetary system, bank funding becomes a policy tool. Where banks must borrow national currency from a public authority, it signifies a shift towards more direct governmental control over the money supply and bank lending. Banks would need to demonstrate their lending activities' viability and social utility to secure funding, aligning their operations more closely with public policy objectives.

With banks no longer creating money and the money supply being managed by a National Monetary Authority, the traditional model of fractional-reserve banking would be altered. If banks are funded directly by a government authority instead of through customer deposits, the risk of bank runs or deposit flight diminishes significantly. Banks would no longer be as vulnerable to sudden withdrawals, fundamentally changing the nature of liquidity risk management.

Banks would need to recalibrate their asset and liability management strategies. Without the need to maintain significant liquid assets to guard against deposit flight, banks might focus more on their assets' long-term sustainability and profitability. However, this would also mean that banks' ability to create credit is more directly tied to the policy decisions of the Monetary Authority, potentially reducing their operational flexibility. Looking at it through a different lens, such influence is needed to move society towards more sustainable and socially responsible goals.

Deposit insurance schemes, which insure a maximum amount of deposits in the event of a bank failure, are key government guarantees to maintain depositor confidence and prevent bank runs. This insurance is a critical component of financial stability in the current banking systems of many countries, as it reduces the incentive for depositors to withdraw funds in a crisis. These deposit insurance schemes would no longer be required as the deposits are now direct liabilities of the *Central Government* under the new monetary framework.

This new system would likely lead to a more utility-like banking model, focusing on serving public interest over profit maximisation. The role of banks would pivot more towards being conduits for government-directed funding, with a reduction in speculative and high-risk activities. Furthermore, it would simplify the monetary system's operations, allowing policymakers to expend less resources on containing the banking system's fragility, giving them the policy space to concentrate on addressing more pressing social and environmental concerns.

Evolution of Credit Risk

Credit risk, a fundamental concern for financial institutions, refers to the risk of loss due to a borrower's failure to make payments on any debt. Traditionally, banks manage credit risk through a variety of mechanisms. These include thorough creditworthiness assessments, diversification of the loan portfolio, setting credit limits, securing collateral, and regularly monitoring loans. A critical component of managing credit risk is adherence to capital adequacy rules, which require banks to hold a certain percentage of their assets as capital. These rules, established under international frameworks like Basel III and Basel IV, are designed to ensure that banks can absorb a reasonable level of losses before becoming insolvent.

The new system could lead to a re-evaluation of capital adequacy frameworks to account for lower liquidity risk, as discussed in the previous section. Since the risk of bank runs and liquidity crises is mitigated by the direct provision of funds from a public authority, the rationale for holding certain types of capital reserves might change. However, capital adequacy would still be crucial for covering credit risks associated with lending activities. With bank runs relegated to an obsolete threat of the past, credit risk will become the primary concern for banking institutions.

Under the proposed monetary system, where banks obtain funding from a public authority, the criteria for credit allocation might shift. Banks may face new mandates to prioritise socially beneficial and environmentally sustainable projects. This shift could alter the risk profile of the banks' loan portfolios, potentially increasing the focus on sectors that align with public policy goals. Over time, this is likely to lower the utilisation of the funding limit provided by the Monetary Authority because loans will no longer be optimised for return on risk capital.

Several factors will contribute to this shift. For example, with the implementation of a public Monetary Authority, banks may be mandated to lend towards projects that align with specific public policy goals, such as environmental sustainability or social welfare. These sectors might have a different level of demand for credit than more traditional or commercial ventures. Consequently, the overall demand for loans from banks could decrease, leading to lower utilisation of the funding limit provided by the Monetary Authority.

Moreover, the public authority's involvement in funding banks would likely require stricter oversight and regulatory requirements. Banks may face more rigorous criteria for loan approvals, including stringent evaluations of their lending activities' social and environmental impacts. This increased regulatory scrutiny could slow down the lending process and reduce the volume of approved loans, thus lowering the utilisation of the funding limit.

There are also implications for a permanently altered risk aversion even with existing capital adequacy rules. Banks would still need to manage their credit risk effectively, but there is a shift towards lending in sectors with different risk-return profiles. The apparent change is that the free ride of lending to the sovereign government by funding with cheap deposits will end. By focusing their lending activities on the non-government sectors, banks will have to adopt a more cautious approach to lending. This risk aversion, coupled with the need to adhere to capital adequacy requirements, could lead banks to be more selective in their lending, thereby reducing their utilisation of the available Monetary Authority funding.

Additionally, government control over the money supply through its Monetary Authority includes the power to regulate the amount of funding available to banks and the interest rate charged for using this facility. This centralised control could lead to a more conservative allocation of funds, especially if the Authority prioritises macroeconomic stability (e.g., controlling inflation) over aggressive credit expansion. The overall impact of public policy objectives cannot be understated; not only has the Government reduced its cost of funding, but the banks will become users of government funding and must align with policy objectives. The result is that banking operations might shift focus from profit maximisation to achieving social and environmental outcomes. This could result in banks pursuing fewer but more impactful lending opportunities, focusing on the quality of loans and their alignment with these objectives rather than the quantity of loans.

The nature of credit risk could change as banks' lending priorities shift. If banks lend more to projects with social or environmental goals, which might have different risk-return profiles than traditional loans, this could alter banks' overall credit risk profile. For example, a new emphasis on infrastructure lending would look markedly different than the current focus on housing mortgages. Similarly, consumer debt will likely shrink as priorities shift towards more sustainable finance and as national income is more fairly distributed.

In the new system, capital adequacy rules might evolve to incorporate considerations for environmental and social risks, reflecting a broader understanding of what constitutes "risk" in the context of sustainable finance. For example, a lending activity with an environmental risk exposure may become subject to charges against the bank's risk capital. This change would align the banking sector more closely with environmental sustainability and social responsibility goals.

While the current capital adequacy regime can continue to operate during a transitionary period, the proposed reforms to the monetary system would significantly alter the relevance of many of the existing capital adequacy rules. It will initially increase the bank risk budgets for credit risk because liquidity risk becomes negligible with deposits being replaced by government funding. However, new lending constraints will eventually surface as funding limits become a policy tool for controlling the national money supply. The Monetary Authority will need to utilise this new policy tool to ensure that the transition to the new monetary framework does not trigger excessive credit growth as banks' credit risk appetites grow to offset the reduction of liquidity risk.

This transition to a system where the state controls money creation, coupled with directives to fund projects aligned with specific policy goals, would necessitate rethinking traditional credit risk management practices. While these changes offer the potential for a banking sector more aligned with public and environmental interests, they also pose challenges for assessing, managing, and regulating credit risk. The evolution of capital adequacy rules and credit risk profiles would ensure that banks remain resilient and effective under this new monetary regime.

The Future of Managing Interest Rate Risk

Interest rate risk is the risk that changes in interest rates will adversely affect a bank's financial condition. This risk arises because the interest rates banks pay on liabilities (like deposits) and the interest rates they earn on assets (such as loans) are subject to fluctuation over time. Banks manage this risk through asset-liability matching, ensuring that their assets' and liabilities' maturities and interest rate sensitivities are aligned. For instance, a bank might use fixed-rate loans (bank assets) to match fixed-rate deposits (bank liabilities) or use interest rate derivatives and other financial instruments to hedge its exposure to interest rate movements.

Under the proposed new monetary system, where money creation is centralised and controlled by a public Monetary Authority, interest rate risk management dynamics would change substantially. The US Greens specify that the currency issued by the Monetary Authority can have different tenors as deemed necessary by the Monetary Authority. This means that the Monetary Authority will have the power to set interest rates across the yield curve for various maturity dates. It is crucial to note that the yield curve will remain an essential feature of the new monetary system, and it will continue to guide the price of borrowing by providing a base rate before other risks are accounted for.

Rates on fixed-term deposits can inform the yield curve just as market forces today inform the yield curve for zero-risk gilts or treasuries at different maturities. With a public authority controlling money creation, interest rates can be set more directly as government policy rather than indirectly by market forces. The result is that the current monetary policy tool of raising and lowering the overnight rate will cease to be the primary tool for managing the money supply, leading to greater predictability in interest rates and less collateral damage to businesses and homeowners. This tool becomes unnecessary because the Monetary Authority has direct control over the level of the Revolving Loan Facility. The new framework reduces some aspects of interest rate risk for banks but could introduce new political or policy-driven risks if interest rates are not aligned with inflation rates.

The Green Party of England and Wales has advocated for a policy for fixed-rate mortgages throughout their terms, aiming to provide borrowers with predictability and protection from interest rate fluctuations. Under the new system, this policy is easily implemented without exposing the lenders to undue risk. Banks would manage the long-term interest rate risk associated with holding large volumes of fixed-rate loans by borrowing at matched maturities from the Revolving Loan Facility at rates set by the Monetary Authority. Banks would be free to compete with each other on pricing mortgage rates at levels sufficiently above the base rates to offset the additional credit risk. If policy rates remain stable over time, there will be a diminished role for interest rate swaps and other hedging strategies to manage interest rate risk.

If commercial banks are funded directly by the Monetary Authority instead of through customer deposits, their reliance on interbank markets for short-term funding will naturally diminish. The Revolving Loan Facility will supplant the interbank lending market and existing central bank liquidity facilities. The Monetary Authority can also be used to shape the yield curve, as borrowing by banks will need to be matched with loan books across different maturities. In other words, the interest rates that the Monetary Authority charges on different tenors will form the new yield curve used to price loans by banks. This will reduce the risk of bank exposure to interest rate fluctuations, changing the nature of banks' interest rate risk management practices.

Investment banks, which engage in activities like underwriting securities and advising on mergers and acquisitions, might see a change in demand for their services based on how the new monetary system affects corporate financing and investment strategies. However, the core functions of investment banks are insulated from interest rate risk management, which is more of a concern for commercial banks.

Yield curve control also aligns with the Greens' objective of fostering a more socially equitable society. This is a common goal long advocated by many MMT economists, who assert that there are no operational constraints for the central bank to set rates for the entire yield curve. However accurate this operational description may be, societal perceptions and the current political structures often impede the recognition of government debt as a form of money. This book, aligning with the monetary reform plan of the Green Party, proposes that the *Central Government* should directly issue term deposits, thereby formalising the process of money issuance and removing political barriers that hinder state control over the yield curve.

The Greens and MMT economists agree that the current system of managing excess demand in the economy – by raising interest rates to a sufficiently high level to bring about a recession – is not aligned with the interests of poorer citizens. The volatility of market-driven interest rates also translates into higher lifetime mortgage costs for borrowers. The Monetary Authority can provide consistency and stability in the credit market by controlling policy rates across all tenors. This stability is crucial for lower-income borrowers, who are often the most vulnerable to economic fluctuations and interest rate volatility.

However, the Green Party diverges in its advocacy for a revamped monetary structure. It envisions the establishment of a Monetary Authority as the principal depository institution, relegating banks to the status of borrowers from the Revolving Loan Facility. In this proposed framework, the Monetary Authority would assume the responsibility of setting interest rates for its Revolving Loan Facility across the yield curve, thereby directing monetary policy for bank lending rates. Such a system would not only make credit more accessible but also more affordable for lower-income segments of society, offering a more equitable approach to monetary management. The Revolving Loan Facility yield curve differs from the yield curve on deposits; the first is used to set monetary policy on lending, while the latter can also be used for monetary policy objectives like managing depositors' propensity to save.

The Greens also stress the importance of limiting interest rates and lending to manageable levels, including for mortgages and small business loans, with ceilings on the proportion of debt to the property's value and borrower's income. The Monetary Authority can play a more direct and pivotal role in protecting citizens from predatory lending practices and empowering economically disadvantaged individuals. Policy rates set by the Authority can be designed to encourage lending to underprivileged sections of society at lower interest rates. This could take the form of targeted lending programs or incentives for banks to extend credit to traditionally underserved communities. This access to affordable credit is essential not only for immediate financial relief but also for enabling long-term improvements in living standards.

It is important to note that there needs to be more documentation on which path the Greens will take to manage interest rate markets. Any monetary reform must address the gap created in the absence of gilts or treasuries to derive a base rate for bank lending for different maturities. Deposits offered at varying tenors are one way to set rates, which can inform rates for the Revolving Loan Facility, but this will result in a market-driven and upward-sloping yield curve as depositors will have a preference for accessing money today and will have an influence on what future rates should be. An alternative approach would grant the Monetary Authority more flexibility over future lending rates for the Revolving Loan Facility, allowing these rates to diverge from the yield curve on deposit rates. This separation is pivotal as it recognises that the mechanisms for controlling the cost of money in lending activities should be distinct from those influencing depositor savings behaviour.

In the reformed monetary system where banks primarily source their funds from the Monetary Authority instead of individual depositors, it becomes imperative for banks to align the terms of their funding with the long-term, fixed nature of their mortgage assets and other fixed-term loans. A bifurcated approach to interest rate management – distinguishing between rates for depositors and lending facilities – allows for a more targeted and effective implementation of monetary policy. It will enable the Monetary Authority to modulate lending rates to support broader economic objectives, such as promoting sustainable growth, without being unduly influenced by short-term market sentiments or depositor preferences for saving.

Capital Markets and the Role of Investment Banks

Capital markets play a crucial role in the global financial system by facilitating the raising of capital for private enterprises. They encompass the markets for stocks (equity) and bonds (debt), enabling companies to access funding beyond what they could obtain through traditional bank loans because they access funding from a larger number of investors. Investment banks are key players in these markets, acting as intermediaries that help businesses raise funds through public equity offerings (IPOs) and the issuance of debt securities. In equity markets, investment banks assist companies in going public or issuing new stock. They underwrite these offerings, meaning they purchase the shares from the company and sell them to investors, bearing the risk of the sale. In the debt markets, investment banks help issuers sell bonds to investors, providing a vital service for businesses and governments needing to raise large sums of capital.

This process differs significantly from the loan business of commercial banks. While commercial banks extend credit primarily through the creation of loans, which appear on their balance sheets as assets, investment banks facilitate access to capital markets. They do not typically hold the securities they help issue as assets but earn fees for their underwriting, advisory, and brokerage services. This process is not without its risks, as investment banks underwrite the issuance process. Therefore, they must have sufficient capital to buy any securities they underwrite that are not absorbed by the market.

Both the Green Party of the US and the Green Party of England and Wales advocate separating commercial and retail banks from speculative investment banks. Moreover, the proposed monetary reform aims to manage the money supply at the state level, which is determined by the Revolving Loan Facility limits set by the Monetary Authority. The credit creation process will continue to create deposits, but the rate of this money growth is now constrained by usage limits for each bank as determined by the Monetary Authority – taking into account capital adequacy, inflation and environmental or social objectives set by the Government. Investment banking activities do not involve an expansion of balance sheets to extend credit. The aggregate currency and deposits on the liability side of the Government's balance sheet do not change as a result of a bond issuance or an IPO. The money simply moves within the non-government sector from one account to another. Separating investment banking activities from the credit creation process ensures that any significant failure of an investment bank has minimal impact on the level of deposits in the system created through credit.

One example of a situation where the functions of investment banks can interfere with the provision of credit is the severe and sudden contraction of credit and money following the 2008 collapse of the mortgage securitisation activities of full-service banks. As the market's appetite for Mortgage-Backed Securities (MBS) plunged, many banking institutions underwriting these activities found themselves in breach of capital adequacy limits. Banks were forced to withdraw credit to reduce charges to risk capital, and that withdrawal of credit precipitated a sudden and self-reinforcing contraction in the privately issued money supply. The deflationary period continued until a sufficient level of government deficit spending offset the credit contraction with state-issued money.

The limits on policy rates and the creation of non-profit public sector banks will ensure that borrowers avoid a significant increase in funding costs. Still, the proposed new monetary system will likely increase demand for investment banking services because free markets shift financial activities to the least regulated financial institutions. Banks can no longer rely on cheap deposits for funding as users of money. Much of this cheap funding source for banks currently comes at a lower rate than the central bank's base rate on bank reserves. If the new system leads to tighter regulations and higher costs for commercial bank loans, companies will increasingly turn to capital markets for financing. This shift will result in a more active role for investment banks in facilitating capital raising through public equity and debt issuance.

While the direct impact on investment banking might be less pronounced than on commercial banking, increased regulation could still affect aspects of investment banking, such as securities trading, risk management, and compliance requirements. The Green Party of England and Wales addresses this potential problem by stipulating that "investment banks should take the form of partnerships rather than limited companies."[24] This was the traditional model that was abandoned in favour of limited liability corporations, which increased the capacity of these financial institutions to raise capital and left the burden of failure on the taxpayer, following in the same pattern of Neoliberal financialisation that privatises profits and socialises losses. A return to the partnership model for investment banks would prevent excessive risk-taking and create long-

---

24 Green Party of England and Wales, "Economy," last amended 2023, accessed 22 November 2023,

https://policy.greenparty.org.uk/our-policies/long-term-goals/economy.

term incentives for successfully managing investment banking activities under the new regime.

The new monetary system could lead to broader changes in the economic landscape, including shifts in clientele, interest rates and investment appetites. For example, if public policy initiatives prioritise specific sectors (like green technology), investment banks may find a growing market for underwriting and advisory services in these areas. The financial regulatory environment could become more stringent under the new system to alleviate this sector's failure risk.

Systemic Risk and the UK's Unique Position in Underwriting Banking Activities

Systemic risk in the financial sector refers to the risk that the failure of a significant financial institution or a series of events could trigger a collapse of the entire financial system, leading to severe economic consequences. In the UK, the Government plays a pivotal role in underwriting the activities of the banking sector, effectively acting as an insurer against bank failures. This role includes mechanisms such as deposit insurance schemes and potential bailouts using taxpayer funds. However, this contingent liability, essentially an insurance policy for the banking sector, is not explicitly accounted for on the Government's books. It represents a significant off-balance-sheet financial commitment and a risk borne by the UK taxpayers, especially in providing support to privately-owned banks, many of which are foreign-owned.

This arrangement grants an exorbitant privilege to these banks, as they can operate with the implicit understanding that they will be rescued in case of severe financial distress, often referred to as the "too big to fail" doctrine. This privilege can encourage risk-taking behaviour, contributing to systemic risk, as banks may engage in more aggressive financial activities with the knowledge that their losses can be socialised.

Post the 2008 GFC, it is arguable that the austerity measures adopted by successive UK administrations were primarily driven by the substantial public funds and resources allocated to avert a catastrophic collapse of the existing monetary system. According to the National Audit Office (NAO), the UK Government spent a total of £133 billion to provide loans and capital to stabilise the banks during the financial crisis from 2007 to 2010, falling gradually to £32 billion on the eve of the pandemic.[25] This considerable allocation to the financial sector was counterbalanced by reductions in government expenditure on the non-financial private sectors, significantly contributing to the anaemic growth during this period.

The Green Party's proposed reforms promise to substantially revise this disproportionate exposure to systemic risk and shield taxpayers from the socialisation of financial sector losses. Transitioning to a framework where a public Monetary Authority oversees the creation and allocation of money and where banks receive direct funding from this authority would fundamentally alter the traditional model of depository institutions. The systemic risk will be significantly reduced as banks will no longer rely on interbank lending for liquidity provision, and investment banking activities will be prohibited from merging activities with retail banking operations.

Under this new paradigm, retail banks would operate as utilities, primarily providing payment services and extending credit to the public. This transformation of depository institutions into banking utilities, emphasising their fundamental roles, will mitigate the risk-taking behaviours that expose taxpayers to contingent liabilities in events of default. The new monetary framework would lower these institutions' overall liquidity, credit, and interest rate risks. Interbank exposures would be substantially reduced as the funding model shifts from a decentralised bank-to-bank network to a more centralised, stable structure anchored by the Revolving Loan Facility. This reorientation from banks being creators to users of money empowers policymakers to prioritise the environment, societal welfare and financial stability over profit maximisation.

---

25 National Audit Office, "Taxpayer support for UK banks: FAQs," last updated November 2020, accessed 23 November 2023, https://www.nao.org.uk/taxpayer-support-for-uk-banks-faqs.

Furthermore, the Green Party is advocating the removal of the limited liability status from investment banks and instituting a partnership model. This change would dampen the incentives for these institutions to externalise the costs of their high-risk activities onto the public. Such a measure would promote more cautious and risk-aware behaviour, aligning the banks' interests with the long-term health of the financial system. Investment banks must exercise greater prudence in their operations, bearing direct responsibility for their losses.

These proposed reforms aim to establish public control over the excessive financialisation of the economy, where financial markets, banking institutions, and financial wealth disproportionately influence political and economic policies and outcomes. While promoting capitalism, excessive financialisation often impedes competition and overlooks economic activities' social and environmental ramifications. It fosters monopolistic tendencies and predatory pricing of public goods and unduly influences politics, education, media, and the functioning of democratic institutions. By restricting the scale and extent of the financialised economy and emphasising sustainable, productive investments, the financial sector's propensity to precipitate economic crises can be significantly reduced.

Such reforms would diminish the likelihood of UK taxpayers being compelled to salvage failing banks. With a banking sector resembling utilities and investment banks assuming their own risks, the contingent liabilities currently implicit in the Government's backing of the banking sector would be substantially lowered. These reforms would safeguard UK taxpayers from the perils of systemic financial crises and diminish the moral hazard inherent in the current system. The financial system would evolve to become more resilient, transparent, and aligned with the long-term economic interests of society.

Restoring Public Ownership of Public Assets

As the book details in Chapter Six, selling the state's real assets to reduce its financial liabilities is accounting trickery to convince the electorate that the Government is financially prudent. Looking at the national debt in isolation, without accounting for the real assets that the Government owns as a result of its deficit spending, leads to the irresponsible destruction of the state's wealth. It prevents politicians from building the infrastructure that we desperately need for real and sustainable development of the nation. The privatisation of critical infrastructure such as railways, electricity, and water utilities in the United Kingdom was a central tenet in Neoliberal policies, but the results present a compelling case for the re-evaluation and subsequent reversal of these privatisation initiatives. The Green Party's advocacy for moving towards public ownership of these services is not merely a political stance but is underpinned by economic rationale and social welfare considerations, elements that are central to this discussion.

Chapter Six elaborates on why these utility companies failed to reduce costs or protect the environment. Moreover, creating an elaborate web of administrative and regulatory oversight justified taxes above the high prices paid to private utility providers. Taxpayers continue to absorb catastrophic losses for insolvent entities running vital infrastructure. The outcome exhibits the same pattern as other areas of the Neoliberal platform: profits are privatised, and losses are socialised. In the case of utilities, the Government cannot just walk away because these are essential services and constitute a fundamental human right.

Infrastructure development is one area where greening the economy must involve the public sector more directly. Even without monetary reform, the Government's funding cost is what it pays in interest on gilts. The private sector can never fund at those rates because they expose investors to a risk of loss, requiring additional returns in the form of an equity risk premium and a credit spread for debt financing. Furthermore, this risk can never be offloaded by the Government because it will always be responsible for providing these public services in the event of default. To begin fixing the problem, the Green Party of England and Wales has advocated for nationalising public infrastructure companies.

The privatisation of the railway system in the UK was predicated on the belief that market forces and private sector efficiency would lead to improved services and infrastructure development. However, empirical evidence over the years suggests a divergence from these expectations. Instead of enhanced efficiency, the system has been plagued by rising fares, inconsistent service quality, and underinvestment in infrastructure. The complexity introduced by the system's fragmentation has led to inefficiencies in operations and increased transaction costs, which are ultimately borne by the general public. Therefore, the economic logic for nationalising railways rests on the need to reintegrate the system, streamline operations, reduce redundancies, and focus on service quality and affordability, which are more aligned with public transportation's social utility nature.

Similarly, the electricity sector's privatisation has raised critical issues concerning pricing, service reliability, and investment in sustainable energy sources. The driving assumption that private ownership would result in lower prices and innovative practices has yet to materialise to the extent anticipated. Instead, concerns about profit maximisation have taken precedence over long-term investment in renewable energy and infrastructure resilience. Nationalising this sector could facilitate a more coordinated approach to energy policy, prioritising long-term environmental sustainability and energy security over short-term profits. It would enable the implementation of comprehensive strategies for transitioning to renewable energy sources, a crucial step in addressing climate change and its associated risks.

The privatisation of water utilities presents the most direct case for re-nationalisation, given water's status as a fundamental human right and its sensitivity to environmental risks. Commercialising water services has increased prices, raising concerns about equitable access to this essential resource. Moreover, issues related to environmental stewardship, particularly in managing water resources and treating wastewater, have emerged. Public ownership of water utilities would ensure more equitable access and place greater emphasis on sustainable water management practices, aligning the operation of these utilities with environmental and public health objectives.

In each of these sectors, the shift to private ownership has often led to an overemphasis on financial returns to investors in the form of dividends and interest at the expense of broader social and environmental goals. This outcome aligns with the critique of excessive financialisation, where the primary focus shifts from serving the public interest to maximising shareholder profits. Nationalisation presents an opportunity to realign these sectors with their fundamental public service objectives, ensuring that they operate in a manner that prioritises general welfare, equitable access, and sustainable practices.

Therefore, the economic argument for nationalisation transcends ideological predispositions towards market or state control. It is rooted in a pragmatic assessment of the outcomes of privatisation and the need to realign these critical sectors with their inherent social and environmental responsibilities. The case for moving towards public ownership, as advocated by the Green Party, finds its justification in the pursuit of a more equitable, sustainable, and socially responsive economic system.

Chapter Nine

Transitional Hybrid System

I n the intricate transition process to the new monetary framework, it is prudent to allow for a period where the existing and proposed systems coexist, functioning in parallel. The design of the new monetary framework allows for this parallel operation of new and legacy monetary systems, in which depositors are free to choose where their money accounts are situated. The Monetary Authority's Revolving Loan Facility will stand ready to offset any bank funding gaps caused by deposit outflows from bank money to state money. This approach ensures a smooth and gradual shift, minimising disruptions to the financial ecosystem. This chapter delves into the multifaceted operational challenges encountered during this transition, focusing on regulatory and compliance hurdles and the evolution from established payment systems to those orchestrated by the newly formed Monetary Authority.

The parallel operation of the two monetary systems begins with the establishment of the Monetary Authority, which introduces depository services to the public to compete with existing banking services. Deposits held at the Monetary Authority, being government liabilities, are inherently risk-free and fully insured. This new structure encourages the general public to gradually shift their deposits to the Monetary Authority, thereby reducing their dependency on traditional bank deposits and increasing the banks' reliance on funding facilitated through the Monetary Authority's Revolving Loan Facility.

Concurrently, the traditional method of government debt issuance through gilts is phased out, supplanted by a direct currency issuance model. The government would introduce fixed-term deposits for non-government sectors needing risk-free financial assets at longer maturities. This allows the Monetary Authority to maintain the system's stability and offer an alternative to gilts required by the financial sector for operational purposes, such as meeting collateral requirements. These changes must be implemented progressively, allowing for minimal disruption and enabling the system to stabilise under the new regime.

During this transition, the Monetary Authority assumes the roles and responsibilities traditionally held by the BoE, encompassing liquidity provision and bank reserve management. This transition continues until the entire transfer of deposits to the Monetary Authority is completed. The government must determine an appropriate deadline to complete the transition to the new monetary system and disband the legacy structures. As the transition evolves, bank reserves will be transferred to the Monetary Authority, and the rate paid on excess reserves will become the Monetary Authority's policy rate paid on deposits. The Monetary Authority's policy decisions, including setting deposit rates, the cost of utilising the Revolving Loan Facility, and managing legacy BoE facilities, play a pivotal role in shaping the monetary landscape. Ultimately, the traditional role of the BoE in managing bank reserves becomes obsolete as banks transition to utilising deposit accounts at the Monetary Authority.

In this transitionary period, ensuring the uninterrupted operation of existing payment systems is crucial. The Real-Time Gross Settlement (RTGS) system, managed by the BoE, remains a central component in settling interbank balances and facilitating transactions from other payment systems such as Clearing House Automated Payment System (CHAPS), Bankers' Automated Clearing Services (BACS), and Faster Payments. The RTGS system ensures secure and efficient fund transfers between financial institutions and is vital in managing banks' reserve accounts. Further complications must be considered when transitioning from RTGS for reserve management to the newly instituted Monetary Authority's payment system to transfer and clear funds between the new deposit accounts. The RTGS can be integrated into the Monetary Authority's payment system and expanded to include settlement between other non-bank users of the Monetary Authority's payment system.

Furthermore, the UK's extensive use of domestic and international payment systems necessitates a seamless integration with the global financial network, mainly through the SWIFT system. Domestically, these payment systems are regulated by the UK's Payment Systems Regulator: BACS, CHAPS, Cheque & Credit, FPS, LINK, Mastercard, Visa Europe (Visa), and Sterling Fnality Payment System. Several layers of highly integrated networks facilitate funds transfers between individuals, businesses, and financial institutions. These systems, bolstered by technological advancements in digital wallets and mobile payment technologies, ensure rapid, secure, and reliable transactions, vital for the country's financial stability and economic activity.

Regulatory oversight ensures that these systems operate in a secure and trustworthy environment, maintaining domestic and international confidence. Throughout this transition, the regulatory landscape, overseen by entities such as the Financial Conduct Authority (FCA), must adapt to the evolving monetary framework, maintaining the integrity and stability of these crucial payment systems. The parallel monetary operations will allow the FCA the flexibility to resolve any unintended consequences of operating under the new monetary framework. This regulatory adaptation is paramount in managing the complex shift towards a new monetary paradigm, ensuring the smooth functioning of the domestic and international financial systems. Stringent regulatory frameworks and oversight mechanisms currently underpin the UK's payment system. The BoE also plays a pivotal role in ensuring the stability and integrity of these payment systems, and its regulatory responsibilities must be transitioned to other regulatory bodies.

Local Payments Under the New System

The Green Party's advocacy for reforming the UK's monetary system marks a paradigm shift in the processing and management of local transactions.

In this new framework, where a public Monetary Authority controls the creation and supply of money, there would be significant changes to the operational landscape of local transactions. The Monetary Authority emerges as the pivotal entity overseeing and facilitating all local financial transactions in the new framework. This centralisation is not merely an administrative change; it represents a strategic move towards enhancing transactional efficiency, reducing operational costs, and broadening equitable access to financial services. A key ambition of this model is to streamline transactional processes, ensuring they are user-friendly and readily accessible to the entire populace, irrespective of their socioeconomic status.

The reconfigured monetary system proposes a radical departure from the traditional role of banks. Rather than acting as autonomous entities that create money through lending practices, banks would transition to serving as conduits for the distribution of funding supplied by the state. This shift would likely yield a more uniform and straightforward framework for handling routine transactions, such as bill payments, salary deposits, and retail purchases. Although the UK is quite advanced in its options for various payment systems, there are hidden costs to outsourcing payments to private financial intermediaries. Even payment systems that appear to be cost-free for both customer and vendor must use bank accounts that function as a low-cost source of funding for banking operations, effectively paying depositors a negative risk-adjusted return.

Technological innovation stands at the forefront of this new system. The Authority must spearhead the development of a unified digital platform tailored to manage a high volume of transactions with utmost security and efficiency. This platform should incorporate advanced payment methodologies, including digital wallets and mobile payment solutions, aligning with the evolving technological inclinations of consumers. The idea of running a public digital payment platform with account services for the general public is not new, and it has been researched extensively as Central Bank Digital Currencies (CBDC). The concept of running a CBDC is identical to running a state-currency system under the Monetary Authority, with non-material differences in the roles of the institutions sponsoring them.

A cornerstone of the proposed system is its commitment to financial inclusion. By centralising control over the money supply and its distribution channels, the system positions itself to better cater to the financial needs of historically underserved or unbanked communities. Initiatives could include more accessible banking services, simplified transactional procedures, and educational programs to enhance financial literacy about the protections offered under the new payment system. This inclusion has been typically served by physical cash transactions, which the new money system should continue to support. The new system is agnostic to ideological views on the use of physical cash transactions, and it must be stressed that Libertarians who champion private ownership and a small state are inadvertently giving up their liberties by supporting the same institutions at the forefront of making physical cash transactions more difficult.

The oversight of the Monetary Authority would also ensure the minimisation of transaction fees, in stark contrast to the current system's often variable and substantial fees across different banking and financial services. As alluded to previously, many of these costs are hidden from the current system's users, serving only to enrich the financial oligopoly that controls the nation's payment systems. The new approach will lessen the financial burden of transactions on individuals and businesses and reduce the economy's excessive financialisation.

Under the new monetary system, the Authority can directly implement strategies to stimulate local economic growth, such as easing access to credit for small enterprises or nurturing community-based financial projects. The control of the money system will free government resources to address societal challenges and achieve more inclusive prosperity. Such measures for credit provision could cultivate a more localised, community-centric financial ecosystem, thereby propelling economic progress at the grassroots level.

In essence, local transactions under the new monetary system would be characterised by increased central oversight, heightened efficiency, and a strong emphasis on accessibility and financial inclusion. The transition to this system represents a significant shift from the traditional model of banking and finance, with a clear path to creating a more equitable and user-friendly financial environment for all the nation's citizens.

International Payments in the New Framework

International transactions, crucial in an increasingly interconnected global economy, require robust systems to manage the complexities of cross-border payments. The Society for Worldwide Interbank Financial Telecommunication (SWIFT) is a pivotal player in this domain, facilitating secure and efficient international financial transactions. Founded in the 1970s, SWIFT has become the standard for international banking communications, linking banks, financial institutions, and corporate clients worldwide.

SWIFT provides a standardised messaging system through which financial institutions communicate transactional instructions for various financial services, including fund transfers, securities trades, and other types of transactions. Its network spans over 200 countries and territories, featuring thousands of member institutions. The system's standardisation enables seamless interactions between banks with different systems and protocols, a fundamental requirement for smooth international financial operations.

Membership in SWIFT is open to any regulated financial institution that can meet the organisation's stringent requirements. These requirements are geared toward ensuring the network's security, reliability, and efficiency. By becoming members, these institutions gain access to a trusted and universal platform for international financial communications, which is critical for executing global transactions.

SWIFT has many advantages for global transactions. The efficiency and security of SWIFT are key to its widespread adoption. The network uses advanced encryption and identification techniques to ensure the integrity and confidentiality of messages. This high level of security is essential in mitigating risks such as fraud and unauthorised access, which are particularly pronounced in international transactions. One of the significant advantages of SWIFT is the reduction of transactional errors and delays. By providing a standardised and universally recognised messaging format, SWIFT minimises miscommunication and discrepancies arising from differing banking protocols across countries. This standardisation ensures that transactions are secure, quick, and reliable.

SWIFT is indispensable in facilitating international transactions, offering a secure, standardised, and efficient platform for financial communication across borders. Its ability to adapt to the changing demands of global finance and maintain rigorous security standards will continue to be crucial in supporting international trade and finance. As the world economy becomes ever more integrated, the role of systems like SWIFT in managing the complexities of cross-border financial transactions becomes increasingly vital.

However, the use of SWIFT is not without its costs and complexities. The need for intermediaries in the SWIFT network can sometimes lead to additional charges and increased transaction times, particularly for more complex or less common routing paths. These factors, coupled with the evolving landscape of international banking regulations, require continual adaptation and upgrading of the system.

In the context of the new monetary system proposed by the Green Party, handling international transactions would necessitate a reimagined approach, especially given the shift in the domestic financial landscape. This new framework, characterised by a public Monetary Authority controlling money creation and supply, would have profound implications for the operation of international transactions. Fundamentally, there is no barrier for the Monetary Authority to operate as a member of the SWIFT network. Any unforeseen challenges can be resolved during the transitionary period in which international transactions can continue in the parallel operation of the existing monetary system.

This parallel operation is necessary because the role of the public Monetary Authority in international transactions would be pivotal. Unlike the current decentralised system where commercial banks play a significant role in facilitating cross-border transactions, the Monetary Authority could centralise and streamline these processes. However, this raises questions about its capacity and infrastructure to handle complex international financial transfers, which often involve navigating various regulations and foreign exchange considerations.

The ultimate goal of integrating the Monetary Authority's operations with global payment systems is to join an existing international payment network, like SWIFT, to facilitate cross-border transactions. This would allow the Authority to leverage established systems and protocols while ensuring secure and efficient international transfers. Alternatively, the Authority could explore the creation of new bilateral or multilateral agreements with other countries or monetary authorities to establish direct transaction channels, which could offer more control over international payment processes.

A notable consideration is this new system's impact on UK businesses' competitiveness in the global market. The ease and cost of conducting international transactions are crucial factors for businesses engaged in import-export activities. The new system would need to ensure that UK businesses can efficiently and cost-effectively participate in global trade by connecting the newly established local payment with the existing international payment networks. This might involve measures to reduce transaction costs and streamline cross-border payment processes.

Moreover, the shift to a public Monetary Authority system could influence foreign investment dynamics. The Monetary Authority's policies on international financial transfers could either encourage or deter foreign investment, depending on how international investors perceive them. Allowing for a time-limited transitionary period to operate a hybrid monetary system will gradually enable deposits and transactions to shift to the Monetary Authority. Ensuring transparency and stability in these policies would be crucial to maintain investor confidence.

International transactions in the new monetary framework would require a thoughtful blend of integration with existing global systems and innovative approaches to manage cross-border payments. The public Monetary Authority would play a central role in this process, necessitating robust infrastructure, transparent policies, and a keen understanding of international financial dynamics. The success of this new approach would hinge on its ability to facilitate secure, efficient, and cost-effective international transactions while supporting the UK's broader economic and trade objectives.

Technological Integration and Innovation

The transition to a new monetary system, as proposed by the Green Party, demands significant technological integration and innovation. This necessity stems from modernising the existing financial infrastructure to support the envisioned changes in money creation, distribution, and transaction processing under public authority. A cornerstone of this transition is the development of a robust digital platform managed by the public Monetary Authority. This platform must be capable of handling a wide range of financial activities, from basic transactions to more complex financial operations. It requires state-of-the-art technology to ensure high processing speeds, throughput, data integrity, and security. With its decentralised and tamper-evident ledger, blockchain technology could potentially be utilised to achieve transparency and security in transactions. Moreover, the platform must be scalable to accommodate future growth and flexible enough to integrate with emerging financial technologies.

Given the central role of the Monetary Authority in the proposed system, ensuring the highest levels of cybersecurity is paramount. This involves implementing advanced encryption techniques, secure communication channels, and continuous monitoring systems to guard against cyber threats. Regular audits and updates would be necessary to keep pace with the evolving nature of cyber risks.

The transition to the new system will require integration with the current banking infrastructure. This is a fundamental necessity for a phased implementation and the ability to operate with international payment networks and banking systems. This integration includes adapting existing banking software and systems to interface effectively with the new central platform. It must also ensure that legacy systems in commercial banks are compatible with new protocols and processes set by the Monetary Authority.

To ensure wide accessibility, the technological framework should include the development of user-friendly interfaces for both individual consumers and businesses. This effort would involve creating intuitive web portals, mobile applications, and possibly even offline solutions to ensure inclusivity, particularly for those with limited access to technology. Households should be able to view their deposits, set up direct debit payments, transfer funds, and perform any banking transaction as they would through their banking portals. The Green Party's proposal for establishing a People's Bank, operated as a public service and owned by the taxpayer, removes barriers for households preferring traditional interactions with banks.

Support for financial inclusion should be prioritised by allowing non-digital interactions with banks and using Treasury-issued cash in the economy. The UK Greens and US Greens do not take a position for or against physical cash in the economy. The advocacy for financial privacy and freedom is prominent among the right-wing parties, and it is a hallmark of Libertarian politics, with any centralisation being viewed with suspicion of potential abuse by an empowered state. However, as stressed previously in this text, the monetary framework is agnostic to using paper money; it is a matter of political choice if we implement a completely transparent and digital system or guarantee privacy protections for transactions, including cash ones. Creating private platforms that facilitate small-scale transactions efficiently and affordably is in the national interest because the informal economy will find alternative platforms and payment systems to evade oversight. The ultimate purpose of oversight is financial stability and informed management of the money supply, not to be confused with surveillance of every transaction in the monetary system as a tool for law enforcement and tax collection. The power of fiscal and monetary policy – along with its control of inflation or deflation – is diminished when the informal sectors of the economy move transactions to alternative currencies that guarantee privacy.

Real-time data analysis and reporting under the new framework becomes increasingly crucial for public scrutiny of fiscal spending because of its direct impact on money creation and inflation levels. The public Monetary Authority would require advanced data analytics capabilities for real-time financial system monitoring. This capability is crucial for informed decision-making, policy formulation, and risk management. Technologies such as machine learning and AI could play a significant role in analysing transaction patterns, predicting trends, and identifying potential risks.

Existing compliance and regulatory reporting infrastructure can be utilised for the banking system. As the new framework reduces overall risk for the banks and the taxpayer, a phased rollout of the new monetary system can work under existing capital adequacy rules. As deposits begin to shift to the Monetary Authority, banks will start utilising the Revolving Loan Facility to fund their operations, and funding liquidity will decrease over time. Compliance checks for depositors and borrowers will continue to function under the current rules, but it is important to note the Monetary Authority's dual function as a regulator and financial services provider. The Monetary Authority's provision of depository services means that it will also undertake the responsibilities for compliance checks previously performed by banks to ensure that these accounts are not used for illicit activity by nefarious actors. Technology must support compliance and regulatory reporting requirements and ensure that the monetary system adheres to national and international financial regulations and standards.

Transitioning to the new monetary system under the Green Party's proposal requires a comprehensive technological overhaul. This overhaul encompasses the development of a robust digital infrastructure, enhanced security measures, integration with existing banking systems, user-friendly interfaces, support for financial inclusion, real-time data analytics, and compliance mechanisms. The success of this transition hinges on the effective use of technology to create a secure, efficient, and inclusive financial environment.

A Central Bank Digital Currency without a Central Bank

In the context of the new monetary framework proposed by the Green Party, introducing and designing a payment system modelled after a Central Bank Digital Currency (CBDC) could play a transformative role. A CBDC, while initially envisioned as a depository and payment service operated by the central bank, can also be the mechanism with which the non-government sector accesses deposits at the Monetary Authority. While the name implies the existence of a central bank, its conventional name is irrelevant to its role, and very little is changed in terms of the operational objective of a CBDC. Effectively, the CBDC will represent a digital form of a nation's currency, issued and regulated by the public Monetary Authority. Its implementation requires careful consideration of various technological, economic, and social factors to ensure it aligns with the overarching goals of the new monetary framework.

To ensure accessibility, a CBDC in the new framework must be designed to provide ease of access for all citizens, irrespective of their socioeconomic status or technological proficiency. This means creating multiple access points, including digital wallets, mobile applications, and even offline solutions for areas with limited internet connectivity. The Green Party's platform includes the creation of a People's Bank, which can be utilised to provide traditional banking services as an additional layer on top of a centrally operated CBDC infrastructure.

Existing designs for a CBDC not only provide the security and frictionless transaction capability of digital money but can also address privacy concerns while continuing to comply with Anti-Money Laundering (AML) and Counter-Terrorism Financing (CTF) standards. Privacy in a CBDC system can be guaranteed or enhanced through various technological and policy measures. However, it is important to note that complete anonymity, similar to cash transactions, is challenging to achieve in practice. Even cryptocurrencies purporting to be anonymous are traceable and identifiable at the point of entry or exit into mainstream financial systems. Implementing tiered levels of anonymity based on the type of transactions can balance privacy and regulatory compliance concerns.

Strict data access controls – where only relevant entities, like regulatory bodies, have access to transaction data under specific circumstances – will ensure that transaction data is not abused by private interests or sold for marketing purposes. In a sense, the Green Party shares concerns about privately-run payment systems with advocates for physical cash; the current monetary system has left society with increasingly digital and privately-run payment systems, which are continuously surveilled for marketing and profit-motivated purposes. People unknowingly sign away their rights to privacy with credit cards, loyalty programmes, and other private payment systems. The driving concern for the Greens has always been the restoration of balance between the corporate interests – who are now in complete control of payment systems – and the interests of the general public. From this perspective, a democratic state stands as the only reliable guarantor of privacy, and legislation is the best tool we have to protect and enforce it.

A future CBDC payment system should be compatible with existing financial infrastructure and systems, allowing seamless integration with banks, payment processors, and other financial services. The scale of the required technological infrastructure must be sufficient to handle the high transaction volumes that the entire banking system currently undertakes. Providing real-time data processing at that scale will require significant government investment in high-capacity servers, secure communication networks, and data centres capable of handling time-critical transaction processing at a national scale. The system should be built on a scalable platform to accommodate future expansions and integrations with new technologies. Interfacing with other systems includes interfacing with users who may want to continue to access their deposits using external software or a bank platform. Providing multiple user interface options for accessing and transacting with the CBDC system should cater to a wide range of users, from tech-savvy individuals to those with limited digital literacy.

In designing a CBDC within the new monetary framework, the primary objective is to create a digital currency system that is secure, efficient, and accessible while also aligning with the broader goals of economic and social policy. The successful implementation of a CBDC would represent a significant step forward in modernising the financial system, potentially setting a precedent for other nations considering similar reforms. It can be the primary account-keeping tool for managing deposits at the Monetary Authority, or it can function as a specific type of current account among a range of account types made available by the Monetary Authority.

Evolving Regulatory Regime

The previous section on Technological Integration and Innovation briefly presented the compliance and regulatory reporting infrastructure. Specifically, the Monetary Authority's dual function as a regulator and financial services provider will necessitate an evolution in the regulatory regime, including transferring the BoE's regulatory responsibilities. Through its subsidiary, the Prudential Regulation Authority (PRA), the BoE supervises banks, building societies, credit unions, insurers, and major investment firms. While its primary focus is on these institutions' financial soundness and resilience, aspects of AML controls may intersect with its regulatory scope, particularly in the context of overall risk management. As the UK and US Greens propose, implementing a new monetary system necessitates a comprehensive re-evaluation of the existing regulatory and compliance structures. This is crucial to ensure the system's integrity, efficiency, and alignment with national and international financial standards.

The transition to a monetary system governed by a Monetary Authority requires the establishment of a robust regulatory framework. This framework must address the unique characteristics and risks associated with a public entity's direct control of money supply and distribution. Regulations should cover aspects such as issuing digital currencies, oversight of banking operations under the new system, and managing cross-border transactions. They must ensure transparency, protect against financial crimes, and maintain financial stability. While the new system may primarily focus on domestic monetary control, adherence to international financial norms and practices is vital. This includes compliance with standards set by bodies like the Financial Action Task Force (FATF) and the Basel Committee on Banking Supervision. The system must be designed to prevent money laundering, terrorism financing, and other illicit financial activities, adhering to global anti-money laundering (AML) and counter-terrorist financing (CTF) standards.

Previous sections have also addressed challenges in integration with global financial systems. The UK's monetary system does not operate in isolation; hence, the new system must be capable of integrating seamlessly with the global financial ecosystem. This is particularly important for maintaining smooth international trade and investment flows. Regulatory measures should facilitate cooperation and information exchange with international financial institutions and regulatory bodies.

Also important are the protections of individual rights and financial inclusion. An essential component of the CBDC or any centralised payment system operated by the Monetary Authority is the protection of consumers within the bounds of the compliance and regulatory framework. Regulations should ensure that consumers' rights are safeguarded, especially concerning privacy, data security, and fair access to financial services. The framework should promote financial inclusion, ensuring that the new system does not marginalise or exclude certain groups from accessing financial services. Effective oversight mechanisms are crucial for the successful functioning of the new system. This involves not only regular monitoring of financial activities but also the enforcement of regulations.

These objectives can be achieved in one of two ways: 1) the establishment of a new entity to become an independent regulatory body and 2) the empowerment of existing institutions to oversee the system's adherence to the established rules and norms. The Financial Conduct Authority (FCA) is currently the primary regulator for financial services firms and financial markets in the UK. It plays a significant role in overseeing financial institutions' adherence to KYC and AML regulations. The FCA sets the standards and requirements for financial institutions to prevent money laundering and financial crimes, ensuring that firms have appropriate systems and controls in place. The FCA could be utilised for oversight over the depository services provided by the Monetary Authority. Its monitoring and compliance reporting of depository services would become a component of the audit and control system for operations under the new framework.

The Greens also call for the dissolution of the BoE, as monetary policy becomes the domain of the Monetary Authority. However, dissolving the BoE in its entirety requires careful consideration about how to transfer the functions of the PRA. A better option would be to absorb the regulatory functions of the PRA into a new body that allows for continuity in monitoring and enforcing capital requirements as per banking supervision rules. The PRA can continue to assess risk management practices, conduct stress tests, perform audits and onsite inspections, take enforcement actions, and impose penalties on financial institutions when necessary. Other regulatory bodies, such as the National Crime Agency and HMRC, can continue to operate independently in the same way.

Under the new monetary framework proposed by the Green Party, the evolving regulatory regime is crucial in ensuring alignment with economic stability. This regime must adapt to the transformed financial landscape, where the public Monetary Authority assumes a central role in money creation and distribution. Ensuring economic stability in this context involves several key considerations. The public Monetary Authority will need clear, well-defined regulatory guidelines to manage the money supply, control inflation, and respond to economic fluctuations. New rules must be established to support the Authority's ability to implement monetary policy effectively through interest rate adjustments, direct control of the money supply, or other monetary tools. This includes creating mechanisms for transparent and accountable decision-making processes.

Policy rules and guidelines should consider counter-cyclical regulatory measures, taking actions relevant to economic conditions. For example, in an economic downturn, regulations could be designed to encourage lending by increasing the limit on the Revolving Loan Facility; in booming economic periods, more stringent measures could be enforced to cool overheating sectors. The new framework should also empower the fiscal authority to pursue counter-cyclical policy by augmenting automatic stabilisers without being debt-constrained. Welfare and other transfer payments should be designed to increase automatically during downturns and decrease during economic booms.

Economic stability under the new system also depends on effective coordination between monetary and fiscal policies. The regulatory framework should facilitate a harmonious relationship between the Monetary Authority and government fiscal bodies to ensure that monetary and fiscal policies are aligned and mutually reinforcing. This coordination is essential for addressing broader economic challenges such as unemployment, income inequality, and sustainable growth.

The regulatory framework must also be adaptable to global economic trends and shocks. Given the interconnected nature of the global economy, regulations should be responsive to international financial developments, ensuring that the UK's monetary system remains robust in the face of global economic changes. Arguably, the new monetary system will empower the Government to respond to global challenges more efficiently and effectively by removing the constraints imposed under the current system.

Chapter Ten

The Fiction of GDP

U p to this point in the text, the ratio of national debt to GDP has served as a tool for gauging fiscal feasibility and governmental capacity because it is the estimate everyone is familiar with. However, as previously critiqued, this metric is far from flawless. Our analysis has highlighted inherent imperfections, particularly concerning the numerator's composition and the widely misunderstood role of the Government in the economic growth paradigm. We have delved into the misunderstandings of the national debt, specifically by examining how it is influenced by the consolidation of the central bank's assets and liabilities within the *Central Government*'s balance sheet.

This exploration has also shed light on the fact that the approach to funding government expenditure is essentially a policy choice. We illustrated how the Treasury, in essence, already possesses the authority to issue its currency, a power that significantly reframes the conversation around fiscal capacity and monetary sovereignty. The ongoing use of the debt-to-GDP ratio serves our discussion because it is the most accessible and familiar tool to illustrate the common fallacies and misconceptions surrounding the effects of privatisation and government spending on fiscal capacity.

Previous discussions surrounding the national debt to GDP ratio have predominantly focused on critiquing the numerator – the national debt component. However, to fully grasp the intricacies and implications of this ratio, a thorough examination of its denominator, the GDP, is equally vital. The following sections of this text are dedicated to a comprehensive analysis of the GDP component, aiming to illuminate the misunderstandings that often lead to misdirection in political and economic discourse.

Many global Green parties criticise the current methodology for calculating GDP as inherently flawed. This chapter endeavours to deconstruct the reasons underpinning this viewpoint. We will delve into the mathematics of calculating GDP as a measure of economic activity, scrutinising the harmful political choices that reveal a lack of conceptual understanding of its methodologies. In doing so, we aim to expose the biases that stem from these misunderstandings and prevent society from achieving everything that it has the excess capacity to do.

One of the critical aspects we will explore is how GDP, in its current form, inadequately captures the full spectrum of economic activities and fails to account for critical dimensions of societal well-being and environmental sustainability. For instance, GDP does not differentiate between sustainable and unsustainable economic activities, nor does it account for the depletion of natural resources or ecological degradation. This oversight results in a skewed understanding of economic prosperity, often at the expense of long-term environmental and social health.

Moreover, we will examine how the exclusive focus on market transactions in GDP measurement overlooks significant non-market activities, such as unpaid domestic work and volunteer services, which are vital to the functioning of societies. This omission presents a narrow and incomplete picture of economic reality, particularly in terms of labour contributions and societal value.

Chapter Eleven will discuss alternative approaches and indicators that could provide a more holistic and accurate representation of economic health, reflecting both human and ecological considerations. By presenting these critiques and alternatives, we aim to underscore the need for a more comprehensive and thoughtful approach to economic measurement, one that aligns more closely with the values and objectives of sustainable development and social justice. The Greens are right to challenge how society accounts for economic output, and their efforts to reshape how we conceptualise and assess economic progress are warranted. It is a call to move beyond the narrow confines of GDP-centric thinking and to embrace a broader, more inclusive understanding of economic and societal well-being.

Debt to GDP Ratio: Unravelling the Fallacy of Composition

Before we address the inherent weaknesses of GDP as a metric, let us engage in a mathematical thought experiment to challenge the conventional wisdom of using the Government's debt-to-GDP ratio for policy decision-making. To provide context, Prime Minister Rishi Sunak recently endorsed the slogan "long-term decisions for a brighter future" at a conference. However, we will demonstrate that even elementary algebra reveals how every incremental increase in government spending can reduce the much-feared government debt-to-GDP ratio when it hovers around 1:1 in a high-tax country like the UK.

Consider a recent dispute between the conservative government and the British Medical Association (BMA) – a UK trade union and professional body for doctors. The Sunak government is described as "digging in on its final pay offer of a 6 per cent uplift for consultants."[26] As high-income earners, these consultants contribute significantly to tax revenues, particularly at the higher marginal rates for every pound of government-funded income. For the 2023/24 tax year, any marginal earnings over £50,270 are subject to a 40% income tax and an additional 2% employee National Insurance contribution. Earnings above £100,000 trigger the withdrawal of the personal allowance, leading to an effective marginal tax rate of 60% between £100,000 and £125,140. For simplicity, we will omit the effects of employer National Insurance contributions.

---

26 Ireland, Ben. "Doctors warn Government they are prepared to strike until next general election." British Medical Association, 4 October 2023. Accessed 29 November 2023. https://www.bma.org.uk/news-and-opinion/doctors-warn-government-they-are-prepared-to-strike-until-next-general-election.

Economic output is measured in both the Gross Domestic Income (GDI) and the GDP. Both approximations may persistently disagree about the precise level of economic output due to the different data sources used in their computations, but they are close approximations of the nation's income. GDI measures all incomes earned from the production of these goods and services, while GDP measures total expenditure on a country's finished goods and services. Measuring expenditures is conceptually equivalent to an income measurement of economic output because any spending activity corresponds to an income somewhere in the economy. To illustrate the effects of the increase in government spending on NHS consultants, let us revisit a fundamental economic equation; the formula for GDP is:

$$GDP = C + G + I + (X - M)$$
$$where,$$
$$C = Consumer\ Spending$$
$$G = Government\ Spending$$
$$I = Investment$$
$$X = Exports$$
$$M = Imports$$

This is an accounting identity, meaning that each pound sterling spent by the Government adds a pound to GDP, while each pound taxed does not directly subtract from GDP. The methodology treats income to the Government, or taxation, as income to the nation, measured in the same unit of account that comes into existence by deficit spending. Government spending also has a multiplier effect on *Consumer Spending* and *Investment* due to the velocity of money – the rate at which money circulates and is re-spent in the economy. In other words, the £1 in extra government spending circulates during the year multiple times, albeit at diminishing rates due to desired *Saving*. The money added to the economy as government dis-saving becomes the non-government sectors' *Saving*, and it continues to add to nominal GDP in the following years as the additional money re-circulates.

To illustrate what happens in the first year, assume the Government grants an additional £1,000 to the NHS consultants, taxed at a marginal tax rate of 42%. Assuming the marginal propensity to consume is

90% of after-tax income – a 10% saving rate – the impact on the Government debt-to-GDP ratio is as follows:

$$\frac{+/- \; Government \; Debt}{+/- \; GDP} = \frac{\begin{array}{c} Government \; Spending: +1000 \\ Taxes \; on \; Consultant \; Income: -420 \\ Taxes \; on \; Consultant \; Spending: -104 \\ \hline Government \; Spending: +1000 \\ Consultant \; Spending: +522 \end{array}}{} = \frac{+476}{+1522}$$

The income and consumption taxes collected that same year reduce the initial government spending in the numerator of this ratio. GDP increases by £1,000 in G and £522 in C. The 10% saving rate leaves £522 of the post-tax income to be spent in the economy, attracting a further £104 in taxes on the additional spending (assuming a 20% tax rate). The net effect is an increase of £476 in government debt and a £1,522 rise in GDP. This calculation exposes the flaw in the political narrative that equates increased government spending with a higher debt-to-GDP ratio under all circumstances, and it reveals the flaw in using GDP as an indicator for determining the nation's capacity for fiscal policy.

Let us further calculate the effects of this initial spending in subsequent years, assuming a 90% marginal propensity to spend and that the additional net income from the increase in *Consumption* in year 1 is re-spent only once in the following year. In this hypothetical low velocity of money, 90% of £522 is spent (re-circulated) in the economy. This £470 in spending generates additional taxes of £94 and lowers the debt to £382 in year 2. The schedule in Figure 25 highlights the impact on GDP and national debt in the eight years following the initial government outlay. By year 8, the debt is self-liquidating, given the tax rates and assumptions made about the saving rate and velocity of money.

Figure 25: Impact of Hypothetical Government Spending on National Debt over Time

Year	GDP	Debt
1	£1,522	£476
2	£470	£382
3	£423	£297
4	£381	£221
5	£342	£152
6	£308	£91
7	£277	£35
8	£250	-£15

This exploration illustrates a severe mathematical deficiency in our political discourse that government spending is assumed to increase the national debt to GDP ratio in every case. Even when using a low multiple for the velocity of money, the methodology illustrates that a larger government budget should not be feared for a highly taxed economy like the United Kingdom. For simplicity and consistency, we ignore the effects of inflation to make the arithmetic relationships more apparent by consistently measuring the increase in debt and GDP in nominal values.

In this example, for every £1 of net government spending on increasing consultant salaries, £3.20 is added to GDP in the first year. Crucially, the actual impact is likely more substantial due to the multiplier effect. The Carnall Farrar study estimates that for every £1 increase in NHS spending, including for lower-salaried staff, up to £4 is added to GVA. The study correlates long-term illness, workforce participation, and median income with economic output, noting that austerity measures have exacerbated long-term illness despite the end of the COVID-19 pandemic. As of October 2022, 2.46 million working-age adults are off work due to long-term illness. Empirical evidence suggests that investment in the NHS, particularly in primary care, is linked to reduced emergency department visits and non-elective admissions, indicators of poor health that affect workforce participation. Curiously, the Conservatives continue to practice this metaphorical bloodletting to deepen a self-inflicted wound.

This exercise demonstrates the fallacy of assuming that what is true for a part (the numerator of the debt/GDP ratio) is also true for the whole. Philosophically, this is known as the fallacy of composition, a concept Keynes famously termed the paradox of thrift. In reality, increasing NHS consultant salaries not only lowers the Government debt-to-GDP ratio but also has broader, positive implications for healthcare service capacity, addressing backlogs that impact workforce participation and overall economic productivity.

Unaccounted Economic Output

Over the years, GDP has become an indispensable metric in domestic and international spheres, gaining prominence as the most pivotal economic indicator worldwide. This metric's integration into global structures is profound; it serves as a critical determinant for international loan eligibility and forms the foundation of national accounting practices. The reliance on GDP transcends mere data collection, influencing a broad spectrum of policy decisions and strategic planning.

GDP's utility extends to offering key economic insights, aiding governments in rationalising and directing public expenditures towards projects and interventions poised to stimulate further GDP growth. However, as illustrated in the previous section, this aspect is often misunderstood when assessing the limits of public expenditures. Government spending is the most direct tool for regulating demand in an economy, and it underscores the significance of monetary reform in shaping macroeconomic policies, particularly those aimed at fostering economic expansion and infrastructure development.

Moreover, the communications power of GDP cannot be overstated. It encapsulates economic progress into a single, comprehensive figure, offering an ostensibly clear indicator of national prosperity. The perception is straightforward: the faster and higher the GDP grows, the better the country's perceived economic condition. This simplicity in interpretation lends GDP an unmatched persuasive potency in public discourse.

The prevailing political narrative, especially in the latter half of the 20th century, revolved around the axiom that GDP growth is good. This philosophy, underpinned by the pursuit of economic growth, has been instrumental in elevating workforce participation, but it also elevates non-government debt levels when GDP-maximising strategies are pursued at all costs. Fluctuations in GDP – whether increases or decreases – have become central to the narrative around which governments structure their policies and strategies. This metric shapes public perception and policy priorities, often becoming the benchmark against which a government's economic competence is assessed.

The pervasive influence of GDP growth has implications for how governments prioritise their agendas and allocate resources. It often drives a focus on short-term economic gains, sometimes at the expense of long-term sustainability, environmental considerations, and equitable social development. A particularly striking manifestation of this skewed focus is observed in the context of gender equality.

The professional trajectory often demanded by the modern workforce – characterised by continuous, uninterrupted employment – poses unique challenges for women, particularly those who choose to become mothers. The traditional career ladder, with its linear and unyielding progression, fails to accommodate the realities of maternity and child-rearing. As a result, women frequently face career setbacks or are compelled to make difficult choices between professional aspirations and familial responsibilities.

Despite numerous initiatives aimed at bridging the gender gap, the current economic framework, heavily influenced by GDP metrics, inadvertently exacerbates gender inequality. Women disproportionately shoulder the burden of unpaid work, including caregiving and household management. They often find their economic contributions undervalued when seeking to re-enter the formal workforce, and they are entirely unaccounted for in GDP calculations. This systemic oversight overlooks a significant portion of societal active contribution to labour, predominantly undertaken by women. Unsurprisingly, certain occupations, like early-year education, are predominantly staffed by women. While the number of male workers in the UK childcare sector has increased, it remains very low at 7.4%. Within this figure, just 1.8% of nursery nurses and assistants and 4% of childminders are male.[27]

To understand how GDP accounts for unpaid work, let us consider a hypothetical scenario involving two households, A and B, and two individuals, Ann and Betty. This situation, depicted in Figure 26, offers an insightful look into the impact of unpaid domestic work on economic indicators.

Figure 26: Unpaid Work Scenario

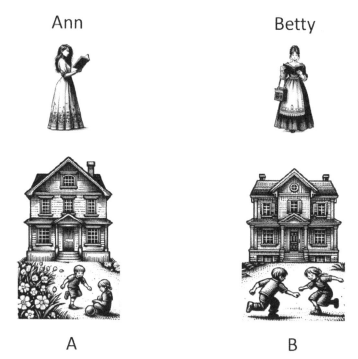

Household B employs Betty as a full-time nanny for two children, compensating her with an annual salary of £20,000. In contrast, Ann

---

27 Education Policy Institute, "The early years workforce in England," 17 January 2019,

https://epi.org.uk/publications-and-research/the-early-years-workforce-in-england.

performs similar childcare duties for her children in Household A without financial compensation, rendering her work invisible in GDP metrics. The disparity in how their labour is accounted for in economic metrics offers a stark illustration of the shortcomings of GDP as a comprehensive measure of economic activity.

In Household B, Betty's employment as a nanny and her £20,000 salary directly contribute to GDP. This economic transaction is straightforward: Betty renders a service and receives a salary, which she uses for consumption or savings. After accounting for taxes of £2,827, Betty's take-home pay amounts to £17,173. Assuming she saves 10% of this and spends the remaining 90%, her consumption contributes £15,456 to the economy. The government further benefits from £3,091 in taxes from her spending. Thus, Betty's gross contribution to GDP, considering her salary and subsequent consumption, amounts to £35,456, which generates £5,918 in total taxes.

Conversely, in Household A, Ann's childcare work, though identical in function to Betty's childcare work, remains uncounted in GDP calculations, and it does not generate any additional tax revenue. Her contribution to GDP will be her spending on consumption, which may be smaller than Ann's because of her circumstances. However, the omission of her work underscores a significant blind spot in economic measurements, where substantial contributions to societal welfare and family well-being are disregarded due to their non-financial nature.

Extending this analysis further, Figure 27 presents an absurd yet instructive hypothetical scenario: Ann takes a job at Household B, earning £20,000, and hires Betty to perform her previous unpaid role in Household A. While economically irrational, this scenario demonstrates how transitioning unpaid work to paid employment can affect GDP figures. In this scenario, Ann's new income contributes £20,000 to GDP, of which £2,827 are government tax revenues. However, after accounting for taxes and the additional money flows where Ann's entire salary goes to pay Betty, there is no net gain in economic activity. Instead, Ann either reduces her consumption to offset the tax burden or incurs debt while attempting to validate her economic productivity. This paradox highlights a fundamental flaw in the GDP model – it favours monetised economic transactions over vital yet unpaid contributions, leading to distorted perceptions of economic health and productivity.

Figure 27: Paid Work Scenario

This hypothetical scenario, while unrealistic, serves as a poignant illustration of the limitations inherent in GDP as a measure of economic activity and societal well-being. The situation illustrated here, wherein no rational individual would willingly diminish her standard of living, time with her children, and financial stability solely to be acknowledged as part of the workforce, underscores the inadequacy of GDP in capturing the true breadth of economic contributions, particularly those of women.

Unpaid work, encompassing a range of activities from caregiving and household chores to various forms of non-market labour, is indispensable to the economy and society. Yet, traditional GDP calculations fail to account for such contributions. This omission leads to a significant underestimate of actual economic output, disproportionately affecting women, who are more likely to engage in unpaid care work. The result is a skewed economic narrative that overlooks a crucial segment of labour underpinning the healthy functioning of society.

Moreover, many women face challenges characterised by disrupted career trajectories and a lack of support in a system that prizes uninterrupted formal workforce participation, stemming directly from an economic framework overly fixated on GDP growth. This framework often neglects the invaluable non-monetary contributions made by those engaged in unpaid labour. This oversight not only perpetuates gender stereotypes but also upholds systemic barriers that impede women's comprehensive economic participation.

This overreliance on GDP as a primary economic indicator conceals significant sectors of economic activity due to their non-market nature. It is an oversight that extends to various realms, including the underground economy, volunteer work, bartering of goods and services, and environmental externalities. While these unmeasured sectors are often dismissed as acceptable, marginal errors in economic analysis, they constitute a substantial portion of economic activity, casting doubt on the reliability and comprehensiveness of GDP as a metric. In the UK, for instance, estimates suggest that the underground economy – encompassing illicit activities and legal production concealed to evade taxes and regulations – ranges from 10% to 12% of GDP.[28] [29] Estimates from 2006 indicate that unpaid household work contributes an additional 63% to the unmeasured portion of GDP.[30]

---

28 Friedrich Schneider, Andreas Buehn, and Claudio E. Montenegro, "Shadow Economies All over the World: New Estimates for 162 Countries from 1999 to 2007," Policy Research Working Paper 5356 (World Bank, July 2010), 24.

29 Friedrich Schneider and Colin C. Williams, *The Shadow Economy* (London: Institute of Economic Affairs, 2013), 12.

30 Office for National Statistics, "Household satellite account, UK: 2015 and 2016," 2 October 2018, https://www.ons.gov.uk/economy/nationalaccounts/satelliteaccounts/articles/householdsatelliteaccounts/2015and2016estimates.

The limitations of GDP are not merely statistical; they have tangible policy implications. The failure of GDP to encapsulate vast swathes of productive activity, particularly in non-market domains, undermines the accurate evaluation of an economy's true productive potential. This blind spot can lead to policy misdirection, with initiatives disproportionately focused on stimulating growth in already saturated market sectors. Meanwhile, the potential for growth and development in neglected non-market areas, which could significantly contribute to a more holistic understanding of national income, remains unexplored.

The underestimation of non-market activities in GDP calculations reflects a broader issue in economic policymaking. Traditional models overlook the intricacies and nuances of economies, particularly the roles played by informal sectors, voluntary work, and home-based activities. Confronting this challenge necessitates a fundamental shift in how economic contributions are measured and valued. There is an urgent need to adopt a more inclusive approach to economic metrics that acknowledge and quantify the worth of unpaid labour. Implementing such an approach would offer a more accurate depiction of economic contributions across gender lines, facilitating the development of policies that bolster gender equality in the workforce and at home.

This call for change advocates for a departure from the traditional reliance on GDP as the singular indicator of economic prosperity. Instead, it calls for a broader, more holistic perspective on economic health, integrating gender equity as an essential element of societal advancement and collective well-being. The reorientation towards a more inclusive and equitable economic model is not just a matter of fairness but a critical step towards realising a society that truly values all forms of labour and contribution.

Distribution of Income Among Residents

GDP, a proxy for economic growth, has long been regarded as a pivotal metric in assessing a country's economic health and prosperity. However, an overemphasis on pure GDP growth, without factoring in distributional impacts, can propagate an illusory view of societal well-being. In fact, GDP can give a wrong signal about how well an economy is doing despite purporting to be the all-encompassing measure of economic might. This disconnect stems from GDP's inability to capture how income and wealth are divided within an economy. Per capita GDP provides an average figure but obscures underlying disparities. In cases where national income accrues disproportionately to wealthy corporations and individuals, aggregate GDP growth paints a misleading picture of living standards for most citizens.

GDP per capita, which measures a country's GDP divided by its population, is a widely used indicator of average material living standards. However, it is subject to various statistical limitations as a *mean* value that does not capture the shape of the income distribution. GDP per capita can be disproportionately pulled upwards by a minority of high-income residents, blinding policymakers to how this income is distributed among the population. Therefore, countries with high income inequality can have a deceptively high GDP per capita that does not translate to proportional improvements for most citizens.

For instance, Ireland has one of the highest GDP per capita figures globally, at US$104,039 in 2022.[31] However, this headline achievement has not translated into high incomes for most of the populace. In Ireland's case, the outsized influence of highly profitable multinational corporations is pivotal in inflating GDP figures. Multinational tax optimisation strategies and intellectual property asset-shifting to Ireland significantly overstate underlying domestic economic activity. In 2015, the GDP of Ireland jumped 26% because of a jump in depreciation when multinationals moved a large block of intellectual property into the ownership of resident affiliates. Even metrics such as Gross National Income (GNI), which exclude profits going to foreign owners, were not accurately measuring the output of Ireland's

---

31 World Bank, "GDP per capita (current US$) - Ireland," 2022, accessed December 10, 2023,

https://data.worldbank.org/indicator/NY.GDP.PCAP.CD?locations=IE.

economy because undistributed profits are also included in GNI even when their shareholders are mostly non-resident.[32]

These distortive effects of multinationals are not unique to Ireland, but the country provides an extreme example of generalising about the economic well-being of the residents of an economy and their per capita output estimates. Other countries that host many multinationals may also face significant distortions when using growth indicators like GDP and GNI. Reforms agreed by OECD countries phased out these multinational tax avoidance schemes by mandating a minimum 15% global tax on multinationals. However, this is only 2.5% higher than Ireland's 12.5% tax rate before the changes took effect. At the end of 2023, Ireland continues to host many of these large multinationals because its taxes remain lower than the global average of 24%.[33]

The Central Bank of Ireland publishes an adjusted figure, GNI*, which subtracts the income of re-domiciled companies, such as depreciation on aircraft leasing and on imported intellectual property. In 2019, GNI* reached a level 40% below GDP; in most countries, GDP and GNI are about equal. Using the GNI* yardstick instead of GDP, Ireland's prosperity ranking in the EU declined substantially from first place to twelfth. The presence of these multinationals also increases the cost of living for the local Irish population, reducing its rank from 2nd to 12th in the EU after Luxembourg when adjusting for living standards. In fact, despite appearing to be a healthy economy and paying the 2nd highest per capita contribution to the EU budget, Ireland's actual individual consumption per capita is 95% cent of the EU average.[32]

---

32 Patrick Honohan, "Is Ireland really the most prosperous country in Europe?" Economic Letters, vol. 2021, no. 1 (February 2021), https://www.centralbank.ie/docs/default-source/publications/economic-letters/vol-2021-no-1-is-ireland-really-the-most-prosperous-country-in-europe.pdf.

33 Lisa O'Carroll and Richard Partington, "What the Irish tax deal means for multinationals?" The Guardian, 7 October 2021, accessed 10 December 2023, https://www.theguardian.com/world/2021/oct/07/why-is-ireland-key-to-taxing-multinationals.

High-profile investments and profits attributed to multinationals have not fully translated into proportional citizen welfare enhancements. Ireland's rank in quality-of-life indices accounting for health, environmental quality, income equality, and subjective well-being is strong but not commensurate to its high GDP per capita. Persistent deprivation and inequality challenges highlight the limitations of GDP per capita in reflecting income distribution. Despite consecutive years of robust GDP growth, Ireland's deprivation rate, which tracks the inability to afford basics like food, clothing, and utility bills, remains elevated for vulnerable groups. Significantly, consistent poverty, which combines relative income poverty and deprivation, has remained elevated in Ireland over the three years leading up to 2022, defying the strong economic expansion as measured by GDP per capita, which increased from $85,420 to $104,039 in the same period.[34] Figure 28 illustrates the disconnect between GDP per capita figures and the actual well-being of the majority of Ireland's population, as measured by the proportion of individuals in poverty.

---

34 Macrotrends, "Ireland GDP Per Capita," accessed 10 December 2023,

https://www.macrotrends.net/countries/IRL/ireland/gdp-per-capita.

Figure 28: Poverty and Deprivation Rates in Ireland 2020-23[35]

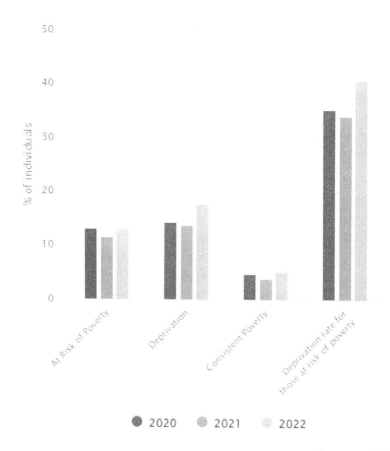

Source: CSO Ireland

Highcharts.com

The apparent paradox of increasing GDP per capita alongside persistent poverty and inequality underscores why governments must look beyond aggregate GDP for progress indicators. Sustained GDP growth on its own is insufficient for fostering broad-based societal prosperity. To

35 Central Statistics Office, "Survey on Income and Living Conditions (SILC) 2022," chart, 22 February 2023,

https://www.cso.ie/en/releasesandpublications/ep/p-silc/surveyonincomeandlivingconditionssilc2022/poverty/.

overcome these limitations, economists increasingly advocate for alternative economic indicators such as inclusive wealth, which accounts for human capital, environmental resources and physical capital. However, alternative metrics alone cannot redress underlying disparities without supportive policy frameworks. Based on Ireland's experience, it is vital to monitor income and wealth inequality and adjust tax policy to provide more equitable outcomes. Progressive taxation that demands greater contributions from corporations and those with the highest incomes and wealth is essential to ensure this illusory prosperity materialises in actual progress for Ireland's population.

The case of Ireland is an extreme example of how an excessive focus on GDP growth in isolation can propagate inequality and deprivation by obscuring the uneven distribution of income and wealth within an economy. Ireland demonstrates these dynamics, where seemingly exceptional GDP per capita performance has not fully translated into proportional welfare improvements, especially for vulnerable groups. Alternative metrics and policies explicitly targeting distributional impacts are vital alongside GDP growth maximisation. Economic growth remains foundational for raising prosperity, but harnessing its benefits equitably should be the ultimate policy priority.

Contribution of Mayhem and Destruction to GDP

In a hypothetical scenario where an extraterrestrial intelligence encounters Earth, they might find our societal constructs puzzling, particularly our obsession with maximising GDP points. Nations, divided by arbitrary geographical boundaries, engage in a relentless pursuit of winning this game of GDP growth, often disregarding the actual impact on well-being and the environmental cost, including shared air, ocean pollution, and ecosystem degradation. The irony would not be lost on these observers; societal distress, fear, destruction, suffering, crime, war, and insecurity paradoxically contribute to what substitutes for an indicator of economic progress.

GDP, which emerged in the interwar period and solidified post-WWII, initially served a practical purpose, especially in quantifying military production during an existential threat. However, this metric is increasingly leading us astray in the contemporary era, masking the essence of our humanity and failing to question the ethical and environmental costs of our actions. We have long been captivated by the allure of GDP, which supposedly encapsulates the health of our economy, progress, and success.

The societal implications of this GDP-centric view are stark. Every crime, for instance, contributes to GDP growth through expenditures on surveillance, security, policing, and incarceration. GDP increases when victims must repurchase stolen or damaged goods, even when there is a real loss to society. Yet, does a society riddled with crime truly signify prosperity? Similarly, wars and their cascading effects – from refugee crises to border security – inflate GDP, but at the cost of shattered lives and perpetuating cycles of conflict.

Environmental destruction further highlights the shortcomings of GDP as a measure. Activities like deforestation and resource extraction boost GDP but externalise ecological costs. Disaster responses contribute to economic activity, yet this growth stems from loss and despair, not from constructive development. While necessary, GDP contribution from rebuilding infrastructure post-disaster represents a reactive measure rather than a proactive investment in sustainable growth and a preventative attitude to managing environmental risks.

Often lauded for increasing efficiency, privatisation paradoxically elevates GDP even if it delivers inferior services at a higher cost. The privatisation of healthcare, for example, may increase GDP through higher insurance claims and out-of-pocket spending, yet it often leads to reduced access and quality of care. The expansion of administrative processes in privatised sectors, while contributing to GDP, comes at the cost of increased societal spending without proportional value gain. Privatisation has been hailed as a saviour of inefficient systems, and its advocates point to the rise in GDP as proof that financialised public services are making nations richer. In reality, it is more of an accounting trick that blinds us to the actual losses of privatising essential public services such as education, healthcare, and basic utilities.

Our societal vices, too, fuel economic growth indicators. Products detrimental to health, like cigarettes and vape products marketed to our youth, contribute to GDP, paradoxically benefiting the economy in the short term and feeding demand for public and private healthcare expenditures in the long term. Advertising for harmful products feeds mindless consumerism and directly adds to GDP, while the consequential environmental and health degradation remains unaccounted for.

This critique leads us to question the very nature of our societal values. Is a society that measures value by spending and consumption genuinely thriving? The current crossroads present an opportunity to redefine our path – not just economically but in the broader context of our societal ethos. The time has come to move beyond the narrow confines of GDP worship. We must embrace a new metric that prioritises human well-being, environmental sustainability, and social justice, a metric that reflects the true prosperity of a society, not just its economic output.

Chapter Eleven

Indicators for a Better Future

The concept of genuine progress has its roots in the early critiques of GDP as an inadequate measure of prosperity and societal well-being. Historically, the architects of GDP and Gross National Product (GNP), John Maynard Keynes and Simon Kuznets, cautioned against using national income as a sole measure of a nation's welfare. Kuznets, in particular, lamented in a report to the US Senate in 1934 that GNP was an inadequate measure for the welfare of a nation, and he urged for a more comprehensive approach. Kuznets cautioned against equating GNP growth with economic or social welfare, underscoring the need for a more holistic conception of national prosperity. In *The General Theory*, Keynes also argued that GDP is an incomplete measure of economic welfare as it does not account for the distribution of wealth, the quality of life, and the environmental impact of economic activities.

However, the post-World War II era witnessed an unprecedented surge in production globally, celebrated as indicative of collective advancement. Accelerating GDP expansion was equated directly with societal progress, overriding its inventors' warnings regarding its overly narrow focus on market-based metrics.

The backlash against growth began in the late 1960s and had its roots in the hippie culture that revolted against the institutional growth model. Increasingly through the 1970s and 1980s, scholars highlighted uneconomic growth, where GDP rises via means counterproductive to welfare. Characterised by heightened inequality, weakened social cohesion, industrial accidents, and ecological decline, uneconomic growth was an outgrowth of narrowly fixating on GDP aggregates while ignoring human and ecological impacts.

In Counting for Nothing, Marilyn Waring highlighted that GDP fundamentally discounted women's immense economic contributions by excluding unpaid work. Feminist economists underscored this severe limitation by demonstrating that unpaid household labour constitutes over 50% of productive work hours globally, none accounted for in GDP. Meanwhile, detrimental activities like oil spills, war preparations and tobacco consumption perversely register as additions to GDP. Such distortions – highlighted by the uneconomic growth critique – powerfully conveyed the need for economic indicators aligned with societal prosperity, not merely monetary transactions in the marketplace. By disregarding sustainability and welfare, GDP's laser focus on maximising production increasingly came at the steep price of eroded well-being.

Concurrent with the uneconomic growth critique, ecological economists like Gene Odum and Herman Daly popularised the "threshold hypothesis" regarding exponential GDP expansion. The hypothesis holds that as macroeconomic systems expand beyond optimal scale relative to containing ecosystems, the rising ecological and social costs of additional growth overwhelm welfare gains. Essentially, the threshold hypothesis contends that GDP increases foster collective prosperity only until the heightening externalities linked with relentless exponential GDP growth diminish net welfare. These crucial perspectives spotlighted the urgent need for indicators assessing genuine economic progress aligned with social and ecological prosperity.

As the Neoliberal market-centric school of thought took over academic and political discourse, GDP became the primary yardstick for the success of their policies. Yet, as we have seen in Chapter Ten, much of this success is attributed to accounting gimmicks. For example, the methodology will yield an increase in GDP when a state-owned infrastructure asset is privatised, even if it yields lower benefits and higher costs than the taxes previously used to fund its operations.

The Climate Emergency Necessitating Better Metrics

The 21st-century context of climate emergency and extreme inequality heightens the need for comprehensive indicators assessing genuine economic progress holistically linked to human and ecological prosperity. Modelling reveals that relentless global GDP growth drives projections of environmental ruin incompatible with organised human societies. Yet GDP growth remains the supreme indicator of success within policy paradigms, creating a paradox where GDP numbers can climb amidst markedly declining prosperity and multiplying climate disasters. In effect, GDP fails to signal the systemic risks accumulating via growth-obsessed frameworks until reaching crisis levels threatening civilisational collapse.

In this context, adopting more holistic indicators offers potential course correction by revealing the divergence between progress as conventionally defined and real welfare improvement amidst sustainability crises. Comprehensive indicators make explicit the increasing welfare losses from ecological unsustainability and inequality accompanying GDP expansion unrecognised in production-focused statistics. Implementing new metrics can spur an essential political debate on whether ever-rising consumption and GDP should constitute economic success within planetary boundaries. This transformation necessitates moving from GDP's production focus towards indicators that directly assess sustainable welfare and create an economy fostering thriving communities within ecological limits.

Living Standards Indicators vs GDP

Exploring living standards indicators versus GDP is an essential discourse within the Green Parties' wider agenda, transcending the sole focus on climate emergency to address various social challenges inherent in the growth-centric GDP model. This necessitates critically evaluating existing indicators that emphasise per capita well-being, offering a more nuanced and human-centric understanding of societal progress. These indicators, such as median household income and healthcare accessibility, shift the focus from the aggregate economic output to the lived experiences and quality of life of individuals.

GDP, long regarded as the primary gauge of a nation's economic vitality, has shown significant limitations in reflecting the holistic state of societal well-being. Recognising these shortcomings, there has been a movement towards developing alternative measures integrating a broader spectrum of human, ecological, and societal factors. These alternative indicators aim to capture a range of critical dimensions overlooked by GDP, including non-market activities like volunteer work and home care, the ecological impacts of economic activities, subjective measures of personal happiness and fulfilment, and the robustness of social infrastructure.

The intrinsic value of these alternative indicators is in their ability to provide a comprehensive view of economic health, which encompasses not just the traditional metrics of income and production but also considers the distribution of wealth, the sustainability of growth, and the overall welfare of society. These measures are particularly relevant in the context of sustainable development, as they align more closely with the principles of equity, ecological balance, and long-term viability.

To illustrate, indicators like median household income offer insights into the actual financial health of a typical family, shedding light on income disparities that aggregate GDP figures may mask. Access to healthcare, another crucial indicator, reflects a society's commitment to ensuring the well-being of its citizens, going beyond the economic metrics to evaluate the quality and universality of health services.

Each of these alternative indicators has its specific strengths and limitations, and their applicability varies depending on the particular facet of economic health under scrutiny. For instance, measures of personal happiness can reveal societal contentment and mental health trends, but they may not adequately capture economic disparities or environmental sustainability. Similarly, indicators focusing on income distribution are vital for understanding economic equality but might not fully encapsulate ecological or healthcare-related aspects of societal well-being.

Genuine Progress Indicator

By the late 20th century, the chasm between swelling GDP and faltering prosperity indicators became too glaring to ignore. This led to the development of GPI by Redefining Progress in 1994, aiming to provide a holistic measure of a nation's welfare, taking into account natural, social, human, and human-made capital. GPI acknowledges the cannibalisation of social and natural capital to sustain GDP growth, highlighting the erosion of real wealth that conventional indicators like GDP overlook.

From the early 1990s onward, several initiatives sought to conceptualise genuinely sustainable prosperity indicators to address GDP's limitations. A notable attempt was the research on sustainable economic welfare indicators by Daly and John Cobb, who developed the Genuine Progress Indicator (GPI) in 1995. a growing awareness of the limitations of GDP as a measure of societal progress. Developed as an alternative or supplement to GDP, GPI emerged from ecological and "green" economics, aiming to factor in the environmental and carbon footprints produced or mitigated by businesses. This shift was partly influenced by the recognition that GDP, while an important measure of economic output, was not designed to assess human well-being or ecological sustainability. The GPI's emphasis on sustainable economic welfare marks a significant departure from GDP's focus on output, recognising the importance of long-term planning and the costs associated with growth.

The conceptual framing of GPI aimed to distinguish between economic activities that enhance collective prosperity versus those diminishing equitable welfare. Methodologically, GPI was formulated as a macro-level indicator adjusted from GDP by incorporating comprehensive social, economic and environmental data. When comparing GPI and GDP, the most significant difference lies in their treatment of costs and benefits. GPI considers factors like income distribution, unpaid household work, cost of underemployment, cost of crime, personal consumption weighted for inequality, the value of higher education and volunteer work, services from consumer durables and public infrastructure, reduction in leisure time, loss of farmland/wetlands/forest cover, resource usage, and cost of pollution in its calculations. For example, while GDP might count crime as a benefit due to the associated economic activities (like property repairs and legal fees), GPI views it as a cost due to its detrimental impact on people's lives. Similarly, GPI values volunteer work and education, which GDP often overlooks, as they do not involve monetary transactions. This approach results in a more realistic assessment of an economy's health, where factors like low crime rates, educational pursuits, and environmental stewardship are deemed beneficial.

This multidimensional methodology enables the assessment of human, social, natural and human-created capital essential for holistic prosperity. Crucially, GPI deductions for factors like environmental degradation aim to capture the real long-term welfare losses from ecological harm and resource depletion overlooked in GDP's transaction-focused calculus. The indicator's comprehensive framework thus provides policymakers with superior insight into connections between economic policies, societal objectives and sustainable well-being outcomes.

Following GPI's emergence, the indicator has undergone broad international analysis to assess its strengths relative to GDP in evaluating economic performance, human development and ecological sustainability. In their groundbreaking research, Clifford Cobb and co-authors utilised the GPI to demonstrate that while the US GDP doubled between 1950 and 2000, the GPI peaked around 1978 and subsequently declined by over 45%. This divergence powerfully underscores that GDP growth post-1970s has fuelled rising inequality, heightened consumerism and ecological decline rather than holistic prosperity. Curiously, it coincides with the beginning of the market-led reforms that followed in the backlash against the welfare state.

Analyses from European countries underscore similar trends. In Austria, while per capita GDP tripled between 1955 and 1992, GPI peaked in 1975. GPI decreased by 30% over the next seventeen years, highlighting welfare reductions from factors like pollution, car accidents, and loss of farmlands/wetlands after Austria's GDP peak.[36] In Italy, GDP grew consistently between 1950 and 2003, but GPI diverged markedly from the late 1970s onward, plateauing while GDP accelerated. The gap highlights that higher production has delivered diminishing returns in Italy, considering rising costs like youth unemployment, income inequality, household debt, and ecological damage unaccounted for in GDP.[37] Reorienting policy based on GPI evidence of climbing social and environmental costs amidst GDP expansion could have spurred essential course correction.

Comparative studies utilising GPI further demonstrate its utility as a policy tool. Analysis of Thailand and Vietnam found that despite Thailand's higher GDP per capita, Vietnam had comparable human development and welfare outcomes at considerably lower economic and ecological costs as measured by GPI.[38] This insight enables targeting higher value areas for continued development while minimising unsustainable welfare reductions.

Most significantly, GPI studies reveal that GDP and holistic prosperity diverge considerably beyond threshold levels as costs of economic expansion frequently overwhelm welfare gains. Across high, middle and low-income economies, empirical evidence shows strong links between GPI peaks and a subsequent decrease in general welfare, heightened inequality, and persistent ecological unsustainability. GPI findings powerfully spotlight that exponential GDP-centred models are fundamentally incompatible with social, economic and ecological prosperity except temporarily during initial industrial consolidation phases.

---

36 Engelbert Stockhammer, Harald Hochreiter, Bernhard Obermayr, and Klaus Steiner, "The index of sustainable economic welfare (ISEW) as an alternative to GDP in measuring economic welfare," *Ecological Economics* 21, no. 1 (1997): 19-34, https://doi.org/10.1016/S0921-8009(96)00088-2.

37 Valentina Niccolucci, Federico M. Pulselli, and Enzo Tiezzi, "Strengthening the threshold hypothesis: Economic and biophysical limits to growth," *Ecological Economics* 60, no.4 (2007): 667-672, published 2006.

38 M. Clarke and S.M.N. Islam, "Diminishing and negative welfare returns of economic growth: an index of sustainable economic welfare (ISEW) for Thailand," *Ecological Economics* 54, no. 1 (2004): 81-93.

Kubiszewski's 2013 study synthesised GPI estimates for 17 countries over the 1950–2003 time period. Figure 29 displays GDP alongside GPI estimates for the US, UK, and the 17-country aggregate. What is notable is how closely GPI matches the experiences and perceptions of the population. In the UK, despite a continued rise in GDP during the austerity measures of the late 1970s and 1980s, the GPI time series captures the actual experience of well-being for the general population. The US and global data highlight the 21st-century context of climate emergency and extreme inequality, where GPI stagnated despite continuous GDP expansion. This reality requires political action that rapidly advances beyond the narrow conceptions of progress that have exceeded ecological limits to deliver equitable human betterment.

Figure 29: GDP vs GPI Divergent Trends[39]

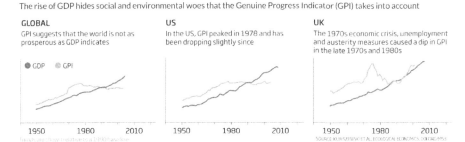

The criticisms of the GPI in economic measurement primarily revolve around its methodological complexities and the potential subjectivity in assessing non-market goods and services. The GPI is designed to account for both the benefits and costs of economic production, including social and environmental factors, which makes it more complex and potentially less straightforward to measure than GDP. One significant critique is that GPI considers some types of production as having a negative impact. In contrast, GDP measures the entirety of

---

39 Ida Kubiszewski, Robert Costanza, Carol Franco, Philip Lawn, John Talberth, Tim Jackson, and Camille Aylmer,

"Beyond GDP: Measuring and achieving global genuine progress," *Ecological Economics* 93 (2013): 57-68.

production at a given time, thus making GDP more straightforward to measure than GPI.

However, while critics correctly identify potential methodological challenges and concerns over practicality and comparability with GDP, the criticisms extend to the difficulty in defining and measuring well-being and the challenges in combining various incommensurable factors into a single index. It is worthwhile to identify negative economic activity in GDP, a measure of income that counts even negative occurrences like natural disasters as positive if they lead to increased economic activity. It fails to consider factors such as poverty, greenhouse gas emissions, or the societal costs of air pollution. GPI, in contrast, offers a more thoughtful measure by subtracting factors harmful to society and the environment. Moreover, there is a concern about GPI's vulnerability to political manipulation due to its subjective nature, but GDP is not free from political manipulation and has become the primary tool for obfuscating the state's responsibility in maintaining its citizens' well-being.

The comprehensive empirical evidence reveals that while GDP possesses restricted utility regarding market transactions, analysed in isolation, it obscures connections between policy, sustainability, equity and real prosperity. In contrast, GPI demonstrates both conceptually and via time-series data how GDP-centred models engender increased externalities eroding long-term welfare. Therefore, the Green Party of Canada has advocated for complementary usage of indicators like GPI that account for sustainability and social costs alongside conventional economic aggregates.[40] Compared to GDP utilisation alone, this combined framework enables transparent linkage between policy choices, growth metrics and societal outcomes across interconnected ecological, human, and economic realms.

---

40 Green Party of Canada, "Green Party of Canada Statement on the Inflationary Crisis," 5 October 2022, accessed 2 December 2023, https://www.greenparty.ca/en/statement/2022-10-05/green-party-canada-statement-inflationary-crisis.

The complementary approach provides decision-makers with more balanced insight on whether national frameworks promote mere swelling of throughput or holistic betterment of people and the planet. For instance, the divergences between many GDP and GPI trends in many countries in Daly's study – including the US, UK, Austria, Germany and Sweden – clearly show that significant welfare reductions accompanied production acceleration after 1980 due to unchecked negative externalities. Such signals are essential for growth policy aligned with sustainable prosperity rather than the continued ecological overshoot endangering long-term social welfare.

Indicators fundamentally deliver signals and create alignment between goals and outcomes. Misaligned signals blind policymakers to compounding issues being exacerbated rather than solved. Therefore, pairing GDP with indicators like GPI that quantify sustainability and equity costs fosters alignment between decisions, development models and real societal advancement amidst planetary boundaries. Adopting holistic economic indicators creates an imperative for re-evaluating the aims underpinning policy. The question the Greens rightfully raise is: does improving lives equitably within ecological limits better constitute success than accelerating consumption and throughput?

The Happy Planet Index

The Happy Planet Index (HPI), as delineated in the analytical works of the New Economics Foundation and endorsed by figures like Herman Daly, one of the pioneers in the development of the Genuine Progress Indicator (GPI), emerges as a compelling alternative to conventional economic indicators. This index proposes a quality-of-life approach to measuring national success, transcending the traditional boundaries of economic metrics.

At its core, the HPI assesses the efficacy of nations in fostering long, fulfilling lives for their citizens while minimally impacting the environment. This index amalgamates three fundamental components: life expectancy, experienced well-being, and ecological footprint, each offering a unique perspective on a nation's development and quality of life.

Life expectancy is the component that reflects a nation's health infrastructure and the general accessibility of healthcare services. Prominent figures such as Sam Altman, Peter Thiel, Jeff Bezos, Larry Ellison, Paul F. Glenn, Dmitry Itskov, Sergey Brin, and Larry Page have invested heavily in research aimed at combating ageing and prolonging life, underscoring the universal recognition of longevity as a key metric of progress.[41] In the contemplation of wealth and its significance, there comes a pivotal juncture where the accumulation of material riches loses its relevance if the lifespan to relish them is insufficient. Ageing is a poignant reminder that time is a precious commodity that cannot be bought or sold. It is a finite resource that we must use wisely and cherish, and no matter how wealthy or powerful one may be, time is a great equaliser that cannot be controlled or manipulated. Perhaps not surprisingly, the HPI considers life expectancy a marker of progress that provides insight into a nation's basic health infrastructure and accessibility.

Experienced well-being is the HPI component that moves beyond mere longevity to encompass the quality of life at all stages. It gauges well-being through responses to the "Ladder of Life" questionnaire from the Gallup World Poll, which asks individuals to rate their current life satisfaction on a scale of 0 to 10. This subjective measure provides insight into the actual lived experiences of the population, recognising that a long life devoid of fulfilment and happiness is an incomplete measure of a nation's success.

The third component of the HPI is a nation's ecological footprint. In stark contrast to GDP, the HPI incorporates this finite resource as a critical measure of environmental impact. This metric quantifies each resident's average environmental burden, calculated through the land area required to sustain their consumption and waste absorption. It serves as a sustainability metric, juxtaposing well-being against environmental efficiency.

---

41 Julian Koplin and Christopher Gyngell, "The rich are pouring millions into life extension research, but does it have any ethical value?" Science X, 11 April 2023, https://phys.org/news/2023-04-rich-millions-life-extension-ethical.html.

The HPI score is derived by multiplying life expectancy with experienced well-being and dividing this product by the ecological footprint. This formula favours nations that support long, contented lives for their citizens with minimal environmental cost. The index's highest possible score is 100, with higher values indicating greater efficiency in achieving sustainable well-being. Figure 30 displays the top 5 highest ranked countries in the 2019 HPI report.

Figure 30: 2019 HPI Score Top 5 Rankings[42]

RANK	COUNTRY	Life expectancy	Wellbeing	Ecological footprint	HPI SCORE and change since 2014
1st	COSTA RICA	○ 80.3 years	○ 7.00/10	● 2.65 gha/p	62.1 (-1.2)
2nd	VANUATU	● 70.5 years	○ 6.96/10	● 1.82 gha/p	60.4 (+0.8)
3rd	COLOMBIA	○ 77.3 years	○ 6.35/10	● 1.90 gha/p	60.2 (+2.7)
4th	SWITZERLAND	○ 83.8 years	○ 7.69/10	○ 4.14 gha/p	60.1 (+2)
5th	ECUADOR	○ 77.0 years	● 5.81/10	○ 1.51 gha/p	58.8 (-1.4)

The HPI framework marks a significant departure from traditional economic indicators like GDP, offering a novel lens to evaluate national progress. Unlike GDP, which primarily accounts for economic output, the HPI integrates environmental sustainability, positioning the ecological footprint as a pivotal measure. This approach encourages nations to strike a balance between elevating citizen well-being and preserving ecological integrity for sustained societal functioning. By incorporating conservation into its framework, the HPI directly correlates environmental stewardship with improved well-being outcomes.

Furthermore, the HPI focuses on the qualitative aspects of life, assessing the actually experienced quality of life rather than inferring well-being from financial prosperity alone. It employs direct data from individuals about their happiness and contentment. This subjective dimension enriches the HPI, complementing the quantitative economic

---

42 "Happy Planet Index," accessed 2 December 2023, https://happyplanetindex.org/hpi.

aggregates typified by GDP, thus enabling more informed policy decisions that reflect real-life impacts on citizens' daily welfare.

The survey also benefits from a universal methodology that can easily be deployed globally, lending itself to straightforward comparisons. The HPI relies on globally available indicators using standardised definitions, making it broadly applicable across culturally diverse country contexts. Life expectancy and ecological footprint data are pulled from UN databases covering nearly all world nations. Experienced well-being originates from the annually conducted Gallup World Poll surveying 99% of the planet's populace. This uniform approach enables performance comparisons and trend analysis irrespective of geographic setting.

The HPI's simplicity and composite structure based on three elements allows for straightforward calculation and understanding. It avoids complex formulae requiring advanced national data-gathering infrastructure and statistical skills for interpretation or replication. This clarity in composition enables transparent communication to policymakers and the public and positions the HPI as an entry point for nations transitioning from GDP-centric to broader well-being accounting frameworks.

However, the HPI is not without its critics. Critiques highlight potential biases in well-being surveys due to cultural differences, the complex interactions among HPI components, and the index's limited direct applicability in crafting specific policies. The subjective nature and simplicity of the HPI can render it an incomplete indicator for measuring a nation's economic well-being backed by hard data.

An essential criticism revolves around the subjectivity of happiness and life satisfaction responses, which vary significantly across cultural and geographic contexts. For example, Latin American nations report higher experienced well-being than ex-Soviet states despite facing greater socioeconomic challenges. Similarly, residents in poorer economies might scale subjective scores relative to lower expectations rather than absolute happiness. Therefore, the HPI must be considered in context rather than as an outright ranking. This relativity in subjective scores necessitates interpreting the HPI within specific contexts rather than as a definitive ranking system.

Furthermore, the HPI's calculation method, which multiplies life expectancy and experienced well-being and then divides this by the ecological footprint, assumes a complete interchangeability of its elements. Yet, real-life scenarios often present contradictions where advancements in one domain, such as increased happiness through high-consumption lifestyles, can exacerbate ecological footprints and compromise sustainability. This potential for intricate interdependencies among the HPI components is not explicitly addressed in its calculation.

The most significant critique lies in the HPI's limited utility in guiding concrete policy measures compared to GDP-based models. While the HPI introduces a pioneering measure of sustainability-adjusted well-being, it does not provide clear guidance on optimal trade-offs between its components or offer actionable targets beyond broad aspirations for simultaneous improvement in well-being and efficiency. This lack of precision limits the utility of HPI scores to guide practical fiscal programs.

In view of the above discussion, the debate over GDP versus the HPI encapsulates a fundamental tension between comprehensiveness and operational precision in economic indicators. While GDP provides a limited but detailed view of economic health, enabling specific economic projections and planning, the HPI offers a broader sustainability perspective but with less direct policy direction. This dichotomy reflects a broader historical trend where social indicators have evolved from targeted, utilitarian metrics to more abstract, philosophical notions as societies advance. Both GDP and the HPI have strengths and weaknesses contingent upon their intended use.

Recent moves, such as New Zealand's adoption of a nationwide well-being budget, signal a growing shift among advanced economies towards integrating broader social and environmental considerations into fiscal planning. For developing nations grappling with basic infrastructure needs and extreme poverty, GDP-focused models prioritising rapid industrialisation may still be most relevant in the short term. However, indices like the Genuine Progress Indicator (GPI), which deduct social and ecological costs from GDP, offer a more data-driven pathway than the HPI to link economic growth with sustainability for these economies.

For wealthier nations with established basic welfare systems, pursuing GDP growth may yield diminishing returns in enhancing actual public life quality while exacerbating environmental strains. Transitioning fiscal policy towards well-being metrics could inject new vitality into societal outcomes. Adopting hybrid approaches that balance GDP projections with weightings for complementary indicators like the HPI, based on national priorities, presents a viable middle ground.

The optimal strategy for national fiscal planning involves a transitional approach where GDP remains a key economic indicator but is increasingly complemented by multidimensional well-being indices like the HPI. The relative importance assigned to GDP versus well-being targets can evolve dynamically, reflecting each country's unique developmental needs and aspirations. Introducing well-being metrics into fiscal planning addresses growing demands for public finances to focus not just on consumption quantity but also on life quality, paving the way for a more holistic understanding of national prosperity.

Green Gross Domestic Product

In addressing the limitations of GDP as a measure of economic health, alternative paradigms such as Green GDP have been introduced, incorporating environmental considerations into macroeconomic assessments. The concept of Green GDP strives to recalibrate growth processes to be more resource-efficient, cleaner, and resilient, which is particularly significant for developing countries. This recalibration involves equating the depletion and degradation of natural resources with the measurement of physical and human capital in economic evaluations. Green GDP seeks to account for environmental costs associated with activities such as resource extraction and carbon emissions, deducting these from the traditional GDP figures. Additionally, it attempts to assign value to non-market environmental assets, such as clean air, biodiversity, and ecosystem services, typically excluded in conventional GDP calculations. By integrating these factors, Green GDP aims to foster sustainable development, aligning economic performance measures directly with sustainability objectives.

However, the practical implementation of Green GDP has faced numerous challenges, including political resistance, methodological constraints, and logistical hurdles. Initial attempts to apply Green GDP in countries like China and the US encountered setbacks due to unreliable valuation techniques, perceived overestimation of environmental damages, and opposition from local governments and industries wary of the potential negative implications on reported GDP figures. For example, the initial estimation of Green GDP in China in 2006 suggested that environmental costs constituted over 3% of the nation's GDP, with an additional annual GDP cost of 1.8% for containing and managing environmental impacts.[43] These figures were met with scepticism, raising questions about the accuracy of such damage assessments. Moreover, the exclusive focus on Green GDP adjustments did not address the intrinsic shortcomings of GDP as a comprehensive welfare indicator. Thus, relying solely on this revised indicator for policymaking failed to deliver genuinely sustainable outcomes.

Acknowledging these impediments, the World Bank initiated a more comprehensive effort to construct a framework for assessing green growth, utilising a broader set of indicators. This initiative, known as the System of Environmental-Economic Accounts (SEEA), transcends the singular focus on Green GDP, advocating for diverse economic and environmental measures. The SEEA, as outlined in the World Bank's 2012 edition, provides a robust and adaptable foundation for monitoring green transitions. It is grounded in internationally recognised accounting principles, definitions, classifications, and standards, facilitating consistent evaluations of changes in environmental assets alongside traditional economic production and consumption activities. This approach moved

---

43 Vic Li and Graeme Lang, "China's 'Green GDP' Experiment and the Struggle for Ecological Modernisation," *Journal of Contemporary Asia* 40, no. 1 (2010): 44-62, http://dx.doi.org/10.1080/00472330903270346.

beyond a concentration on Green GDP alone towards a more versatile dashboard of economic and environmental metrics, and it enabled coherent assessments of stocks and changes in environmental assets alongside economic production and consumption.

The SEEA embraces a capital approach, conceptualising nature as economic and human capital. This approach emphasises natural capital's regenerative capabilities, efficiency, and resilience, which are foundational to human endeavours. Such a perspective is in harmony with broader sustainability frameworks, as exemplified by the Dasgupta Review's focus on the economics of biodiversity.[44] The SEEA's integration with national accounts enables policymakers to make informed choices about the interplay between economic production and environmental regeneration. Furthermore, it allows for a detailed examination of how environmental degradation disproportionately impacts various sectors and communities, thus offering actionable and socially beneficial guidance for sustainable development pathways.

Progressing this green accounting initiative, the World Bank has developed the SEEA Ecosystem Accounting (SEEA EA) methodology. This approach received formal endorsement from the United Nations Statistical Commission in 2021. The SEEA EA extends beyond the physical and monetary asset accounts in the SEEA by incorporating detailed biophysical data about ecosystems. This methodology concentrates on ecosystem services, biodiversity, and the array of benefits that humans derive from nature. It characterises ecosystem assets using tangible measures and ascribes monetary value to these assets, employing valuation methods based on exchange values, cost-based revealed preference, or stated preference techniques.

Crucially, the SEEA EA balances the negative impacts of economic production on nature with the positive contributions of ecosystems to

---

44 Anantha Kumar Duraiappah and Deborah Rogers, "The Intergovernmental Platform on Biodiversity and Ecosystem Services: opportunities for the social sciences," Innovation: The European Journal of Social Science Research 24, no. 3 (2011): 217-224, http://dx.doi.org/10.1080/13511610.2011.592052.

human activities. By accounting for the degradation and depletion of environmental assets, this approach enables the formulation of policies that promote sustainable usage and conservation. Concurrently, quantifying critical ecosystem services – including carbon sequestration, air filtration, flood control, recreational opportunities, and aesthetic value – underscores nature's integral role in underpinning social and economic outcomes. The delineation of these provisioning, regulating, habitat, and cultural services constructs a persuasive argument for investment in ecosystem restoration on par with expenditures on physical infrastructure.

The SEEA EA extends its utility by offering broader indicators that resonate with global sustainability objectives, such as the United Nations Sustainable Development Goals (SDGs). A notable innovation within this suite is the introduction of Gross Ecosystem Product (GEP), which aggregates the overall value of final ecosystem services. By juxtaposing the trends of GEP against traditional GDP metrics, policymakers and analysts can glean more profound insights into the true sustainability of an economy and its strides towards greener operational models. The SEEA EA thus moves beyond a singular reliance on GDP, advocating for a multifaceted approach that incorporates a range of indicators covering produced, human, social, and natural capital. This diverse array of metrics enables a tailored approach to policy formulation, sensitive to the unique ecological, social, and economic nuances of different regions.

Critically, the World Bank is at the forefront of developing more rigorous methodologies for evaluating nature's tangible and intangible contributions to human well-being. With its Wealth Accounting and Valuation of Ecosystem Services (WAVES) initiative, the Bank is pioneering innovative valuation methods such as opportunity cost, replacement cost, damage avoidance expenditure, and geospatial analysis. This initiative has led to the development of national ecosystem accounts in various countries across Latin America, Africa, and the Asia-Pacific region. WAVES also promotes the exchange of knowledge and expertise across regions, continuously improving valuation methodologies and guiding investments in natural capital accounting on a global scale. This ongoing commitment of the World Bank to refine its green growth frameworks exemplifies its dedication to incorporating sophisticated economic valuations of environmental resources in policy decision-making.

However, the World Bank acknowledges that more than merely introducing green growth policies is needed to engender meaningful transformations. The successful implementation of these policies is contingent on broader governance reforms, including the establishment of responsive economic institutions and political willpower for enacting sustainability regulations. Measures such as financial inclusion, strengthening property rights, and fortifying the rule of law are instrumental in garnering public and private support for green fiscal and monetary policies. These policies include initiatives like carbon taxes or incentivising sustainable infrastructure through favourable lending rates. Thus, the World Bank advocates for comprehensive strategies combining growth-enhancing economic reforms with ecologically sustainable practices customised to suit local conditions.

Moving forward, the World Bank's ongoing development and refinement of tools like Green GDP and the SEEA ecosystem accounting framework represent a sophisticated and pragmatic approach to integrating environmental sustainability into economic policy-making. This multifaceted methodology enables a balanced consideration of economic and ecological trade-offs, facilitating human development that is harmonious with ecological regeneration. By placing a monetary value on the diverse benefits provided by nature, the World Bank underscores the imperative of investing in conservation and restoration, thereby fostering enduring prosperity. Furthermore, the Bank's efforts in propagating the adoption of green accounting through platforms that enhance valuation techniques and demonstrate the practical impact of policies solidify its role as a leader in establishing globally recognised standards for measuring inclusive green growth. Consequently, the SEEA methodology emerges as a superior alternative to traditional GDP, guiding public policy towards judicious and sustainable development.

The Environmental Performance Index

The Environmental Performance Index (EPI), developed collaboratively by Yale and Columbia Universities, represents a critical tool for enhancing the policymaking landscape, especially in contemporary challenges that demand a balance between economic prosperity, social equity, and environmental stewardship. As an adjunct to GDP, this index provides an elaborate and nuanced framework for sustainability measurement. It encompasses a broad spectrum of indicators pertinent to environmental health, air quality, biodiversity, and resource management, with a significant emphasis on climate change mitigation and adaptation strategies. The EPI's comprehensive structure, comprising 40 distinct indicators spread across 11 categories, yields insight into national environmental performance and policy efficacy that traditional economic metrics such as GDP fail to capture.

In stark contrast to GDP, which primarily focuses on quantifying consumption and production flows, the EPI employs a capital-based approach, assessing how countries are either depleting or conserving their natural capital over time. This methodology resonates deeply with the principles of sustainable development that underscore the interconnectivity of economic, social, and environmental pillars, as championed in international frameworks like the UN Sustainable Development Goals (SDGs). Consequently, the EPI's focus on capital offers a more accurate gauge of the long-term sustainability of growth and development trajectories.

Its intrinsic alignment with established, science-based sustainability targets and planetary boundaries sets the EPI further apart from GDP. The index's proximity-to-target methodology facilitates rigorous evaluations against global and localised sustainability thresholds, encompassing greenhouse gas emissions, air pollution, deforestation, and water usage. This multi-faceted approach unveils policy gaps in sustainability that remain obscured within GDP statistics, thereby guiding governments towards critical areas that require immediate and effective intervention.

The broad, forward-looking perspective offered by the EPI is absent in GDP statistics. When used in tandem, these measures provide complementary insights; GDP delivers key economic information, while the EPI adds crucial context regarding environmental health and human well-being. Their combined use in policymaking can foster more balanced, ethically sound, and sustainable outcomes.

At both national and international levels, the EPI is invaluable as a tool for guiding policy direction. By distinguishing leaders and laggards in sustainability performance, it helps identify replicable best practices and points to areas needing urgent attention. The granular nature of the EPI's data enables the development of bespoke policies that cater to the specific environmental challenges of individual countries. For instance, the exemplary performance of countries like Switzerland in the EPI rankings, attributable to their effective climate change policies and robust environmental health protections, can serve as a model for developing nations formulating their sustainability strategies. The EPI also illustrates that factors beyond wealth, such as Costa Rica's high ranking due to strong environmental stewardship, suggest that political commitment and governance play a significant role in achieving sustainability goals.

The EPI's latest reports underscore the critical need for intensified global efforts in climate change mitigation to achieve net-zero emissions, as recommended by scientific consensus. This quantitative evidence highlights the inadequacy of current policies in meeting essential targets like the Paris Agreement's 1.5 degrees Celsius warming limit, urging policymakers globally to strengthen their sustainability commitments and actions. Figure 31 displays the top 10 countries in order of EPI score, highlighting the impact of Europe's efforts to target environmental performance and green energy.

Figure 31: 2022 EPI Rankings[45]

COUNTRY		RANK	EPI SCORE	10-YEAR CHANGE	
FILTER BY REGION:	ALL REGIONS ▾				
Denmark		1	77.90	14.90	
United Kingdom		2	77.70	23.00	
Finland		3	76.50	21.00	
Malta		4	75.20	25.40	
Sweden		5	72.70	15.80	
Luxembourg		6	72.30	13.50	
Slovenia		7	67.30	8.60	
Austria		8	66.50	7.20	
Switzerland		9	65.90	8.20	
Iceland		10	62.80	4.40	

While the EPI marks a significant advancement in environmental accounting, it is not without limitations. Data gaps, particularly in developing countries, in areas such as biodiversity, agriculture, and water use, affect the precision of policy guidance. Additionally, the EPI is yet to fully encapsulate the transboundary impacts of sustainability, a crucial factor in an interconnected global environment. Despite these challenges, the EPI team is actively engaged in enhancing the index and integrating new data sources and analytical techniques. Recent developments include the incorporation of indicators projecting progress towards net-zero emissions and improved air and water quality metrics. Efforts are also underway to incorporate the sustainability impacts embedded in international trade, using advanced multi-regional input-output models. These ongoing enhancements demonstrate the EPI's flexibility and evolution in response to emerging research, a trait less evident in more static economic indicators like GDP.

While the EPI does not supplant the vital economic insights provided by GDP, it offers additional sustainability context for balanced,

---

45 Yale University, "Environmental Performance Index 2022 EPI Results," 2022, Mountain View, CA,

https://epi.yale.edu/epi-results/2022/component/epi.

ethical policymaking. Its detailed framework, which evaluates environmental performance against science-based targets, provides a forward-looking perspective crucial for practical policy guidance. The EPI equips policymakers with a comprehensive, multi-dimensional view, enabling informed decisions that concurrently promote economic growth, social equity, and environmental sustainability. It shifts policy focus to previously overlooked sustainability issues, urging coordinated action at both local and global levels to address time-sensitive challenges such as climate change.

The Social Progress Index

The Social Progress Index (SPI) has arisen as a necessary complement to the GDP metric, addressing its notable deficiencies as a measure of societal progress. Over recent decades, a growing chorus of academics, global leaders, and institutional authorities have underscored the limitations of GDP as the sole indicator of a nation's advancement. This critique has inspired the development of the SPI, an alternative indicator designed to provide a more nuanced understanding of prosperity and sustainability, thereby enriching the information base for informed policy-making.

Fundamentally, GDP quantifies the market value of newly produced goods and services within a given period. However, its design is not attuned to assess broader societal outcomes such as health, education, equality, leisure time, environmental quality, and overall subjective well-being. GDP's conceptual framework harbours several limitations that render it an incomplete measure of living standards. Notably, an economy geared towards rectifying social challenges may display a high GDP, primarily if substantial investments are channelled into defensive expenditures like prisons, security systems, mental healthcare, and drug rehabilitation programs. While contributing to economic output, such expenditures often signal uneconomic growth that fails to enhance human prosperity meaningfully.

Moreover, GDP overlooks crucial aspects such as wealth distribution and inequality. Per capita GDP, for instance, reveals little about how resources are allocated between the affluent and the impoverished. Consequently, two societies with identical aggregate GDPs may exhibit stark disparities in access to essential services and opportunities across different income groups. As discussed in previous chapters, GDP disregards unpaid work – such as household and volunteer work – significantly contributing to family and community welfare. This oversight highlights GDP's limitation as merely a flow measure of immediate economic output, failing to act as a comprehensive metric encapsulating sustainable, long-term prosperity.

GDP's narrow focus on market transactions further limits its efficacy as an all-encompassing gauge of social progress. This focus excludes consideration of activities that deplete natural capital and ecosystem services, which are essential for future generations' well-being. Activities such as deforestation, fossil fuel extraction, soil degradation, and practices eroding biodiversity and ecological stability are paradoxically counted as positive contributions to GDP despite their detrimental impact on long-term sustainability.

Structurally, the SPI is organised around three core dimensions: 1) basic human needs, 2) foundations of well-being and 3) opportunity. Each dimension is integral to the comprehensive assessment of societal advancement, diverging from the growth-centric focus of GDP. Basic human needs are evaluated as society's effectiveness in fulfilling the essential prerequisites for its citizens' survival and basic living standards. It encompasses crucial elements such as nutrition: ensuring access to adequate food supplies; water: gauging the availability and quality of water resources; housing: assessing the adequacy and safety of shelter; and healthcare access: measuring the reach and quality of medical services.

The second dimension builds upon the foundational needs by expanding target factors into the components necessary for sustaining prosperous and resilient communities. This includes ecosystem protections, which assess the preservation and management of natural environments; access to education, taking into account the availability and quality of educational resources and opportunities; communication channels, including the accessibility and freedom of information flow; and health and safety aspects that scrutinise the overall well-being and security of the community. This dimension reflects the quality of life beyond mere survival, indicating a society's commitment to fostering environments where individuals can thrive.

The third dimension of opportunity explores the extent to which societies facilitate the realisation of individual potential, irrespective of personal backgrounds or circumstances. It examines the degree of social inclusion, assessing how well societies integrate diverse groups and mitigate inequalities; personal freedom, evaluating the liberties and rights enjoyed by individuals; and social capital, measuring the strength and quality of community networks and relationships. This dimension is pivotal in understanding how societies empower citizens to contribute to and benefit from communal and national progress.

These three dimensions, encompassing over 50 specific indicators, collectively offer a multifaceted approach to evaluating social progress. The SPI thereby provides a holistic measure that extends beyond economic output to encompass a broader spectrum of societal development. This approach is critical for understanding the full scope of a nation's progress, allowing for a more nuanced and comprehensive assessment than what is provided by traditional economic indicators alone. In its aggregated form, the SPI becomes an instrumental tool for policymakers and stakeholders, guiding them in addressing the diverse aspects of societal advancement and ensuring a balanced approach to national development.

Unlike GDP per capita, SPI scores relate strongly to income inequality, allowing policymakers to identify access deficiencies across socioeconomic strata. Countries exhibiting high SPI performance generally sport relatively equitable income distribution and resource access between rich and poor citizens. Conversely, nations with high GDP but substantial wealth concentration among economic elites tend to lag SPI leaders. These insights into distributional equity provide crucial guidance for policymakers to target interventions promoting inclusive development rather than aggregate growth alone.

Furthermore, SPI indicators better reveal many welfare-enhancing conditions that GDP neglects. For example, among the SPI's health and wellness measures are suicide rates, obesity prevalence and perceived mental health, which link much more tightly to overall subjective well-being than GDP growth trends. This perspective on income inequality and access across various socioeconomic strata illuminates the disparities in resource distribution and quality of life, often obscured by GDP metrics. Countries with high SPI scores generally exhibit a more equitable allocation of wealth and resources, in stark contrast to nations where high GDP coexists with concentration of wealth.

Figure 32 depicts global rankings on a map, with darker shades indicating higher SPI scores. The overall score for each country is based on tiered levels of aggregation that include health, safety, education, technology, rights, and many more measures. Such leading SPI countries as Norway, Denmark, and Finland forge strong social cohesion and community ties that foster public goods like interpersonal trust, which are vital for prosperity. Meanwhile, Qatar and Singapore score among the absolute GDP per capita leaders yet rank near the middle on the SPI, exhibiting how sheer economic wealth absent other social foundations is an incomplete recipe for widespread welfare. Also notable is how the SPI score in the US did not keep pace with its economic output as measured by GDP. Policymakers can utilise these specific SPI components to guide decisions supporting mental/physical health, social capital, and economic development.

Figure 32: 2022 Social Progress Index Rankings Map[46]

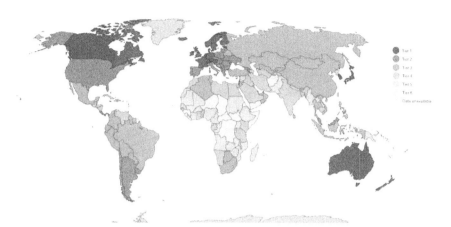

Additionally, GDP entirely ignores sustainability, biodiversity and natural capital preservation, while SPI indicators directly track ecological footprints, greenhouse gas emissions, sanitation access and water quality. These gauges of environmental stewardship are increasingly vital foundations of sustained prosperity absent in GDP statistics. For instance, New Zealand and Switzerland score much higher on sustainability metrics than rapidly growing GDP leaders like China and India, signalling that setting policies merely to maximise economic expansion jeopardises stable social progress. Tracking SPI environmental indicator trajectories will enable superior policymaking and balance growth against stability.

Many social welfare-enhancing conditions like equitable resource distribution, health/social capital and ecological sustainability are poorly reflected in GDP. The SPI framework covers these multidimensional components of shared prosperity underrepresented by pure output metrics. Policymakers attuned to SPI indicators can craft superior decisions targeted at inclusive, sustainable human development rather than short-term growth alone. Analysis of GDP alongside SPI statistics surfaces several

46 Social Progress Imperative, "2022 Social Progress Index Results," accessed 6 December 2023, https://www.socialprogress.org/global-index-2022-results; J. Harmacek, P. Krylova, and M. Htitich, 2022 *Social Progress Index Data* (Washington, DC: Social Progress Imperative).

examples where high economic growth absent corresponding social progress highlights the need for policies specifically addressing human welfare.

The US represents a prime case where GDP offers an excessively rosy picture masking social deficiencies prioritised by the SPI framework. Impressive GDP expansion has not prevented the prevalence of negative social outcomes in America from rising relative to peers. Among 35 OECD countries, the US ranks 28th in life expectancy, tied for 30th in obesity rate, 26th in overall poverty and exclusion, and 30th in environmental quality and biodiversity protection. However, only four nations in this group boast higher GDP per capita than America. High levels of income inequality and inadequate healthcare access deficiencies likely contribute to disproportionate social dysfunction in the US relative to national wealth. These SPI insights suggest a misdiagnosis by policymakers of the appropriate cures for American ills, pointing to prescriptions addressing welfare and equity directly rather than assuming a tide of GDP growth alone will lift all boats.

Conversely, Latin American countries like Costa Rica and Chile achieve social progress levels comparable to the EU average despite GDP per capita being significantly below that of leading European economies. Both countries provide nearly universal healthcare and education access, leading to life expectancy, literacy, environmental sustainability, and poverty metrics mirroring the EU's. These SPI trends spotlight that national wealth is not the only path to welfare, and targeted investments in human development can pay social dividends beyond what aggregate economic expansion achieves. Prioritising SPI-focused policies led Costa Rica and Chile to overcome relative income disadvantages to match First World living standards.

Meanwhile, SPI frontier leaders like Norway, Iceland and Finland far outpace global GDP per capita juggernauts like the US, Singapore, and Qatar on comprehensive social welfare. This divergence signals that an economic model maximising mere market output unintentionally sacrifices other prosperity dimensions like equality, leisure time, social cohesion, and ecological sustainability, which are tracked by the SPI framework. Setting policy based on GDP targets alone risks advancing narrowly defined growth divorced from actual population welfare enhancement.

These cases illustrate insights policymakers gain from side-by-side GDP and SPI analysis in crafting balanced, sustainable development policy benefiting society broadly rather than narrow measures of growth. GDP offers no warning signs of eroding social welfare amid US aggregate growth. However, SPI red flags over inequality, healthcare access dysfunction, and institutional distrust appropriately reframe policy concerns. Conversely, SPI achievements in Latin America and Northern Europe, despite GDP handicaps, spotlight social policy successes from which to learn rather than risk misreading income figures alone as the keys to welfare. Comparing GDP and SPI trajectories fosters policies nurturing multidimensional prosperity.

The Social Progress Index complements GDP by capturing numerous fundamental components of health, equality, sustainability and human development, which GDP overlooks. By tracking 50+ non-economic social welfare and sustainability measures alongside traditional GDP, the SPI provides critical data otherwise invisible to policymakers intent on guiding societies toward broad-based prosperity. Optimising decisions by referencing GDP in tandem with SPI statistics can focus policy on nourishment, housing, education, environmental protection, inclusion, and freedom, which are central to the multidimensional quality of life yet easily obscured by aggregate income growth. The Social Progress Index more fully reveals the human impact of the economic activity measured by GDP. Policymakers seeking to craft superior development policies targeting societal well-being in all its dimensions should consider GDP and SPI trends side by side.

The Gini Coefficient

Developed by Italian statistician Corrado Gini, the Gini Coefficient represents a statistical gauge of economic inequality within a country, measured on a scale from 0 to 1 (or 0 to 100%). A Gini Coefficient of 0 denotes absolute equality where every citizen earns precisely the same income. Conversely, an index of 1 (or 100%) indicates maximal inequality wherein a sole individual possesses the entire national income while the rest have none. This metric simplifies complex income distribution data into a single, interpretable figure, facilitating straightforward comparisons within a particular country over time and between different nations. It is why the Gini Index became an instrumental tool in scrutinising the impacts of social and economic policies aimed at curtailing inequality.

While the Gini Coefficient captures critical dimensions of economic equality and sustainability – notably absent in GDP calculations – it has its limitations. The GDP metric, often equated with enhanced citizen welfare, overlooks the unequal distribution of economic benefits, rendering it inadequate as a comprehensive indicator of societal health. The Gini Coefficient, in contrast, sheds light on the disparity between overall economic growth and the well-being of the general population. However, its focus primarily lies in detecting alterations in income distribution around the median, potentially obscuring significant disparities at the extreme ends of the income spectrum.

This is crucial in understanding why the Gini Coefficient does not fully capture extreme poverty in countries with wide disparities between rich and poor. Despite its popularity for providing a simple and singular number to judge a country's success at income distribution, the Gini Coefficient over-represents the middle classes for several reasons. Income groupings used in Gini calculation are often broader in the middle ranges. This essentially lumps more people together in those middle-income bands, overestimating their collective share of total income. The very poor and very rich get placed in smaller buckets at either end. It is also more sensitive to income transfers in the distribution's middle ranges. Large transfers at the ends of the distribution impact the measure less. Therefore, inequality amongst low or high earners gets downplayed.

For instance, the disconnect between economic growth and inequality mitigation in the US is reflected in a rising Gini Coefficient, from 34.7 in 1980 to 41.5 in 2019, the year before the COVID-19 outbreak. With progressive taxation targeting mainly the middle classes, there remains a disproportionate concentration of income and wealth among the ultra-rich that the Gini Index does not capture. However, it is notable that the significant fiscal measures during the pandemic, including expanded transfer payments, significantly reduced the Gini Index to 39.7 by the end of 2020. Conversely, the United Kingdom's Gini Index showed a marginal decrease from 32.8 in 2019 to 32.6 by the end of 2020, influenced by the country's furlough scheme (see Figure 33 and Figure 34).

Figure 33: Gini Index for the US[47]

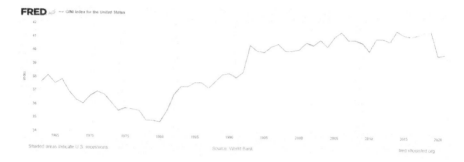

Figure 34: Gini Index for the United Kingdom[48]

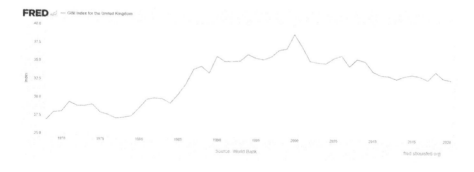

---

47 World Bank, "GINI Index for the United States [SIPOVGINIUSA], retrieved from FRED, Federal Reserve Bank of St. Louis, 6 December 2023, https://fred.stlouisfed.org/series/SIPOVGINIUSA.

48 World Bank, "GINI Index for the United Kingdom [SIPOVGINIGBR]," retrieved from FRED, Federal Reserve Bank of St. Louis, 7 December 2023, https://fred.stlouisfed.org/series/SIPOVGINIGBR.

There are a few key reasons the Gini index fell more sharply in the US than the UK during the pandemic, with the UK's furlough scheme likely playing a role. More generous unemployment benefits were implemented in the US by expanding eligibility, benefit amounts, and duration. This supported incomes for middle and lower-income groups, narrowing inequality. US stimulus payments provided substantial lump-sum transfers to lower-income households, disproportionately boosting their pandemic incomes. The UK relied more on its existing welfare system, and most UK fiscal support came through the job retention scheme preserving existing income relationships. The UK furlough scheme subsidised 80% of wages for retained but idle employees across the income spectrum. Temporarily protecting existing pay hierarchies likely moderated declines in income inequality in the United Kingdom during the pandemic recession, but it did not have the extreme redistributive effects experienced in the US.

Beyond merely signifying economic growth, the Gini Coefficient also sheds light on the quality of growth by highlighting instances where macroeconomic advances are accompanied by increasing inequality. This metric elucidates the nuanced disparities often masked by power imbalances within populations. A comparison between Nordic countries and the US exemplifies this; despite similar GDP per capita levels, the Gini Coefficient exposes the significantly higher levels of inequality in the US, aligning it more closely with developing countries with comparable per capita income.[49] This stark contrast accentuates how reliance solely on GDP figures can obscure the realities of inequality and social exclusion.

Changes in the Gini Coefficient over time provide vital social mobility insights. For example, an upward Gini Coefficient trend amid GDP growth indicates that macro-level gains fail to reach lower strata, directing policymakers to address exclusions urgently. Therefore, rather than a peripheral metric, distribution gauges like the Gini Coefficient constitute foundational indicators exposing economic fissures that enable calibrated policy responses benefiting vulnerable communities. However, the

---

49 World Bank, "Gini Index," 7 December 2023, https://data.worldbank.org/indicator/SI.POV.GINI.

mechanics of the Gini formula, data collection methods, and density of actual incomes for a population all contribute to an overemphasis on inequality amongst middle-income groups rather than the extremes. Analysts must understand this skew and use other metrics to track extreme poverty and deprivation better. Relying solely on the Gini Index risks missing inequality at the ends of the distribution.

The Multidimensional Poverty Index

The Gini Index provides a limited perspective on poverty because it fails to capture the extremes in the income distribution and is limited to monetary aspects. The Multidimensional Poverty Index (MPI), introduced in 2010 through a collaboration between the Oxford Poverty and Human Development Initiative (OPHI) and the United Nations Development Programme (UNDP), offers a rich framework that accounts for overlapping deprivations across health, education, and living standard dimensions on an individual level. This integrated assessment tool enables policymakers to identify the poorest subgroups, understand complex poverty dynamics, and formulate targeted interventions – capabilities not adequately offered by standalone measures like the Gini Index or GDP.

A purely financial conceptualisation of poverty is incomplete, even when income is viewed through an expanded measurement of utility or purchasing power. Poverty manifests in many ways, including capability failures and a lack of opportunity to pursue valued goals and pursuits. The creators of MPI have highlighted the limitations of money-centric measures, arguing that assessments of well-being and advantage should encompass a wider scope of human prosperity. The MPI aligns with this multidimensional perspective, assessing poverty as deprivations in very rudimentary functioning across health, education, and living standards. Its comprehensive design accounts for joint distributions of disadvantages at the micro level, generating actionable insights to guide policy.

The MPI's framework identifies the poor and constructs aggregate poverty measures using a dimensional breakdown that captures the incidence and intensity of poverty. It employs ten indicators across education, health, and living standards, with each dimension equally weighted. These indicators include nutrition, child mortality, years of schooling, school attendance rates, cooking fuel, sanitation, drinking water, housing materials, assets, and electricity. A person is identified as multidimensionally poor or MPI-poor if deprivations in at least one-third of the weighted indicators are experienced concurrently. Data on deprivations each household member faces, rather than proxies like household income or assets, informs the identification. Once the poor are identified, the aggregate MPI value is calculated by multiplying the incidence of poverty (H) with the average intensity across the poor (A). The MPI value thus reflects both the percentage of MPI-poor individuals (incidence) and the proportion of indicators in which they are deprived on average (intensity).

Multidimensional poverty measurement allows for the decomposition of the MPI by indicators and sub-national units, enabling more targeted policy. For instance, poor infrastructural access may disproportionately deprive marginalised social groups, necessitating investments prioritising drinking water and sanitation facilities in remote areas populated by minorities. High child mortality rates often accompany limited access to healthcare facilities and acute malnutrition. By capturing such joint distributions of disadvantages, policy interventions can holistically target the various manifestations of extreme poverty. Such analysis exposes inequality amongst the MPI poor that uniform policy prescriptions tend to overlook. Furthermore, the flexibility to set different poverty cut-offs to align with country-specific priorities and data availability makes the MPI a suitable metric in diverse contexts.

The MPI indicators focus on the most rudimentary human functioning, including core aspects like adequate nourishment, child survival, basic schooling, and sanitation. Deprivations in such acute necessities offer insight into abject failures to secure basic capabilities that facilitate broader functioning. This identification of acute failures that trap populations in extreme poverty is less discernible in traditional monetary metrics of poverty. For example, the MPI reveals that specific segments of the population in India continue to experience extreme poverty rates in a study that ended in 2006. Despite relatively low consumption-based measures of poverty and a visible downward trend in the incidence of poverty rates in the Indian population, the multidimensional analysis reveals the continued prevalence of extreme poverty within different subgroups. The intensity of deprivations is captured by the MPI, highlighting acute failures in public policy.[50]

Moreover, the MPI framework fulfils a key shortcoming of the Gini Index by discerning poverty intensity among the poorest subgroups and enabling progress tracking over time. Its granular attribution of poverty rates enables a more accurate policy strategy for alleviating the hardships of the extremely poor. While income inequality metrics certainly have utility in framing specific welfare assessments, they remain limited to singular monetary attributes and fail to expose inequality amongst disadvantaged populations across multiple fronts. On the contrary, the MPI framework dives deeper to reveal heterogeneity in the multidimensional poverty experienced by vulnerable groups and geographical subsets.

For instance, across 41 developing countries with available disaggregated data, the global MPI identified systematic disadvantaging of discriminated groups, including higher poverty rates amongst ethnic minorities and lower castes.[51] Beyond monetary aspects alone, these inequalities manifest through capability failures across health, education and living standards – including higher child mortality, lower literacy and infrastructural access. Such analysis exposes group inequalities that require dedicated policy efforts, like affirmative action in public services and targeted basic income schemes for minorities.

The framework also enables comparisons between multidimensional poverty levels across sub-national regions, spotlighting

---

50 Sabina Alkire and Suman Seth, "Multidimensional Poverty Reduction in India between 1999 and 2006: Where and How," *World Development* 72 (2015): 93-108, https://doi.org/10.1016/j.worlddev.2015.02.009.

51 Sabina Alkire et al., "Unmasking disparities by ethnicity, caste and gender: Global Multidimensional Poverty Index 2021," Oxford Poverty and Human Development Initiative, United Nations Development Programme, 2021, https://ophi.org.uk/wp-content/uploads/UNDP_OPHI_GMPI_2021_Report_Unmasking.pdf.

within-country geographic inequalities. A child in Sub-Saharan Africa faces greater odds of being MPI-poor and higher average intensities than one in Europe or Central Asia. Tailored poverty reduction approaches responsive to the sub-national pockets experiencing the highest multidimensional poverty are more effective and cheaper to address than directing fiscal responses to a larger but less destitute group. Furthermore, the techniques allow intersectional analysis across subgroups like gender, caste and region – which uncovers particular instances of exclusions of marginalised classes in poorer subgroups. Income-based metrics fail to capture nuances that can crucially guide policy design.

The MPI also enables monitoring of focused investments like decentralised drinking water expansion projects, public transportation, or rural mobile health clinics. Pinpointing specific indicator improvements through robust methodologies exposes impacts on the ground and aids iterative refinements for greater effectiveness of fiscal policy while accentuating accountability. Such empirical policy feedback facilitates the learning required to address complex development challenges related to poverty and human flourishing.

Moreover, the techniques expose the interconnected nature of deprivations that necessitate coordinated cross-sector efforts. Analysis may reveal that sanitation failures underpin both poor child nutrition levels and higher school dropout rates, especially among female children. Tackling these interconnections requires collaboration between national nutrition boards, education ministries and local government agencies funding infrastructural improvements. The MPI framework, implemented through cross-departmental cooperation, can thus spur integrated strategies to address interconnected sources of poverty.

The MPI methodology is not without criticism, and there are many critiques of its limitations. The choice of dimensions and weights that classify a person as MPI poor have been cited as subjective. Aggregating these multiple dimensions into one index is also criticised in favour of partial aggregation, which considers the choices available to the poor.[52] The MPI has also been critiqued for utilising an arbitrary 33% weighting across indicators towards poverty identification, albeit robustness tests revealing limited sensitivity across a range of alternative cut-offs.

However, the MPI methodology does not preclude its users from setting different thresholds to accommodate specific contexts. Policymakers can set other criteria for what is considered poor if they follow some basic principles and guidelines. For example, they can choose different dimensions, indicators, deprivation cutoffs, and weights depending on the availability of data, the indicators' relevance, and the stakeholders' preferences. However, they should also ensure that the MPI is consistent, transparent, robust, and comparable over time and space. Mexico's MPI variant (see Figure 35) excludes indicators like child mortality rates, which are low nationally; however, it includes sanitation and housing quality metrics as policy priorities.

---

52 Martin Ravallion, "On multidimensional indices of poverty," *The Journal of Economic Inequality* 9, no. 2 (June 2011): 235-248, https://doi.org/10.1007/s10888-011-9173-4.

Figure 35: Mexico's MPI Components[53]

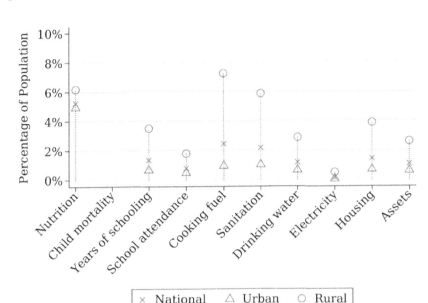

Adaptations like the World Bank's Multidimensional Poverty Measure (MPM) have also been implemented for specific cases. The MPM utilises monetary poverty, education, and basic infrastructure services as the three dimensions for capturing poverty. Monetary poverty is a novel idea of applying an international poverty line based on income – initially set at $2.15 a day.[54] The MPM offers alternate insights and potential policy handles by combining monetary and non-monetary aspects. However, the precise choice of dimensions and indicators remains grounded in judgment calls regarding development priorities. Ultimately, the value of

53 Oxford Poverty and Human Development Initiative and United Nations Development Programme, Global MPI Country Briefing 2021: Mexico (Latin America and the Caribbean), 2021, https://ophi.org.uk/wp-content/uploads/CB_MEX_2021.pdf.

54 World Bank, "Multidimensional Poverty Measure," last updated 30 April 2023, accessed 8 December 2023, https://www.worldbank.org/en/topic/poverty/brief/multidimensional-poverty-measure.

multidimensional poverty statistics depends on the interventions they enable.

Despite criticisms, the MPI framework is invaluable to the policymaker's toolkit in poverty diagnostics that income-centric measures miss. It also exposes interconnections, inequalities, and heterogeneities useful for targeting resource allocation. The technique is a methodological innovation in distilling a complex phenomenon into insightful statistics. Critiques regarding its limited incorporation of some dimensions of well-being are valid, but in the absence of more robust alternatives, the indicator enhances policymaking that focuses solely on growth metrics. Despite methodological debates, the MPI offers a viable tool to expose acute capability failures amongst the extremely poor. Its country adaptations highlight local priorities in basic requirements to inform policy towards ensuring more equitable access. While eliminating poverty undoubtedly necessitates sustained improvement in well-being and social progress, measures like the MPI can guide policy to ensure human development keeps pace across populations consistently left behind.

The Human Development Index

The United Nations Development Programme's Human Development Index (HDI) incorporates health, education, and income dimensions into its framework as a solution to the gaps missed by GDP, and it enhances policy decisions targeted towards advancing human development. Introduced in 1990, the Human Development Index (HDI) was developed as an alternative to GDP for evaluating development outcomes. HDI measures the average achievements of a country in three fundamental dimensions: health, education, and standard of living. Health is measured by life expectancy at birth, education is measured by expected years of schooling and mean years of schooling, and standard of living is measured by Gross National Income (GNI) per capita, adjusted for purchasing power parity (PPP). These metrics are aggregated using a geometric mean to calculate HDI scores between 0 and 1, facilitating comparisons across countries and over time. The HDI conceptualises development as expanding human capabilities and freedoms, and it emerges as a multidimensional alternative to the growth-centric GDP model for assessing a nation's development.

Published annually by the Human Development Report Office (HDRO), the global HDI categorises countries into different tiers of human development. Alongside this global HDI, the HDRO introduces ancillary indices that delve into inequality, gender disparities, and poverty, all rooted in the HDI's foundational framework. Regional and national HDI adaptions have also emerged over the years. Figure 36 illustrates HDI's emphasis on these human development metrics, where the impact of the pandemic far outweighed the Global Financial Crisis in its assessment of societal well-being. Despite the economic hardship, the human-level development metrics heavily weighted to educational and health outcomes are less sensitive to economic crises than pandemics.

Figure 36: 2022 Human Development Index[55]

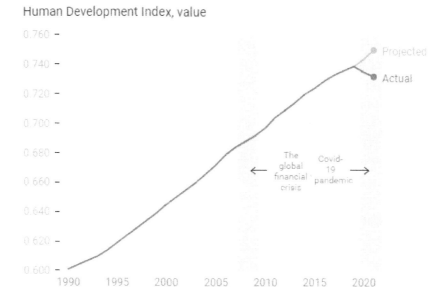

Human Development Index, value

Note: The period of the global financial crisis is indicative.

Source: HDRO calculations based on data from UNDESA (2022a) and (2022b), UNESCO Institute for Statistics (2022), United Nations Statistics Division (2022), World Bank (2022), Barro and Lee (2018) and IMF (2021) and (2022). • Created with Datawrapper

The HDI offers multiple advantages over GDP that address some of GDP's limitations. HDI's inclusion of health and education metrics covers key aspects affecting quality of life beyond just income levels. This is crucially important when contrasting countries with predominantly privatised healthcare and education systems against those with public systems. As detailed in Chapter Ten, economies with privatised public services often show inflated GDP figures, which do not necessarily correlate with the benefits received from these essential services. Through its cross-country comparisons, the HDI uncovers human development variances that GDP differences fail to explain, thereby shedding light on the profound

---

55 United Nations Development Programme (UNDP), *Human Development Report* 2021-22, 2022,

http://report.hdr.undp.org.

impacts of sociopolitical choices. When utilised alongside GDP, HDI offers invaluable context, illustrating the extent to which economic advancements are translated into tangible human development outcomes.

Despite its merits over GDP, applying HDI also requires methodological care. The HDI's streamlined approach, though easy to interpret, risks simplifying the intricate nature of human development. The equal weighting assigned to each of its dimensions – health, education, and income - invites scrutiny, particularly given the potentially varying marginal returns across these areas. Furthermore, challenges emerge from the limited availability and varying quality of underlying health and education data, which is essential for constructing and comparing HDIs. Additionally, the diverse methods employed in national and regional adaptations of the HDI can complicate both cross-country comparisons and sub-national assessments.

Indian and Brazilian regional-level HDI statistics illustrate how national-level statistics may not reveal distributional inequalities within a country. The HDI is typically calculated at the national level, but some countries do calculate HDI at a more granular level. For example, in India, the NITI Aayog releases a sub-national HDI for the different states and union territories.[56] Similarly, in Brazil, the United Nations Development Programme (UNDP) and the Institute for Applied Economic Research (IPEA) released the Municipal Human Development Index (MHDI), which calculates the HDI for each of Brazil's 5,565 municipalities.[57] Moreover, condensing multiple indicators into a single index can lead to ambiguity in policy guidance on addressing specific shortfalls. Thus, applying HDI warrants careful attention to its functional form, weights, data sources, and

---

56 NITI Aayog. SDG India Index & Dashboard 2020-21: *Partnerships in the Decade of Action*. New Delhi: NITI Aayog, 2021. https://niti.gov.in/sites/default/files/2021-06/SDG-India-Index-3.0_27-Jun-2021.pdf.

57 D. V. S. Pereira, C. M. M. Mota, and J. A. G. Miranda, "Municipal Human Development Index for Brazilian Cities Based on ELECTRE TRI-C," in 2013 *IEEE International Conference on Systems, Man, and Cybernetics*, (2013): 736-740, doi: 10.1109/SMC.2013.130.

role within wider policy conversations on measuring multidimensional concepts like well-being.

HDI's utility becomes particularly evident in cross-country analyses, offering more nuanced insights into human welfare than GDP alone. Consider the comparison of Gross National Incomes, adjusted for purchasing power parity (PPP) in US dollars, between countries with distinct economic profiles. For instance, despite Kuwait's far higher Gross National Income per capita ($52,920 in 2017 PPP) than the UK's ($45,225 in 2017 PPP), the UK achieved a higher HDI score of 0.929 than Kuwait's HDI score of 0.831. This discrepancy primarily stems from markedly different health and education outcomes in the UK, such as a higher life expectancy (81 years versus 79) and greater mean years of schooling (13.4 years versus 7.3 in Kuwait).[58] Such contrasts underscore the value of HDI in highlighting the societal choices and priorities that shape how national income translates into human well-being.

The HDI lens carries significant implications for policymaking aimed at advancing human development. HDI identifies areas where countries underperform or overperform their economic standing across health, education and income, pointing to sectors requiring policy attention. Changes in HDI can reveal policies' human impact regardless of their influence on economic production. Therefore, they can help direct fiscal budgets towards inclusive development policies in disadvantaged regions or demographic segments. Sub-national HDIs are key to uncovering distributional inequalities within countries, allowing for localised policy actions suited for human development needs in different regions within countries.

The HDI lens carries significant implications for policymaking aimed at advancing human development. HDI identifies areas where countries underperform or overperform their economic standing across health, education and income, pointing to sectors requiring policy attention.

---

58 United Nations Development Programme, "Human Development Index (HDI)," *Human Development Reports*, accessed 8 December 2023, http://hdr.undp.org/en/content/human-development-index-hdi.

Changes in HDI can reveal policies' human impact regardless of their influence on economic production. Therefore, they can help direct fiscal budgets towards inclusive development policies in disadvantaged regions or demographic segments. Sub-national HDIs are key to uncovering distributional inequalities within countries, allowing for localised policy actions suited for human development needs in different regions within countries.

As an indicator of social progress, the Human Development Index is a meaningful complement to GDP for public policy guidance on advancing human welfare, and governments should closely monitor HDI alongside GDP to formulate appropriate social policies, evaluative mechanisms, and expenditure plans centred on human well-being. HDI is a critical counterbalance to the purely economic GDP perspective by encapsulating crucial health and education dimensions, revealing policy impacts on human lives, and promoting progress-oriented decision-making. However, applying HDI warrants careful attention to its limitations around data constraints, weighting dilemmas, and role within broader policy dialogues on the complex concept of societal well-being.

Epilogue

In recent times, we have observed a burgeoning schism between the populace and its governing elite, one that has crystallised in the form of populism – a response to socio-economic inequality and perceived collusion between government and corporations. The seismic event of Brexit in Britain is emblematic of such unrest, reflecting not the culmination of solitary disquiet but a profound dissatisfaction with the prevailing Neoliberal policies which have shaped societal priorities for decades. The narrative peddled, one that conversely assigns immigration policy as the solitary scapegoat for all of Britain's economic ills, diverts from the reality of a nation grappling with stark socio-economic contrasts, rendered all the more conspicuous by the steely grip of austerity measures that continue to plague our nation.

The impact of Neoliberal ideology – subservient as it is to market freedom and deregulation – has palpably steered Britain towards intensifying societal divides. From the state's approach to social housing to education and healthcare, markets have rendered society's fundamental rights more susceptible to the whims of every budget squeeze to hide the failures of privatisation that stripped the state of its real assets.

Privatisation across utilities has ostensibly failed in its purported mission to curtail costs and safeguard environmental sanctity, instead rendering the asymmetry between risk and finance, where private management's profitability marginalises the wider societal obligations. This philosophy entrenched within the Thatcherite vision inadvertently spawned a financial sector characterised by the abstraction of wealth and extractive mechanisms that concentrate wealth and power in a few hands. The envisaged competition that was to foster market diversity instead ushered in monopolistic practices and nudged society towards environmental negligence and societal disregard.

The paean to government debt reduction, hailed by many as a hallmark of financial prudence, masks the profundity of taxpayer asset loss through privatisation. Despite a backdrop of high national debt, the audacity of Britain's social welfare investments post-WWII stands in stark contrast to modern fiscal cuts to institutions such as the NHS. This embodiment of social equity, anchored within the Rawlsian notion of fairness, underscores the right to healthcare as a collective societal duty. Yet, the current economic trajectory inches Britain perilously towards the more privatised model of American healthcare, incurring risks that materialise emerging market-driven health disparities, even as investments in the NHS have consistently demonstrated their multiplicative effects on economic growth.

Yet, in this story, we are coming to a juncture where the choice to build a better future is presented by the Green Party of England and Wales. They have set our gaze upon the storied landscape of historical monetary practices to transport us beyond the myopic focus on the national debt and GDP, dissecting its flawed construction and the misleading narratives it engenders. We unearth these instances where the state-money framework found practical application: from the Song Dynasty with its private government-issued currency to the American Colonies' use of Colonial Scrip. These moments in time demonstrate the viability of state-backed monetary systems against modern ideological criticism. The case for paper money, as espoused by Benjamin Franklin – a tool to sustain the economic vitality of the Revolutionary War even amid depreciation – sheds light on an unappreciated facet unacknowledged in contemporary debates.

Standing in opposition to building its green and equitable future, society is shackled by imagined constraints about affordability, despite the rise of Modern Money Theory to fill the gap where Keynesians once stood to yield power in the halls of government. The question of affordability for the Green Party comes down to a choice in the type of currency system we use, proposing an overhaul of the architecture of modern bank money. In this regard, the Greens have moved beyond discourse to untangle the veil surrounding the interconnections between existing fiscal ideology and the actual monetary operations within sovereign nations. The scrutiny of conventional wisdom on money creation, interrogating the fabric of monetary policy, is set against an ever-evolving dogma that resists seeing sovereign money as anything but debilitating debt.

To overcome the resistance to fiscal activism, the Green Party's monetary reform plan promotes a reframing of the common belief by lending new shapes to economic realities. In this new reality, a gilt is no longer government debt when it is held as a fixed-term deposit at a Monetary Authority, despite both being liabilities of the state and the historical recognition of debt as being intertwined with money. In the conventional economic narrative, the transition from barter to fiat money is frequently presented with a beguiling simplicity. In reality, debt and credit are far more primal in socioeconomic interactions than the typical market exchanges society often associates with the foundation of money. Indeed, debt obligation is a prerequisite for the notion of money, exhibiting a crucial alignment with the cyclical and contingent life of seasonal farming. It is here, within these proto-financial promises – a confluence of need, trust, and reciprocity – that money evolved.

In navigating these complexities, one uncovers a synthesis of history, theory, and practical policy implications – a synthesis that underscores the enduring social contract of money, premised on trust and intricately woven through the very tapestry of human social evolution. However, it becomes evident that the monetary system operates as a complex adaptive system, sustained by continuous evolution crucial for stability. In this instance, it becomes imperative for the Green Party to take control over the economic narrative by making the currency-issuing authority of the state a formal practice for funding government spending. With gilt issuance phased out, the power over government spending and the public misconception will be permanently altered. Its monetary reform plan makes formal what Modern Money Theory aims to accomplish but is continuously compromised, with collective illusions often backtracking on progressive policies and subjecting the general public to more austerity measures.

The analysis in this book extends beyond its broad definition of state money to include privately created credit, each influenced by convertibility and assorted risk factors. We are confronted with an architecture of modern money that guarantees redemption of government bonds at maturity at face value and bank deposits hedged against credit risk through deposit insurance and regulation. This contemporary monetary landscape requires navigation through a labyrinth of liquidity risks, regulatory frameworks, and a constant pursuit of confidence in the money's convertibility into that ever-elusive concept of state currency.

With risks to the banking system significantly reduced as the state becomes the sole issuer of money, society will collectively free up resources to tackle social, economic, and environmental challenges. This new paradigm transports us beyond the myopic focus on GDP. It calls for a re-imagination of economic progress metrics, placing at its core the well-being of society and the planet. The Green Party's voice may lay the groundwork for inspiring broader discourse on social challenges and considerations that span a spectrum of indicators for real progress. The prospect of nationalising public utilities is articulated as a Green Party stance not purely as a matter of economic rationality but also as an articulation of social welfare – part of a broader realignment of public policy with welfare, access, and sustainability. Most importantly, the new monetary regime will change the narrative about what society can achieve within its capacity to produce, given the real constraints of inflation and ecological limits. The new monetary role of the government is given sovereign and exclusive legal authority to create money, and its taxation mechanisms act as a compelling retraction method for managing the nation's money supply.

Disclosures

Conflict of Interest Statement

The author certifies that he is affiliated and involved with the Green Party of England and Wales. He is a committed member and monetary reform campaigner, and he has plans to stand as a candidate in his area.

Statement on Use of Artificial Intelligence Tools

At the time of publication, Large Language Models (LLMs) have a limited context window and do not produce research from reliable sources. While they are great tools for providing assistance in articulating a complex idea in a language and tone that can easily be understood, LLMs are prone to fabrications and misrepresentations. In the absence of standards on attribution for LLM usage, this statement is a disclosure of LLM utilisation for editing purposes. Any AI-generated text used in this book was done for editing purposes only and for standardising the text in British English.

The ideas presented in this book are the result of the author's original work, and research sourced from other authors and organisations has been cited appropriately. GPT-4 was used to review and amend grammar and spelling mistakes, rewrite sections to make the ideas more easily understood, and ensure the endnotes and bibliography followed the Chicago Manual for Style format. To ensure that GPT-4 did not generate plagiarised content, the manuscript has been checked by plagiarism checkers.

In addition to LLMs, graphics design was assisted by the use of DALL·E 3 to brainstorm colour matching and design for the book's cover art and the pictograms in figures and diagrams. To ensure that the designs do not violate any copyrighted content, the author used DALL·E 3, which guarantees copyright protections and declines requests that ask for an image in the style of a living artist.

References

Chapter One

Elliott, C.P. "The Role of Money in the Economies of Ancient Greece and Rome." In *Handbook of the History of Money and Currency*, edited by S. Battilossi, Y. Cassis, and K. Yago, Singapore: Springer, 2018. https://doi.org/10.1007/978-981-10-0622-7_46-1.

Graeber, David. *Debt: The First 5,000 Years*, Updated and Expanded. US: Melville House, 2014.

Harl, Kenneth W.. Coinage in the Roman economy, 300 B.C. to A.D. 700. United Kingdom: Johns Hopkins University Press, 1996.

Howgego, Christopher. "The Monetization of Temperate Europe." *The Journal of Roman Studies* 103 (2013): 16–45. http://www.jstor.org/stable/43286778.

Chapter Two

BoE. "BoE balance sheet and weekly report." Accessed 6 November 2023. https://www.bankofengland.co.uk/weekly-report/balance-sheet-and-weekly-report.

Kelton, Stephanie. The Deficit Myth: Modern Monetary Theory and How to Build a Better Economy. United Kingdom: John Murray Press, 2020.

McLeay, Michael, Radia, Amar, and Thomas, Ryland. "Money creation in the modern economy." *BoE Quarterly Bulletin 2014 Q1*. https://www.bankofengland.co.uk/-/media/boe/files/quarterly-bulletin/2014/money-creation-in-the-modern-economy.pdf.

Mosler, Warren. *Soft Currency Economics II: The Origin of Modern Monetary Theory*. U.S. Virgin Islands: CreateSpace Independent Publishing Platform, 2013.

Office for National Statistics. "UK financial accounts experimental statistics flow of funds matrices: 2020." 7 December 2020. Accessed 6 November 2023. https://www.ons.gov.uk/economy/nationalaccounts/uksectoraccounts/articles/ukfinancialaccountsexperimentalstatisticsflowoffundsmatrices/latest.

Office for National Statistics. "UK Economic Accounts: flow of funds." 29 September 2023. Accessed 6 November 2023. https://www.ons.gov.uk/economy/nationalaccounts/uksectoraccounts/datasets/unitedkingdomeconomicaccountsflowoffunds.

Patel, Natu Somabhai, ed. *Financial statistics explanatory handbook*. 2010. Hampshire: Palgrave Macmillan, 2009.

Wang, Joseph. Central Banking 101. US, 2020.

Chapter Three

BoE. "BoE Market Operations Guide." 5 May 2023. Accessed 6 November 2023. https://www.bankofengland.co.uk/markets/bank-of-england-market-operations-guide.

Board of Governors of the Federal Reserve System. *The Federal Reserve System: Purposes & Functions*. 10th ed. 2016. https://fraser.stlouisfed.org/title/federal-reserve-system-5298.

Chapter Four

BoE. "Asset Purchase Facility Quarterly Report – 2023 Q1." 25 July 2023. https://www.bankofengland.co.uk/asset-purchase-facility/2023/2023-q1.

BoE. "BoE balance sheet and weekly report." Accessed 6 November 2023. https://www.bankofengland.co.uk/weekly-report/balance-sheet-and-weekly-report.

BoE. "QE at the BoE: A Perspective on Its Functioning and Effectiveness." *Quarterly Bulletin 2022 Q1*. 18 May 2022. https://www.bankofengland.co.uk/quarterly-bulletin/2022/2022-q1/qe-at-the-bank-of-england-a-perspective-on-its-functioning-and-effectiveness.

Debt Management Office. "Joint Bank-DMO Statement on Gilt Lending." 6 August 2009. https://www.dmo.gov.uk/media/exkogfb4/sa060809b.pdf.

Keynes, John Maynard. How to Pay for the War: A Radical Plan for the Chancellor of the Exchequer. London: Macmillan and Co, 1940.

Keynes, John Maynard. The General Theory of Employment, Interest, and Money. London: Macmillan, 1936.

Panico, Carlo, and Marco Piccioni. "Keynes on Central Bank Independence." *Studi Economici* 118-119-120 (2016): 190-216. doi:10.3280/STE2016-118012.

Chapter Five

Huber, Joseph. "Split-circuit reserve banking – functioning, dysfunctions and future perspectives." *Real-World Economics Review*, no. 80. (2017): 63-84. http://www.paecon.net/PAEReview/issue80/whole80.pdf.

House of Commons Work and Pensions Committee. "Defined Benefit Pensions with Liability Driven Investments." *Seventh Report of Session 2022–23*. 14 June 2023. https://committees.parliament.uk/publications/40563/documents/197799/default.

Moynihan, Jon. "How the Bank broke the Government." *The Critic Magazine*, December/January 2023.

https://thecritic.co.uk/issues/december-january-2023/how-the-bank-broke-the-government.

Chapter Six

Burn-Murdoch, John. "Britain's winter of discontent is the inevitable result of austerity." *Financial Times*, 22 December 2022. https://perma.cc/N9DQ-4KMF.

Carnall Farrar. "The link between investing in health and economic growth." London: NHS Confederation, October 2022. https://www.nhsconfed.org/publications/analysis-link-between-investing-health-and-economic-growth.

Carter, Zachary D. The Price of Peace: Money, Democracy, and the Life of John Maynard Keynes. New York: Random House, 2020.

Department for Levelling Up, Housing & Communities. "Housing supply: indicators of new supply, England: January to March 2023." 29 June 2023.

Gray, John. *False Dawn: The Delusions of Global Capitalism*. Revised edition. London: Granta Books, 2009. Originally published 1998.

Bevan, Gwyn. How Did Britain Come to This? A century of systemic failures of governance. London: LSE Press, 2023.

The King's Fund. "The NHS budget and how it has changed." 20 September 2023. Accessed 29 November 2023. https://www.kingsfund.org.uk/projects/nhs-in-a-nutshell/nhs-budget.

O'Rourke, Kevin. A Short History of Brexit: From Brentry to Backstop. London: Pelican Books, 2019.

Office for National Statistics (ONS), "Healthcare expenditure, UK Health Accounts: 2021," statistical bulletin, released 17 May 2023, https://www.ons.gov.uk/peoplepopulationandcommunity/healthandsocialcare/healthcaresystem/bulletins/ukhealthaccounts/2021.

Organisation for Economic Co-operation and Development (OECD). "Gross domestic product (GDP): GDP per capita, USD, current prices and PPPs." 2023. https://stats.oecd.org/index.aspx?queryid=61433.

Pickard, Jim, Tanya Powley, and Gill Plimmer. "UK rail bailout hits £3.5bn and set to rise further." Financial Times, 18 June 2020. https://www.ft.com/content/24e57a49-03e6-4106-9f7c-b630fdb76e28.

Rawls, John. *A Theory of Justice*. London: Harvard University Press, 2009.

Watling, Samuel. "Why Britain doesn't build." *Works in Progress*, Issue 11, 23 May 2023. https://worksinprogress.co/issue/why-britain-doesnt-build.

Wolf, Martin. "The UK economy has two regional problems, not one." *Financial Times*, 8 March 2023. https://perma.cc/9EAN-53SA.

Chapter Seven

BoE. "BoE balance sheet and weekly report." Accessed 6 November 2023. https://www.bankofengland.co.uk/weekly-report/balance-sheet-and-weekly-report.

Cartwright, Mark. "Paper in Ancient China." *World History Encyclopedia*. Last modified September 15, 2017. https://www.worldhistory.org/article/1120/paper-in-ancient-china/.

"Examination before the Committee of the Whole of the House of Commons, 13 February 1766." *Founders Online*. National Archives. https://founders.archives.gov/documents/Franklin/01-13-02-0035. Originally in: Labaree, Leonard W., ed. *The Papers of Benjamin Franklin*, vol. 13, 1 January through 31 December, 1766. New Haven and London: Yale University Press, 1969, pp. 124-162.

Flynn, David. "Credit in the Colonial American Economy." In *EH.Net Encyclopedia*, edited by Robert Whaples. 16 March 2008.

Humpage, Owen F. "Paper Money and Inflation in Colonial America." *Federal Reserve Bank of Cleveland, Economic Commentary* 2015-06, 2015. https://doi.org/10.26509/frbc-ec-201506.

Michener, Ron. "Money in the American Colonies." In *EH.Net Encyclopedia*, edited by Robert Whaples. Revised 13 January 2011. Originally published 8 June 2003.

Office for National Statistics. "UK financial accounts experimental statistics flow of funds matrices: 2020." 7 December 2020. Accessed 6 November 2023. https://www.ons.gov.uk/economy/nationalaccounts/uksectoraccounts/articles/ukfinancialaccountsexperimentalstatisticsflowoffundsmatrices/latest.

Office for National Statistics. "UK Economic Accounts: flow of funds." 29 September 2023. Accessed 6 November 2023. https://www.ons.gov.uk/economy/nationalaccounts/uksectoraccounts/datasets/unitedkingdomeconomicaccountsflowoffunds.

Chapter Eight

Green Party of England and Wales. "Economy." Last amended 2023. Accessed 22 November 2023. https://policy.greenparty.org.uk/our-policies/long-term-goals/economy.

Green Party of England and Wales. "Greens call for Big Five energy companies to be brought into public ownership to stabilise market and protect consumers." Press release. 17 August 2022. https://www.greenparty.org.uk/news/2022/08/17/greens-call-for-big-five-energy-companies-to-be-brought-into-public-ownership.

Green Party of the US. "The Green New Deal." Accessed 22 November 2023. https://gpus.org/organizing-tools/the-green-new-deal.

House of Commons Library. "Public ownership of energy companies." 28 October 2022. https://commonslibrary.parliament.uk/research-briefings/cdp-2022-0184.

U.S. House of Representatives. "National Emergency Employment Defense Act of 2011." H.R. 2990, 112th Cong. Introduced September 21, 2011. https://www.congress.gov/bill/112th-congress/house-bill/2990/text.

Chapter Nine

Scott, Brett. Cloudmoney: Cash, Cards, Crypto and the War for our Wallets. Random House, 2022.

Huber, Joseph. The Monetary Turning Point: From Bank Money to Central Bank Digital Currency (CBDC). Palgrave Macmillan, 2023.

Payment Systems Regulator. PSR PS 15/1: A new regulatory framework for payment systems in the UK. London, 2015.

Chapter Ten

Carnall Farrar. "The link between investing in health and economic growth." London: NHS Confederation, October 2022. https://www.nhsconfed.org/publications/analysis-link-between-investing-health-and-economic-growth.

Chapter Eleven

Abdallah, Saamah, Sam Thompson, Juliet Michaelson, Nic Marks, and Nicola Steuer. The (un)Happy Planet Index 2.0: Why good lives don't have to cost the Earth. London: New Economics Foundation, 2009. https://base.socioeco.org/docs/the_happy_planet_index_2.0_1.pdf
.

Alkire, Sabina, Adriana Conconi, and Suman Seth. "Multidimensional Poverty Index 2014: Brief Methodological Note and Results." Oxford Poverty and Human Development Initiative (OPHI), University of Oxford, 2014.

Alkire, Sabina, and José Manuel Roche. "Beyond Headcount: Measures that Reflect the Breadth and Components of Child Poverty." OPHI Working Papers 45. University of Oxford, July 2011. JEL Codes: I32, J13, O1. ISBN 978-1-907194-29-0.

Alkire, Sabina, and Suman Seth. "Multidimensional Poverty Reduction in India between 1999 and 2006: Where and How?" *World Development* 72 (2015): 93-108. https://doi.org/10.1016/j.worlddev.2015.02.009.

Alkire, Sabina, et al. "Unmasking disparities by ethnicity, caste and gender: Global Multidimensional Poverty Index 2021." Oxford Poverty and Human Development Initiative, United Nations Development Programme, 2021. https://ophi.org.uk/wp-content/uploads/UNDP_OPHI_GMPI_2021_Report_Unmasking.pdf.

Böhringer, Christoph, and Patrick Jochem. "Measuring the immeasurable – A survey of sustainability indices." *Ecological Economics* 63, no. 1 (2007): 1-8. https://doi.org/10.1016/j.ecolecon.2007.03.008.

Cobb, Clifford, Ted Halstead, and Jonathan Rowe. "The Genuine Progress Indicator: Summary of Data and Methodology." *Redefining Progress*, September 1995.

Daly, Herman. *Ecological Economics and Sustainable Development*. Cheltenham, UK: Edward Elgar, 2007.

De Maio, Fernando G. "Income inequality measures." *Journal of Epidemiology and Community Health* 61, no. 10 (October 2007): 849-852. doi: 10.1136/jech.2006.052969. PMID: 17873219. PMCID: PMC2652960.

Decancq, Koen, and Lugo, María Ana. "Weights in Multidimensional Indices of Well-being: An Overview." *Econometric Reviews* 32, no. 1 (2013): 7-34. https://doi.org/10.1080/07474938.2012.690641.

Edens, Bram, and Hein, Lars. "Towards a consistent approach for ecosystem accounting." *Ecological Economics* 90 (2013): 41-52. https://doi.org/10.1016/j.ecolecon.2013.03.003.

Griggs, D., Stafford-Smith, M., Gaffney, O., et al. "Sustainable development goals for people and planet." *Nature* 495 (2013): 305-307. https://doi.org/10.1038/495305a.

Hasell, Joe. "Measuring inequality: What is the Gini coefficient?" *Our World in Data*. 2023. https://ourworldindata.org/what-is-the-gini-coefficient.

Hsu, A., D. Esty, M. Levy, A. de Sherbinin, et al. The 2016 *Environmental Performance Index Report*. New Haven, CT: Yale Center for Environmental Law and Policy, 2016. https://doi.org/10.13140/RG.2.2.19868.90249.

Exton, Rebecca, and Shinwell, Marc. "Policy use of well-being metrics: Describing countries' experiences." *OECD Statistics Working Papers*, no. 94, SDD/DOC(2018). 6 November 2018. https://one.oecd.org/document/SDD/DOC(2018)7/En/pdf.

Harmacek, Jaromir, Petra Krylova, and Mohamed Htitich. *2022 Social Progress Index Data*. Washington, DC: Social Progress Imperative, 2022.

Hickel, Jason. "The contradiction of the sustainable development goals: Growth versus ecology on a finite planet." *Sustainable Development* 27, no. 5 (September/October 2019): 873-884. First published 15 April 2019. https://doi.org/10.1002/sd.1947.

Keynes, John Maynard. The General Theory of Employment, Interest, and Money. London: Macmillan, 1936.

Lawn, Philip A. "A theoretical foundation to support the Index of Sustainable Economic Welfare (ISEW), Genuine Progress Indicator (GPI), and other related indexes." *Ecological Economics* 44, no. 1 (2003): 105-118. https://doi.org/10.1016/S0921-8009(02)00258-6.

Permanyer, Iñaki. "Using Census Data to Explore the Spatial Distribution of Human Development." *World Development* 46 (2013): 1-13. https://doi.org/10.1016/j.worlddev.2012.11.015.

Ravallion, Martin. "On multidimensional indices of poverty." *The Journal of Economic Inequality* 9, no. 2 (June 2011): 235-248. https://doi.org/10.1007/s10888-011-9173-4.

Schmelzer, Matthias. The Hegemony of Growth: The OECD and the Making of the Economic Growth Paradigm. India: Cambridge University Press, 2016.

Stern, Scott, Jaromir Harmacek, Petra Krylova, and Mohamed Htitich. *2022 Social Progress Index Methodology Summary*. Washington, DC: Social Progress Imperative, 2022. https://www.socialprogress.org/global/methodology.

United Nations. System of Environmental-Economic Accounting 2012: Central Framework. New York: United Nations, 2014.

United Nations Development Programme (UNDP). *Human Development Report 2021-22*. 2022. http://report.hdr.undp.org.

Waring, Marilyn. *Counting for nothing: what men value and what women are worth*. Buffalo: University of Toronto Press, 1999.

Wealth Accounting and the Valuation of Ecosystem Services. *WAVES Annual Report 2018*. 2018. https://www.wavespartnership.org/en/knowledge-center/waves-annual-report-2018.

Wendling, Zachary A., Mathew Jacob, Daniel C. Esty, and John W. Emerson. "Explaining environmental performance: Insights for progress on sustainability." *Environmental Development* 44 (2022): 100741. https://doi.org/10.1016/j.envdev.2022.100741.

Index

Printed in Great Britain
by Amazon

40552525R00162